BARDOT

AN INTIMATE PORTRAIT

JEFFREY ROBINSON

DONALD I. FINE, INC.
NEW YORK

Library of Congress Catalogue Card Number: 94-061915

ISBN: 1-55611-452-4

Manufactured in the United States of America

10   9   8   7   6   5   4   3   2   1

Contents

This Book is for Celine Chelsea
Another Superstar who Changed the World
Love Papa

Il était une fois une rose
un bras qui tenait cette rose
et au bout du bras, Jeffrey.
C'est ainsi que le 10 Décembre
1994 à St Tropez, j'ai découvert
l'homme qui en écrivant ce
livre a pris un terrible risque !
Ce jour là, entourée de chiens
abandonnés que j'essayais en
vain de faire adopter pour
le Noël des animaux, j'ai fait
la connaissance de ce Jeffrey
Robinson que je redoutais et
dont je me méfiais comme de
la peste. Encore un bonhomme
qui écrit sur moi, encore un
procès en perspective, encore
un fouilleur de vie privée, un
saligaud, un opportuniste....
Et puis en l'écoutant, il
m'a apprivoisée, il m'a fait
rire, je voulait adopter tous

II les chiens, les chats.... il avait un charme magique et un humour irrésistible.

Il me racontait mon grand père "le boum" comme s'il l'avait toujours connu, il me racontait mon enfance, ma vie, j'étais fasciné par la vérité et la sensibilité de ses propos.

Je lui fais donc confiance puisqu'il me connait peut être encore mieux que je ne me connais moi-même et je le remercie d'avoir la générosité d'abandonner une partie de ses droits en faveur de la Fondation pour la protection des oiseaux.

A tout de suite, je vous retrouve à la page suivante....

Brigitte Bardot

ST TROPEZ - Mars 94.

Once upon a time there was a rose,
an arm that held this rose,
and at the end of the arm, Jeffrey

That's how, on 10 December 1993, in St Tropez I came across the man who, in writing this book, had taken an awful risk.

That day, surrounded by the abandoned dogs I was vainly trying to have adopted for 'Animals' Christmas', I met this Jeffrey Robinson whom I'd feared and avoided like the plague – yet another guy writing about me, another lawsuit in prospect, another person prying into my private life, a gossip monger, an opportunist . . .

But then, listening to him, he tamed me, he made me laugh, he wanted to adopt the dogs, the cats . . . he had magical charm and an irresistible sense of humour.

He told me stories about my grandfather, 'Le Boum', as if he'd known him all his life, he told me about my childhood, about my life; I was fascinated by the truth and sensitivity of his remarks.

I trust him because he knows me, perhaps better than I know myself and I thank him for having the generosity to donate part of his royalties to my Foundation for the protection of animals.

I'll see you again right away, on the next page.

Brigitte Bardot

St Tropez, March 94

Life One

THE CRAZY YEARS

'I am a woman just like any other. I have two ears, two eyes, a nose and a mouth. I have feelings and thoughts and I am a wife and a mother above all else. But my life is becoming impossible. My soul is not my own any more. Stardom to me is a monster, like the sorcerer's apprentice. I cannot live as I want to. I merely exist underground. If I want fresh air in my home, I cannot open my window because there's a photographer sitting on the roof opposite with a telescopic lens. There is very little in my life that I can call my own.'

Brigitte Bardot, 1960

Chapter One

EXISTING UNDERGROUND

In the provençal dialect of southeastern France, a *madrague* is a heavy rope net that, many years ago, was laid across the mouth of open bays to catch large fish – especially tuna, swordfish and shark. In those days, the Mediterranean was clean enough that big fish would come in close to shore. So these special nets were strung in place – put there to last for ten or 15 years – and secured in the water by huge green glass balls that floated on the surface. When a fish was caught, the weight of it would pull the nearest glass ball under the water – a signal to the net keeper, who lived along the shore, to row out and get the fish. Eventually, the net keeper's cottage also came to be called La Madrague. And, these days, there are dozens of villas with that name, up and down that coast, where net keepers once lived.

It was such a common name that no one thought twice about it, until 1958, when Brigitte Bardot bought a small fisherman's bungalow on the Bay of Canebiers, along the side of the cape that juts out from what was then the tiny, remote fishing village of St Tropez.

Instantly, her Madrague became the most famous of all Madragues. And because it was hers, it automatically surpassed the Elysée Palace and the Chateau of Versailles as the most famous residence in France.

No longer a fisherman's shack, she's built an attractive home there, and since added other buildings to the property – a little cottage called La Petite Madrague and an even smaller, one-room guest cabin called Le Microbus. Still, this is not, by any stretch of the imagination, a movie star's estate. This is not Beverly Hills. Anyway, Brigitte Bardot never wanted anything to do with Hollywood.

La Madrague is a compact, two-storey provençal house, right on the water's edge. There is a large living room, in light colours, dominated by a huge wrap-around white imitation-leather sofa. On one side there's a dining area with a sensational mahogany refectory table – long enough to seat 12 comfortably. On the other side, there is her bedroom, with a large dressing area and bathroom behind it, where she has a gorgeous oval sunken tub. The kitchen is at the rear of the house. Downstairs, there is a guest apartment.

Her home is not extravagantly decorated. But then, deep down, she's never really been a woman with extravagant tastes. And even if there were times in the past when she might have let some excess get in the way – for a time she rode around in a white Rolls-Royce driven by a tall, handsome, ebony-black chauffeur in a uniform to match the car – she is not an extravagant person these days. The house is neat and clean, tended to by a live-in housekeeper, and, in fact, rather sparse. What art she used to own, and what few mementos she once collected from her movie career, have long since been sold to further her work as an animal activist. There are, however, several dozen photos scattered around, many of them in matching red frames, meticulously placed on end tables. A lot of them are of animals – cats and dogs and ponies – past and present. Among the rest are some huge blow-ups – both in black and white and in colour – of her.

Not only is she frightening beautiful in these pictures – like one taken in 1968, where she is Marianne, the symbol of France, draped in a tricolour flag – but they are, at the same time, such gorgeous photographs that living with them like this has little to do with narcissism and a lot to do with sheer beauty.

4

From the dining room and from the living room and from her bedroom too, there are large windows looking out to the bay. The first thing you realize when you stand in her house and stare out of those windows is just how exposed she is to the sea. And, with such easy access, it's hardly surprising that from the moment she moved in, La Madrague became a villa under siege.

In an era before the word 'stalking' became the popular term to describe the danger posed to famous people by obsessed fans, she was stalked and tracked, ferociously so. Swimmers waded ashore here – not unlike a mini-version of the Allied landings that took place a few miles down the coast – to station themselves on her little beach. They waited to take her photo, to speak to her, to try to touch her, to proposition her, to steal her beach towels, to insult her.

And they came in cars and tour buses, to park in front of her gates and wait for her, to try to peek through her fence, to ring her bell, hoping she would open the gate, and to climb over her gate and traipse around her property, hoping that she would welcome them.

And they came in little boats – literally thousands of them making up the annual armada – anchoring less than 50 feet off shore, waiting there to take her photo, or to call to her or just to gape at her.

The tour boats came as well. A two-hour adventure on the bay of St Tropez, with translations in six languages, for only 40 francs. Like those buses that roam Beverly Hills, their loudspeakers blaring outside the stars' homes, the tour boats stopped in front of her house. 'And now, the grand finale, ladies and gentlemen, La Madrague, the most famous villa in France, because it is the home of Brigitte Bardot. And if you're lucky, ladies and gentlemen, you can see her there, in a bikini, on her private beach.'

The guide would tell his passengers everything they wanted to know about her, broadcasting it over speakers so loud that she too could hear his high season spiel six times a day. As he read from his prepared script, the tourists would fight their way to the side of the tiny boat, pressed up against the rails with cameras and binoculars to catch sight of her, as if she was some friendly gorilla living in a cage at the zoo who swung from tree to tree whenever a crowd arrived with bananas.

And as the tourists fought for a better view, the boat would roll to that side. At times there would be so many people leaning over the side taking pictures, causing the boat to list so dangerously that the tour guide would have to promise his passengers, don't worry, please don't worry, we'll stay in front of Brigitte's house long enough for everyone to get their photos. Step back please, one group at a time, please step back. Brigitte's house isn't going anywhere and neither are we. Step back please.

It never ended.

They were there all the time, every day. The crowds and the onlookers and the tourists and the paparazzi.

Everyone came to get their photos, amateurs and professionals, but especially the professionals – hundreds upon hundreds of them from all over the world – swarming St Tropez like the perennial locust plague, taking up positions in front of her gate and on her beach and in her trees and atop nearby telephone poles or just off-shore, spending days and weeks waiting for a sight of her.

*   *   *

The harassment she has known has been both dangerous and ugly.

She's found total strangers camping out on her property, total strangers roaming through her house, and, once, a total stranger in her bed.

One night in August 1964, while she was entertaining guests at a dinner party, a band of thieves came ashore, commando-like in a rubber dinghy, and raided her house, stealing jewellery and cash.

She has had microphones hidden under her dock and people in

the nearby bushes with movie cameras secretly filming her. Total strangers have arrived at her gate bearing flowers, most of them thinking they're being very original when they announce their arrival as a delivery from a local florist. Others have shown up with wine or champagne, most of them thinking that no one before has ever been quite as gallant. One night, a young man arrived with a bottle of champagne and a cake, saying he intended to spend the night with her.

People would sneak in at night to swim in her pool, or to take pictures of themselves making love on her beach, or to use the showers, or to break into La Petite Madrague to use the toilet, or to expose themselves to her. A drunk once made his way into her living room at 5 a.m. installed himself on her couch and sat there, drinking from a bottle of her whisky, waking her by screaming, 'Brigitte, Brigitte, you whore, get your ass out here.'

Her phone would ring throughout the day and also in the middle of the night – she was constantly changing her unlisted number – with people on the other end making aberrant requests, threatening her, muttering obscenities. Sometimes she would get as many as 200 calls a day.

She has also received all sorts of weird things in her mail, including a letter covered in blood. The woman writing to her explained that she'd already slit her wrists and would kill herself if Brigitte didn't send her money.

That attempt at extortion was amateurish. A more serious effort was launched against her in 1961. France's so-called 'Secret Army' – the underground OAS – had pledged to overthrow Charles de Gaulle for his cowardice in abandoning French colonial North Africa. Shortly thereafter, a letter arrived for Bardot threatening that if she didn't make a contribution to the OAS of 50 million old francs ($10,800*) they would blow up La Madrague. Without any hesitation, she turned the letter over to the police, who

---

* Wherever currency equivalents are given, they are based on exchange rates at the time.

promptly put the house under armed surveillance. A few days later, after making the letter public, the police were able to identify the author as a conman who'd written similar notes to other well-known French people and used their money, not to help the OAS, but to buy himself a hotel in Switzerland.

A few years after that she started getting correspondence from a man in prison and, because he seemed pleasant enough, she responded to him. He wanted her advice on how he could learn to play the guitar. Thinking she was doing a good deed for a poor soul, she went out and bought him one of those 'teach yourself the guitar' books, which would show him some basic chords. It seemed innocent enough at the time. But the man took their friendship in a different vein and one day, while being transferred between prisons, he escaped. Before dawn the following morning, man-hunted by the police, he started banging on the front gate at La Madrague, demanding that she allow him to hide in one of her closets.

The police once arrested a guy waiting at the front gate of La Madrague with an Uzi submachine gun. Another time, a crazy threw a suitcase over the gate and inside there was a toy gun. One evening a strange man was hanging around the property and the police arrived in time to chase him away. The next night he was back, this time climbing on her roof, and when they arrested him he had a knife in his hand.

A fellow once forced himself inside her house, hit the caretaker and broke his nose. Another has, for several years running, shown up at her house, convinced that he's been invited. She's had him arrested several times and even offered to pay his fare home. While, some years ago, an American guy arrived like clockwork every summer, expecting to stay there with her. He even had the gall to tell his friends back in the States that he would be with Brigitte and had his mail forwarded to La Madrague.

Once, with friends taking the sun on her beach, a helicopter bearing the insignia of the French National Police flew overhead. Spotting a nude blonde woman, the pilot made a short circle and came back for another look. When the sunbather didn't move, the pilot came back for a third look. Then a fourth look. Then a fifth look. Each time he got more daring, coming lower, trying to attract her attention. Then, suddenly, he was too low and couldn't make his turn and he crashed into the sea.

On yet another occasion, she and friends were on the beach when they noticed an orange crate floating a few dozen yards off shore. Seeing rubbish in the sea had become much too commonplace, so no one in the group gave it a second thought. But an hour later the orange crate was still there, in exactly the same place. Curious why it hadn't floated by, one of Bardot's pals got up and walked into the water to fetch it. Underneath he found a man, in skin-diving equipment, sporting a long-lensed camera.

And then there was the night she was having dinner on the beach with friends when she thought she heard someone rustling in the bushes behind her house. An old chum, the French character actor André Pousse – who earned his reputation as a tough guy not only on the screen but during the war with the French underground – immediately got up and went around to the rear of the house. Stalking the intruder until he spotted a dark outline in the shrubs, he waited for his moment, then pounced, savagely grabbing the man and pinning him to the wall.

'What the hell do you want?' he demanded.

'I'm not hurting anyone.' The young man was petrified by the terrifying force of the furious Pousse. 'I'm not here to hurt anybody. Please. I don't even want to bother anyone . . .'

'What the hell do you want?'

'I was just here for the laundry.' He was scared to death. 'Just her wash. You know, her stuff.'

'What stuff?' Pousse kept him pinned to the wall.

'That stuff.' The fellow tried to point to the laundry line. 'There. That.'

Pousse looked. 'Her underwear?'

'Yes. Yes. That's all I wanted.' He tried to explain, 'I come here to steal her underwear. I cut it in small squares and tape the pieces to postcards and sell the postcards to tourists.'

*   *   *

At times, the only way she could get any peace from prying eyes was either to stay inside or to hang bed sheets across a small section of the beach and hide behind them. She would complain to the photographers, 'I am a prisoner.'

And while she complained – sometimes trying to reason with them, sometimes screaming at them – they would just stand there, taking more pictures.

None of this ever made much sense to her. 'I'd look the same every day. I'd wear the same bikini every day. And the photographers came every day to take more pictures. They never wanted yesterday's picture. One that was just the same, taken a week before, was never any good.'

It was just as bad, if not worse, whenever she left La Madrague. Going with her to a restaurant meant that people from all over the neighbourhood would either come in to stare at her, or congregate outside, waiting for her to pass by. Then they would walk with her along the street.

It was the same when she went into a club. Her arrival was treated like the main event of the evening – while, outside, more crowds would gather waiting for her.

She learned early on not to go anywhere alone. And if she needed to go somewhere and couldn't find anyone to come along, she simply wouldn't go.

One afternoon, while Pousse was at La Madrague, Bardot asked him to take her to a clothing store across from the Town Hall in St Tropez. He tried to beg off, saying shopping wasn't his thing. But she insisted and he gave in because he understood that if he didn't go with her she'd be forced to stay at home. So the two of them drove into town, parked near the port and walked through the empty, narrow streets to the shop.

Pousse thought no one had spotted them.

When they left the shop, no more than 15 minutes later, there were 40 people waiting for her on the curb outside. Word had spread that Bardot was there and Pousse had to make a path for her through the crowd.

At least in St Tropez, when she went somewhere with friends, although it was an inconvenience, she often got away unscathed. At other times, in other places, people tracking her have been absolutely terrifying. There were times when the only way she was able to get out of a hotel or off a movie set was to recruit a stand-in, dress her up to look like Brigitte Bardot and send her through one door so that, when the crowds followed the decoy, she could duck out the back. But that worked only the first few times she tried it. The crowds quickly learned to have all the entrances and exits covered.

'She didn't just suffer from being a star,' comments her chum of more than 30 years, Jo de Salerne, 'it was beyond that. It was infernal. She was hunted like an animal.'

In Italy, a madman twice tried to break into her hotel room in the middle of the night. He managed it the second time, terrifying her until her screams were answered and the police arrived.

In Geneva, on the first night of filming *Vie Privée*, the police had blocked off the area – keeping a huge crowd away from her – but one well-dressed woman somehow got through the security cordon and, when she found Brigitte, she started spitting on her. A few weeks later, still in Switzerland, she was shopping with a friend when a crowd cornered her and pushed the two of them through a jewellery store window.

In Portugal, attending a gala, crowds were so close to the entrance that as she walked in they mauled her and ripped the buttons off her clothes.

In Rome, filming there, someone broke a window in a women's toilet to snap a photo of her.

11

In London, to shoot *A Ravishing Idiot*, 500 people were waiting for her when she arrived on location, so that she couldn't even get out of her car. Hoping to clear the street, the police ordered her chauffeur to drive around the block. Half an hour later the crowd had swelled to 1,000 people and now the police ordered that she be removed from the area immediately. The London street scenes had to be shot in a French studio.

In Paris, doing nothing more than going out to buy a handbag, four carfuls of reporters and photographers followed her into the shop.

In Meribel one Christmas Eve, she was just leaving her apartment to go to midnight mass when an old woman, who'd been waiting outside for her, began screaming 'whore' and 'bitch' and then started throwing stones at her. It was Mary Magdalene all over again.

'Fame is fun for six months,' she says, 'a year at the most, then you get fed up, unless you're particularly stupid.'

Chapter Two

THE BOURGEOISIE

T he way they tell the joke in France, a man is looking to hire an assistant and three young women apply for the job. One is American. One is British. One is French. Unable to choose between them, he decides on a little test, intending to hire the one who comes up with the best answer. He explains to them, 'You are the only woman on a private jet with two dozen young men, all of whom are handsome, virile top-class athletes. The jet crashes in the desert. There is nobody around, except you and the men. What do you do?'

The American woman says right away, 'I can take care of myself. Where I come from, the frontier spirit lives on, so I'd lure all of the guys out of the plane, run back inside, barricade the door and wait until help arrives.'

'Fine,' the fellow says, turning to the British woman. 'And you?'

'Where I come from,' she explains, 'we have a long tradition of chivalry. You know, knights in shining armour and all that. So I'd find one bloke, the strongest among them, and convince him that he had to defend my honour. And I know he would.'

The fellow nods, approvingly. 'All right,' he says to the French woman. 'And you?'

She thinks about it for the longest time.

13

Growing impatient, the man wonders, 'Don't you understand the question?'

The French woman shrugs, 'Of course I understand the question. But what's the problem?'

*   *   *

When Billy and Joe went home to the States from World War II – 'The Big One' they called it in the days when we were still numbering wars – there was always a lot of winking and nudging whenever anyone mentioned France.

'The French', they coyly reminded each other, 'have sex tattooed on their brains.'

They'd seen the light during their two weeks in Paris, after they'd liberated the place and celebrated the German defeat with Mimi or Fifi, or maybe even both of them. Nudge, wink. Hey, these girls are wearing black underwear. What kind of American girl would do that? Holy key-rist, Joe, Cleveland was never like this.

But then, for Billy and Joe, this was the country that gave the world the Marquis de Sade, naked women on playing cards, banned books and the prefix to such words as kissing, postcards, letters and toast.

What they didn't know was how, in medieval times, women in France were completely subservient. Knighthood during the 12th and 13th centuries began the slow process of idealizing women. Troubadours sang of their favours and, in turn, women were pursued to great lengths. Sometime during the 14th century, France's aristocratic sisterhood invented a precursor to women's lib by forming what they called 'Courts of Love' to legislate relations between the sexes. In one case, for instance, the court ruled that a married woman who had refused the advances of a former lover was wrong in doing so. The judges wrote, 'The marriage bond does not exclude the rights of first love, unless the lady has decided to abstain completely from matters of love.'

The same court also decided that in arranged marriages –

something that still goes on today – real love cannot exist. So they encouraged, and perhaps greatly widened, the gap between romantic love and marriage. The next logical step was to turn marital infidelity into a national institution. *Cinq à sept* – five till seven – is what the French do while the British are taking tea and the Americans are shaking martinis. A Frenchman's mistress is free for those two hours because her husband is with his mistress, whose husband is with his mistress. It is, the French believe, a very civilized way of making a marriage work. At the same time, it is a totally acceptable alternative to marital boredom – a safety valve that, according to French logic, prevents divorce.

Napoleon did his bit for the national image when a few of his letters to Josephine turned up as collectors' items in auction houses. He was very explicit in his descriptions of what he liked to do with her. And equally explicit, when he divorced her, in explaining that she had the most beautiful private parts in the world, 'but she lied too much'.

Whereas the rest of the world makes heroes of centre fielders and centre forwards, the French adore their more infamous women. In the middle of the 1970s, instead of giving away dishes with each litre of fuel, a French gasoline company offered its customers small medals that contained historical sketches of history's greatest lovers.

And why not? Their influence was and is undeniable. Marie Antoinette married Louis XIV, not for his money or good looks, but for political gain – it was a marriage that strengthened the alliance between his France and her native Austria. And, although she wasn't born French, the lady quickly adapted. When her marriage still wasn't consummated after seven years – what the king was doing during that time is anyone's guess – she took up *cinq à sept* on a regular basis with any number of officers in the royal guard. She threw herself head first into a life of hedonism and didn't come up for air until she died.

Yet the grand prize for faithfully serving a French chief of state must go to Meg Steinhill. She was the *petite amie* – little friend

– of François Félix Faure. President from 1895 to 1899, Faure was a terrific aficionado of *cinq à sept* and frequently said of Mme Steinhill, 'She could shake any man's loins.'

Unwittingly, the poor man became proof positive of that. During one of their regular, early evening encounters in his office, he died in her arms. Faure is remembered in glowing terms – every city in France has a street named after him – but Mme Steinhill is an authentic hero.

Unlike Anglophones – who seem to have a difficult time accepting marital infidelity in general terms and the cavorting of politicians and public figures in specific terms – few people get upset about such things in France. When they do, it's usually for another reason, as was the case with Mme Caillaux, wife of the French Premier in 1914. The newspaper *Le Figaro* printed some letters the Premier had written to his mistress. Indignant, Mme Caillaux walked into the newspaper office, screamed at the offending editor, 'Leave my husband alone,' and shot him.

The French loved it.

De Gaulle might have been sexless – at least when it came to running around – but his prime minister and successor, Georges Pompidou, certainly wasn't. His name was linked to a scandal involving a photographer who took pictures of well-known people being 'otherwise occupied'. Nor did Valéry Giscard d'Estaing disappoint when he succeeded Pompidou. For months following his 1974 election, he was known to leave the Elysée Palace in the middle of the night, alone, to visit 'friends'. François Mitterand took over the mantle when he succeeded Giscard. Ever since, his name has been romantically linked, true or not, with just about every well-known woman in France.

The fact that French politicians might spend time sexually involved with women to whom they aren't married is understandable, seen in light of the fact that, for so many years, French women had no other means to exercise political power. They didn't get the vote until 1946. They couldn't even open a bank account without their husband or father as co-signatory until 1965.

Out of necessity, French women have been forced to confront the sexual culture that is their heritage. As a result, they do not automatically associate skin with sex. You need merely look at any beach in France to find women of all ages topless, and in some cases, bottomless too. They think nothing of baring their skin because they don't see it as a sexual gesture. They'll sit topless in public all afternoon. They'll get up and walk into the water topless, in full view of the boardwalk or street. But if you approach one of them to make small talk, the first thing they do is put their top back on.

That said, the French woman is a potpourri of contradiction. There is sex. And there is SEX. And the two can be very different. One has to do with love. The other is, traditionally, a prize. The term for sexual experimentation before the wedding is *pratiquer* – to practise, as in 'practice makes perfect'. And, while many foreigners never notice, in most of the better hotel rooms in France there's a wardrobe somewhere with a mirror that can be turned to face the bed. It's there if you know about it – not there if you don't.

In a culture where women have frequently held a place similar to that of the queen on the chessboard – the prize that cannot be taken without a battle – the French woman has learned to be elusive and mysterious, at times totally inconsiderate, at times childlike and seductive. She sulks. She broods. She slams doors. She yanks the prize out of reach, then offers it again, before teasing it out of reach – at least until she is ready to surrender it, on her own terms.

She can be totally at home with her own sexuality, and yet terrified of it. She may want to be cuddled and held and made love to with all the romantic ardour a man can muster. She may want poetry and candles and moonlight. But there seems to be something in her psyche that warns, before you can claim her, she is permitted to be juvenile, silly, nasty, cold,

17

unapproachable, mysterious, unliberated, dependent, brooding, predatory in the way she chooses her suitors, and brutal in the way she rejects them.

And, by God, she does it all with such a unique inbred style that the prize seems well worth the game.

Brigitte Anne-Marie Bardot was born French on 28 September 1934.

*   *   *

It was quite a year.

Cole Porter wrote 'You're the Top', Leopold became King of Belgium, the British Road Traffic Act introduced driving tests, Hitler and Mussolini met in Venice, the Soviet Union was admitted to the League of Nations, Raymond Poincaré died, Winston Churchill warned Parliament of the German air menace, Stalin began his purge with the assassination of Serge Kirov, Japan renounced its treaties with the USA and F. Scott Fitzgerald wrote *Tender is the Night*. Bonnie & Clyde were killed, Ralph Nadir was born, Sophia Loren was born, Edward Elgar died, Frederick Delius died, Marie Curie died, and Yuri Gagarin was born. Frank Capra won the Academy Award for *It Happened One Night*, Al Capone was installed at Alcatraz, the SS *Queen Mary* was launched, the FBI shot John Dillinger, the Dionne quintuplets were born, women wore shorts for the first time at Wimbledon, Max Baer beat Primo Carnera for the world heavyweight boxing title, Franklin Roosevelt devalued the dollar, and Mao Tse-tung began his 'Long March'.

Brigitte came into the world in her mother's bed, in her parents flat on the Place Violet, in the 15th arrondissement — a five minute walk from the Eiffel Tower, just in time for lunch. She weighed 7 lb 11½ ounces. In keeping with well-established bourgeois Parisian custom, the Bardots formally announced Brigitte's arrival in *Le Figaro* — the equivalent proclamation of social status that comes with similar listings in *The Times* of London or of New York.

Soon to be known around the house as 'Bricheton' and 'Bri-Bri', she'd chosen interesting parents.

Anne-Marie Mucel was born in Paris in 1912 but raised in Milan, in the midst of a very lively French community, where she was educated in the cultural pursuits of the era's proper young ladies – notably, music and dance. Called Toty by her friends, she was a good-looking woman with hauntingly dark-green eyes, elegant mannerisms and a strict attitude to behaviour.

Louis Bardot was born in Paris in 1896 and graduated with an engineering degree from the Ecole Supérieure Electro-Technique. Afterwards, his father brought him into the family business, Charles Bardot & Company, manufacturers of liquid air and acetylene. Called Pilou by his friends, he was a tall man who wore his white hair combed back, and offset his linear features with round glasses. He spoke well, but his patrician bearing was deceptive. He was very humorous and considered, by most people, to be good company. Later in life he grew grapes to make his own wine and took up sailing.

The couple met at a dinner party in Milan, early in 1933. Pilou, who'd gone to Italy on business, was sitting at one end of a big table, being funny, as he often was. Because he was older than the others, everyone seemed a bit in awe of him.

Especially Toty.

She summoned up the courage to move from her end of the table to a place next to him, telling this much older man, 'I want to sit closer to the sunshine.'

It was, as the French say, a *coup de foudre* – an instant crush – which quickly blossomed into something much more serious. They were married on 3 August 1933, in Paris, at a Catholic church in St Germain des Prés.

By the time Brigitte arrived, Pilou was chairman and managing director of the family business. His offices were at 39 Rue Vineuse, in the centre of the capital, near the Place du Trocadero – although he spent much of his time at the company factory in the suburb of Aubervilliers. Like most things he did in life, Pilou took his business responsibilities seriously and was at work most mornings by six. But in spirit he was a dreamer and Toty would always say that Pilou went through life with a rose in his hand.

The sort of man who bowed and kissed ladies' hands – a genuine, old school romantic – he always carried a small notebook with him in which he jotted down whatever thoughts flew into his mind. Sometimes it was a little anecdote about the family. Sometimes it was a love letter he'd leave at the side of the bed for Toty to find when she woke up. But most of the time he wrote poetry and wrote it well. Using his family nickname as a *nom de plume*, he published several volumes of poetry, including *Vers En Vrac* – Verse in Bulk – which earned him the Vauquelin Prize from the French Academy of Letters. He also held the Légion d'Honneur and the Croix de Guerre as a veteran of World War I.

Though poetry was his great passion, he soon developed an affinity with a small film camera that he bought when Brigitte was just a year old, and long before she knew that the cinema existed, she was already starring in Pilou's home movies.

Cared for by a succession of nannies, Brigitte's earliest years were orderly and correct. Her first governess was Italian and today she speaks that language fluently. She also speaks English, although she is hesitant to do so, using the excuse that it's too rusty. However, she is clearly more at ease with the language than she admits. Asking for the English translation of the French word *thym* and being told it is thyme, she instantly puns, 'As in, thyme is money?'

From the Place Violet the family, plus a few cats, moved to an apartment along the Avenue de La Bourdonnais, in the shadow of the Eiffel Tower, and then to an even larger flat at 1 Rue de la Pompe, across the Seine in the 16th arrondissement, the quarter known as Passy – the heart of bourgeois Paris. They had nine rooms on the fifth floor, formally decorated with period French furniture. There was an enormously long hallway running straight through the centre of the apartment, from the large entrance hall all the way back to the servants' quarters and the kitchen. The building was grand and solid – it was a very chic address – although the old hydraulic elevator shook the entire apartment.

Looking for Pilou's son and heir, the Bardots tried again. Convinced they'd have a boy, Toty never considered anything but boys' names. When her second daughter was born in May 1938, she and Pilou settled on the most obvious name that came to mind – a combination of Marie, for Toty, and Jeanne, for Toty's mother. So Marie-Jeanne is the name Brigitte's sister was christened with, except that on an official paper someone made a spelling mistake and listed it as Marie-Jane. It hardly matters because, like everyone else in the family, she too got a nickname.

Even today, Marie-Jeanne is always called Mijanou.

'Being Brigitte Bardot's sister', she confesses, 'was never easy. But that didn't start when Brigitte became a movie star, it began when I was an hour old. She recently told me that when I was born she was very jealous. I can understand that. After all, she was the only child for the first four years of her life and all of a sudden I showed up to spoil that for her. What's more, because my parents were hoping for a son, because there was all this expectation that I would be a boy, when Brigitte suddenly saw that she had a sister, when she realized there was another little girl in the house, she wasn't willing to accept that.'

Typical of a first child faced with a baby to rival her parents' affection, Brigitte protected her own territory.

'But then', Mijanou continues, 'she's always been someone who's done that. Perhaps some of it stems from the fact, that where my mother was concerned, there wasn't enough tenderness to share. I'm not saying she wasn't a tender woman. But she was very strict and could be very tough. Like Brigitte, she was filled with contradictions. Looking back, I think that as a little girl Brigitte felt a lack of affection. I know that I did. One result was that we share a dislike for being alone. Neither one of us can live in solitude. I'm certain that comes straight from our childhood. So when I arrived and took a small piece of our mother's affection, because it was already to limited and therefore so vital for Brigitte, it was more than just sibling rivalry. For Brigitte, it was a matter of survival. I was taking her oxygen.'

In those formative years, both girls were sent to Catholic school, and watched over after school by a fearless governess whom they called, somewhat bizarrely, 'La Big.' Because Toty was concerned that her daughters' friends should come from the proper social class and meet her own rigorous standards, the girls weren't exposed to a lot of other children. Brigitte grew up well mannered, quiet and very shy.

By her own admission, 'When I was a little girl, I used to annoy my mother because she would make me pretty dresses and I would refuse to wear them. So she'd punish me, refuse to let me go out if I didn't comb my hair and dressed properly. I've always been disorderly.'

In those days, she saw herself as a homely little girl with thin hair who needed to wear glasses because of astigmatism, who needed to wear braces to straighten her teeth, and who suffered for long periods with allergic rashes. 'I was a very frozen, solemn kind of child.'

Years later, she would be equally critical of her own looks. 'My nose is a very bad nose. When I meet a man it wrinkles up, as if I was sniffing a bowl of milk. My mouth is not a good mouth. My upper lip is heavier and more swollen than the other. My cheeks are too round and my eyes are too small.'

Toty's father was a heavy-set, white-bearded man with a laughing face whose real name was Isidore, who called himself Leon, but who was never called anything except 'Boum Papa' by his granddaughters. He was in the insurance business and stayed in Italy long after his company had asked him to come back to France, because Milan was where La Scala was and Boum Papa loved opera. His wife Jeanne was called 'Mamie' by her granddaughters and she became a major influence on Brigitte's life.

Only nine years older than Pilou, Mamie took extremely good

care of herself and paid a lot of attention to how she looked. She always tried to set an example by being perfectly dressed, perfectly turned out. There was never any doubt that Brigitte was her favourite and that the feeling was mutual. All these years later, longtime friends of the family still speak about Jeanne Mucel with great affection, about how special a woman she was, about how she worshipped Brigitte and about how Brigitte could make her grandmother melt.

Pilou's father, Charles Bardot, was an engineer and metallurgist who passed away in 1941. A few years later, when Pilou's mother Hyacinthe fell ill, she moved into the apartment at Rue de la Pompe where Toty could care for her. And she too had a unique side. At the Paris Exhibition – the 1889 fair for which M Eiffel built his tower – she spotted a large wooden chalet that was on display as a model home in the Norwegian pavilion. She fell in love with it and, quite eccentrically, decided she wanted to own it.

Just about the last style of architecture you expect to find in France, Charles bought it for her as a wedding present. She then had it taken apart piece by piece, transported it to Louveciennes – just outside Paris – where she'd been born, and rebuilt it there.

A stunning old house where Brigitte and Mijanou spent a good part of their childhood – going with their parents every weekend from Easter to the autumn, and also one month each summer – it is, nicely enough, still in the family.

As the girls got older, they began spending winter holidays skiing in Megève and a few weeks each summer in the south of France, often staying with family friends in a small village, not far from St Tropez, called La Croix Valmer. Those friends had a property on the side of a hill, where three white marble homes had been built before the war, then largely destroyed during it. In the middle of fields, surrounded by rose bushes and laurel trees, there were no doors, there were no windows and there was no furniture. They were lovingly remembered as 'delicious and poetic days'. The parents slept in one of the houses, the children slept in the second, while the third served as the communal dining room. The nearby beach was totally empty, just for them.

When they were old enough, both girls were enrolled at Hattemar — a private school school favoured by the Parisian bourgeoisie. It was indicative of the comfort that surrounded their youth. However, the education Brigitte got there left her, she believes, largely unprepared for life in the real world. Among the subjects never discussed was sex. That claim was reinforced many years later by her first husband, Roger Vadim, who loved to tell people that Brigitte was so still naive about such things at the age of 17 that she honestly believed mice laid eggs.

In keeping with their social status, and considering the era, Pilou and Toty brought their daughters up in a formal way, hoping to instil in them a strict sense of Victorian values, which was reinforced by Toty's severe discipline.

And severe is the proper word.

One afternoon, when Brigitte was seven and Mijanou was three, the girls were playing at home when they bumped into a table, accidentally breaking an expensive oriental vase. Toty flew into a blind rage. Brigitte received 50 spankings. Mijanou 25. Toty screamed that this was not their home, that they were living in her home and that if she wanted to she could throw them out. She warned that, at her whim, they could find themselves on the street.

Understandably, the girls were panic stricken.

From that moment on, Toty said, they could no longer use the familiar '*tu*' form for the word 'you' when they spoke to their parents. From that moment on, they would have to address their parents with the formal '*vous*', which is usually reserved for strangers and people who are not friends.

In fact, both girls were so marked by the intensity of the punishment that for the rest of their parents' lives – while they use '*tu*' freely with just about everybody else – they continued to address Pilou and Toty as '*vous*'.

For Brigitte, the incident was a turning point. 'I no longer felt as though we were their children. I didn't feel as if I was in my home, but in my parents' home.'

With one cracked vase, her world had abruptly changed.

'She felt unloved,' notes her second husband, Jacques Charrier. 'She told me, and I know she's told lots of other people, she felt from that moment on she'd lost her parents. And from the way she's repeated that story to so many people, you can see what an important moment it was in her life.'

.   .   .

If she didn't know much about sex, at least by the time she reached puberty she was well coached in other areas – specifically those that her mother believed were more in keeping with the way a young girl from a proper family in the 16th arrondissement should be raised.

Brigitte once remarked, 'My parents wanted me to become a very well-educated, cultured and, I think, rather boring young girl.'

Having herself been a dancer, Toty encouraged both Brigitte and Mijanou to appreciate music and take up dance, and both of them were shipped off to class at the age of seven to study with Marcelle Bourgat, a former star with the Paris Opera. But whereas Mijanou showed little talent, Brigitte proved to be good on her feet and displayed enough natural flair and grace that she quickly progressed to more serious classes.

Friends these days say that if Brigitte was the beautiful one, then Mijanou was the brainy one. But that's not quite true. Mijanou was a very pretty young girl, who turns out – at least according Jacques Charrier – to have been the family favourite. 'Her parents doted on her.'

Because Mijanou was also treated, in many ways, like the son Pilou never had, dance was soon replaced by academia.

'The thing was,' she explains, 'mother decided not to put all her eggs in the same basket. I was especially good at maths, so she prodded me to study.' Mijanou gained her French *baccalauréat* when she was only 15, several years ahead of her contemporaries.

At the same time, Brigitte – who was, admittedly, a lazy student at school – became more and more intent on a dancing career. In 1947, only just 13, she was permitted to take the entrance exam for the distinguished Conservatoire Nationale de Danse. Places were limited and based on very rigid criteria. Several hundred young hopefuls auditioned – almost all of whom were older and more experienced and had received more formal training than Brigitte. Yet she was one of only eight chosen. So for the next three years, three afternoons a week, she studied first with Jeanne Schwartz and then with the brilliant, but tyrannical, Boris Kniaseff.

A curious man, who might well have been slightly crazy, the Russian-born Kniaseff is remembered today as one of the great teachers. He himself had been a star of the Paris stage in the 1920s, coming to it at the age of 24, which is late in life for a dancer. More importantly, he was a man who knew how to mould dancers and, through that unique talent, Kniaseff created an entire generation of stars after the war.

One of the girls he helped to establish – three years Brigitte's senior, who would go from ballet straight into a leading role with Gene Kelly in the film *American in Paris* – was Leslie Caron.

'Brigitte was long and thin and elegant with her gestures. We called her *Bichette* [the French word for doe]. She wasn't very muscular. Nor was she very sure of herself on her feet. But then, she was very young.'

Caron notes that, even though 'Bichette' had such a beautiful dancer's body, 'she was lazy. She wasn't sparkling and fast. She had talent and she had a gorgeous stature. She could have been a wonderful dancer if she'd been willing to work at it. But that would have meant she'd have had to work damn hard. Kniaseff would parade around the studio with a stick in his hand and never hesitated to hit a girl with it if she didn't respond. I recall him practically beating her with it because she was slow and always did it the easy way.'

By being so terribly demanding, Kniaseff transformed Brigitte. He taught her how to move. And that's stayed with her for the rest of her life.

'She has always had the most wonderful walk in the world,' Andre Pousse maintains. 'When she walks by, everyone stops to look. Even now. And that has nothing to do with the fact that they're looking at Brigitte Bardot. She could be absolutely nobody and they'd still look. That's her dancer's training. Everything about her is perfect when she walks.'

French movie star Jeanne Moreau agrees. 'Just watching her walk was just like listening to great music.'

In an odd way, that's presented some unique problems for Bardot. To avoid crowds, she's gone through entire wardrobes of disguises. She's put on wigs and scarves and donned huge glasses to mask her face. But the minute she starts to walk, the instant she takes two steps, crowds of fans and the paparazzi could always tell it was her.

There was no way she could disguise her walk. And part of that is down to Kniaseff. But Christine Gouze-Renal, her friend of 40 years and a woman who produced several films for her, attributes a portion of that to Bardot's innate elegance.

'She is naturally elegant. Incredibly so. It's something I've never seen before with anyone else. You could put the most stupid hat on her head and dress her in the most awful clothes and make her up to look ugly and get her to bend down on her hands and knees and sweep the floor, and she'd still be beautiful, still be wonderful, still be sexy, still be astonishingly elegant.'

The author Simone de Beauvoir spotted that same quality too, very early on, dubbing Bardot the most perfect specimen of the ambiguous nymph.

'Seen from behind, her slender, muscular, dancer's body is almost androgynous. Femininity triumphs in her delightful bosom. The long voluptuous tresses of Melisande flow down to her shoulders, but her hairdo is that of a negligent waif. The line of her lips forms a childish pout, and at the same time those

27

lips are very kissable. She goes about barefooted, she turns up her nose at elegant clothes, jewels, girdles, perfumes, make-up at all artifice. Yet her walk is lascivious and a saint would sell his soul to the devil merely to watch her dance.'

At the beginning of the 1948 season, when Leslie Caron and a few other girls from Kniaseff's class went on to dance with the Ballet de Champs Elysées, Brigitte became a regular feature backstage – always accompanied by Pilou – watching the company work, trying to learn.

Jean Robin, one of the ballet's directors, remembers her very distinctly. 'I certainly do. She was only 13 or 14 years old. I can still see her standing in the wings with her father. She was a stalk of wheat, tall and thin, not very pretty but very timid. She hardly ever spoke.'

Any hope she might have had of finding a permanent place in the company evaporated when the Ballet left for a tour of Egypt later that year. There's no telling what her life might have been like had she been invited to join them, and had her parents allowed her to go. Some people are convinced she would have emerged as a great French ballerina.

As it was, she continued studying with Kniaseff, until her dancing career took a very odd turn.

*   *   *

France after the war was a country slowly waking up from a prolonged and horrible nightmare. Everything had to be rebuilt, not least of all the national psyche. It was a darkness, into which light now came. And after the usual blinking, after the time it took to get used to the sudden brightness, the rebuilding began.

In the midst of a mini cultural renaissance that slowly dawned in Paris – and would come to be known as St Germain des Prés – there was a resurgence of fashion. And in 1948, Toty decided to open a small hat boutique, using two rooms of the flat on the Rue de La Pompe.

One of the new designers she admired was a man named Jean Barthet and, when he mentioned to her that he was planning to launch his first post-war collection, she suggested he might consider putting together a fashion show using a ballet theme. Her idea was that he could introduce each hat with classical music and a dancer instead of the usual model. And, just in case he was interested, she said, she knew the perfect dancer.

So Brigitte was hired.

Each new hat in the Barthet collection, which premiered at an art gallery on the Faubourg St Honoré at the end of January 1949, appeared to music on top of a slightly faltering 14 year old, dressed in a tutu, a black ribbon and a rose corsage. Unfortunately for the 14 year old, she says, 'I felt very silly.'

But that first modelling assignment led to another. Toty had a friend name Marie-France de la Villehuchette, who was editor-in-chief of the magazine *Jardin des Modes*. She heard that Brigitte had done this fashion show, knew that Brigitte danced and rang Toty to say she would be delighted if Brigitte could model for a special supplement the magazine was putting out. Toty didn't mind, Brigitte liked the idea and the layout was published 22 March 1949.

That particular photo spread wound up on the desk of Helen Gordon-Lazareff, the founder and legendary editor of *Elle* magazine. And nothing might have happened with it had not one of the professional models she'd planned on using for a photo session come down with some illness. In a mild panic, needing someone right away, she phoned her friend Marie de la Villehuchette, said she thought the model was stunning and wondered who it was. So, Marie de la Villehuchette gave her Toty's phone number and Helen Gordon-Lazareff dialled it to ask if Madame Bardot's daughter was available at such short notice.

This time Toty had her doubts. It was one thing to help out an old family friend. It was another for a young girl from a proper

Parisian family to get involved in something as commercial as professional modelling. Of course, when Brigitte heard about it she pleaded with her mother to let her do it and, in the face of Brigitte's determination, Toty gave in.

However, she agreed only on condition that Brigitte's name not be used.

Elle magazine paid Brigitte 500,000 old francs ($140) for her profile and silhouette, which appeared on the cover of the 2 May 1949 issue. True to her word, Gordon-Lazareff credited the model's name as simply, 'BB'.

*   *   *

For a girl who was not yet 15 to find herself on the cover of one of France's most prestigious magazines was quite an adventure.

Travelling on a bus one afternoon, she came face to face with a woman reading that edition of *Elle*. The woman didn't recognize the cover-girl in front of her and Brigitte found herself getting angry. To make up for it, she delighted in leading small troupes of her friends home from Hattemar past the neighbourhood newsstands so that she could point to the magazine and gleefully announce, that's me.

And even that might have been the end of the story had the actor Daniel Gélin and his actress wife Daniele Delorme known where to find a babysitter.

They'd given over a room in their flat at 44 Avenue Wagram, not far from the Arc de Triomphe, to a young, handsome, dark-haired friend who was determined to make his career in the movies – a budding scriptwriter who only found enough peace and quiet at their place to write his screenplays when he shut himself in the toilet.

Normally they wouldn't have asked him to babysit their young son Xavier, but they had to go out and they couldn't get anyone else, so he said okay. And while taking care of the Gélin baby, he happened to spot Daniele's copy of *Elle*.

The girl on the cover startled him.

The next day, when he went back to work as the assistant to film director Marc Allégret, he took the magazine with him. Using Allégret's name, he badgered the staff at *Elle* magazine into revealing 'BB's' name and address, and the next thing Toty knew, a letter arrived from Allégret saying he wished to give her daughter a screen test.

Until that point, although Brigitte liked the idea of modelling all right, she was still hoping to dance professionally. But this sounded like fun.

However, Toty had grave reservations about something as crass as film. What's more, the awkward little girl with glasses and braces and eczema was blossoming into a graceful, attractive young woman with a statuesque body. Toty could just imagine what pitfalls awaited a young woman like that in show business. Brigitte would be 16 before her parents would allow her to go out at night unchaperoned. And that was only once a month, and even then she had to be home by midnight.

The ever-protective Pilou was even less convinced about the propriety of this than his wife. 'I will not', he put his foot down, 'have gypsies in my family.'

But Brigitte wanted to go.

When it was clear that her parents were dead set against it, she marshalled her forces and called in heavyweight reinforcements. Mamie immediately went to bat for her, coercing Boum Papa into arguing Brigitte's case. So Boum Papa assured his own daughter that allowing Brigitte to meet a director simply to find out if there was any possibility of film work would not make her a lost child. Which is how his own daughter finally agreed that her daughter could meet this man, Marc Allégret.

An appointment was arranged and Brigitte arrived, with her mother in tow, at Allégret's seventh-floor apartment on the rue Lord Byron, a couple of blocks from the Gelin's place.

It was Allégret's young, handsome, dark-haired assistant who opened the door.

His name was Roger Vadim.

'The first time I saw her she was still 14 and there was no doubt in my mind that she was from another planet. That she'd come from another dimension. I said to myself, my God, this girl is an extraterrestrial.'

Chapter Three

VADIM

Igor Plemiannikov named his son Vadim when the boy was born in Paris in 1928, but French law required a French name – there used to be a list of official names at every City Hall and if you didn't choose a name that was on the list you couldn't get a name – so he stuck Roger onto the front of it and eventually, when Roger was old enough, he dropped the Plemiannikov because it was too difficult to pronounce, and before long everyone else dropped the Roger because his soul seemed more Russian than French, and ever since he's gone through life just being called Vadim.

His father came from Kiev and had fought with the Bolsheviks at the age of 14 before emigrating to France, studying political science and working his way up in the French diplomatic corps to become a Vice Consul. He died of a heart attack at the age of 34, at the breakfast table, in front of his then eight-year-old son.

His mother, Marie-Antoinette Ardilouze, was French, and after her short-lived second marriage Vadim drifted off on his own – now in his late teens – trying to make his way through the world, living by his wits. He wouldn't take a full-time job, so he wrote screenplays and did some magazine journalism and told people that he hoped someday to be a film director.

It was when he went to work for Marc Allégret that he found the father he'd lost.

'Marc was a cultivated, delicate, attentive man who enjoyed being with young people and encouraged them,' Vadim says. 'He was the sort of man who doesn't exist any more, perhaps too delicate and too sensitive to win in a modern jungle.'

Allégret's younger brother Yves was less refined, tougher, had harder edges and because of that was more successful. Yet Vadim agrees that Marc was a better director and probably one of the three or four best film-makers working in France before the war.

'His problem was that he couldn't adapt to the changing style of French cinema. He was overly concerned with little details, very hesitant, incapable of making even the smallest decision. He'd go into a total panic when it came to important decisions.'

It was, however, Marc Allégret, and not Roger Vadim, who discovered Brigitte Bardot.

'Marc was an aesthete, an eclectic man with a good sense for young people. He made a number of important finds. He first brought Gérard Philippe and Michele Morgan to the screen. Later he found Jean-Paul Belmondo and Jean Pierre Aumont. And he didn't only help actors. He helped young writers and, in my case, directors too. The list is very long. He demonstrated that sensibility, that nose he had for talent, when I showed him the photo of Brigitte on the cover of *Elle*. He spotted something immediately. I'd just written a scenario for him called *Les Lauriers Sont Coupées* (The Laurels Are Cut) where the principal role was a young girl in her mid to late teens. He wanted her for that. He was the one who said, if she's as good as I think she will be, we must test her.'

When Brigitte arrived at Allégret's apartment for that first meeting, Toty was determined to see that nothing got in the way of her daughter's dancing career. As it turned out, her cause was greatly enhanced because Monsieur Allégret didn't like Madame Bardot. He found her dominating and didn't appreciate the way she so blatantly tried to shield her still innocent little girl from the clutches of evil bohemia.

Unbeknownst to Toty, Brigitte was struck by Vadim. 'In my

life, I'd never met a man so handsome, so relaxed, so informal. But I never could have imagined that I would have fallen in love with him.'

Now at Vadim's insistence, Allégret agreed to go ahead with the test. To help Brigitte prepare for it, Vadim volunteered to be her coach. They began meeting in the afternoons – at that stage it was all very platonic – until the day before her screen test, by which time she was so nervous that she was breaking out in spots.

The following day, when Allégret watched her in front of a camera, he decided, 'She talks as if she's wearing her mother's dentures and I loathe the way she laughs.' There was no way he could see of turning that girl into a movie actress. But, then, he said the same thing when he tested Leslie Caron for the same role.

What happened next was the first in a long string of odd coincidences, where Brigitte's and Vadim's lives would cross.

When she didn't get the part, Allégret figured that was the end of her. After all, she was just another girl hoping to get into the movies. But Vadim was infatuated. Several years before, he'd begun writing a novel – it was called *The Wise Sophie* – and, in his mind, Brigitte was Sophie.

'It was incredible. She was speaking straight off the pages of my story. When I heard the way she spoke, heard the way she expressed herself as a free spirit, I couldn't believe it. Brigitte speaks in a very particular, in a unique way and that was exactly the same way that Sophie spoke. When I made up Sophie I believed she didn't exist, that she couldn't possibly exist. But here she was. I gave her the manuscript and when Brigitte read it, she recognized herself too.'

He was smitten with her – particularly charmed by her innocence – but was also smart enough to have caught on to her situation. He'd seen her mother in action and knew that Toty wasn't going to permit anyone as slick as him to court her daughter. So for the next several months, he tried to push her

35

out of his mind. Then one Saturday afternoon, sitting around Daniel Gelin's flat alone, slightly depressed and with nothing to do, he started thinking about whom he could call. Gelin's phone had been disconnected and Vadim, who was broke, had only one phone token. He took himself to the local café and started dialling. But none of his pals was in. No one answered. Next he tried some girl friends. None of them was home either. That's when he thought of ringing Brigitte. He guessed that, if her mother answered, she'd hang up on him. But with no one else around, he sacrificed his last token and dialled her number.

It was Brigitte who picked up the phone.

He explained that he was just calling to say hello and she got all excited, saying that her parents were out of town for the weekend, that she was there with her sister, a friend and her grandmother, and then asked, why not come over.

Vadim walked into Brigitte's place – not wearing a tie, and with his hair longer than fashion dictated – and the old lady was anything but impressed. He and Brigitte spent the afternoon together, while Mamie kept a keen eye on him. Not only did she see this 'bohemian' as a threat to her granddaughter's virtue, she also feared he might disappear with the family silver.

Nor were Pilou and Toty thrilled when he showed up again a few days later. His unpressed slacks and uncut hair were only two of the points they had against him. More critical was the fact that he didn't have a real job. That immediately ruled him out of their plans for their daughter's future.

However, Brigitte had her own ideas and, much to her parents' chagrin, Vadim quickly became a regular feature in their lives. Except that by the time she was 15 – now blindly in love with Vadim – she ran smack into the brick wall that was her parents' hankering to protect her from this older, more sophisticated, obviously dangerous man.

Hearing the ideas he was putting into her impressionable head – all about movies and existentialism and sex – Toty and Pilou had every reason to suspect Vadim's intentions. Their eldest daughter didn't want to know what they thought, believing herself capable, even then, of handling this relationship. So the stage was set for a major confrontation.

What particularly troubled Brigitte was that Toty and Pilou always, somehow, seemed to know what was going on. She soon came to believe that whenever her parents objected to Vadim's presence it was because Mijanou had betrayed her, had gone behind her back to tell their parents all of Brigitte's secrets.

For instance, the first time Vadim kissed Brigitte – it was on the Métro – Toty knew all about it within hours of the event and Brigitte was convinced that it was Mijanou who'd announced the news.

These days, the controversy rages on – whether or not Mijanou told Toty about Brigitte and Vadim – to the point of hysterical laughter between the sisters.

And these days Mijanou is willing to confess that, well, perhaps she did tell their parents a few things. Although she denies relating the story of the Métro kisses and steadfastly maintains that the really big secrets were the ones she kept to herself.

'I thought Vadim was terrific,' Mijanou says. 'I found him marvellous. He was always very nice to me. I remember that he was intrigued with my room because it was very modern while Brigitte's room was more conservatively furnished. I also remember, quite distinctly, that there was plenty going on I never told my mother about.'

Such as the afternoon she came home from school to discover, embarrassingly, that her sister and Vadim were in fact – as she puts it – 'a very loving couple'.

*   *   *

At the age of 15, Brigitte announced to her parents that she and 'Vava' would be married.

Faced with such a declaration, Pilou and Toty were not merely shocked, they were driven to denouncing the engagement as momentary foolishness. They gave her every reason in the world to think about other things besides marriage. They wanted her to get her *baccalauréat* – her high school leaving certificate. They wanted her to continue with her dancing. And they stipulated that she not mention marriage until she was 18, because, in their Victorian eyes, marriage was a serious and irrevocable step. It was all the worse that she intended to marry someone so unbefitting.

Vadim's promises to Brigitte that everything would be all right fell on deaf ears. The two began meeting regularly at a small studio apartment owned by his friend Christian Marquand, at 15 rue Bessano, off the Champs-Elysées. She wanted to get married right away. He constantly reassured her – and reassured her parents – that he loved her, but only Brigitte was willing to listen to that.

On those occasions when they couldn't see each other – because Toty or Pilou managed to ground her or refused to let him into the apartment – they wrote to each other, with Brigitte often signing her letters 'Sophie'.

Understandably, Pilou and Toty applied what pressure they could to keep her from making what they believed to be such a serious mistake. Although Pilou took it a bit far when he threatened Vadim with a gun.

He kept a revolver hidden in a cupboard above his desk at home and one night showed it to Vadim, warning him that if he ever touched his little girl, he'd use it.

That Vadim managed to live through those years, Mijanou adds, is proof positive of her loyalty to Brigitte's most intimate secrets. 'Trust me, Pilou's pistol did not have the desired effect.'

* * *

Neither did some vague promise from her parents that she might be permitted to marry her Vava when she was 18.

Brigitte accused her father of being 'an old-fashioned man from the days of the dinosaurs'. But neither Pilou nor Toty would give in. And the harder Brigitte tried to force their hand, the more they resisted.

The major confrontation came a few months after Pilou had shown Vadim his revolver. On his way to spend a few weeks in Nice – he explained that he needed some peace and quiet to work on a screenplay – Vadim stopped at Brigitte's to say goodbye. She announced that her parents were in one of their moods – 'You cannot see Vadim any more' – and that she'd been arguing with them. He tried to reassure her that everything would be all right but she seemed despondent, almost defeated.

That night on the train, he says, a strange feeling swept across him. 'I didn't yet recognize it. I didn't yet know what it meant.' When the train stopped at La Roche Migène, he almost got off to phone her. A week later he received a letter from her that explained his premonition.

Mijanou had got it into her head that she wanted to see the lights of Paris. No one else in the family was interested but the 12 year old made such a nuisance of herself that Toty and Pilou finally consented.

Feeling especially lonely and dejected, Brigitte refused to join them.

So Toty and Pilou and Mijanou left her alone in the apartment and went to see the lights. Legend has it that Mijanou then claimed she was cold and that her parents brought her home to get a coat. It isn't true. Pilou drove his wife and youngest daughter on a quick tour of the lights of Paris and, having decided that they'd seen enough, announced it was time to go home.

The three of them rode the old hydraulic lift upstairs, and walked into the apartment. When Brigitte didn't greet them, Toty called out for her.

There was no answer.

A sulking Mijanou stayed where she was while Pilou and Toty walked down through the long narrow hallway looking for their daughter. They found her in the kitchen, on her knees, with her head in the oven and the gas turned on.

Again, legend has it that she was already unconscious. But Mijanou says that, when her mother screamed, she remembers rushing down the hall and coming into the kitchen to find Brigitte sitting up and talking to her parents.

A doctor was called. He examined the girl, then explained to her parents that, had they been delayed by as little as 15 minutes, Brigitte would have been dead.

*   *   *

Vadim had been in love before. There was a girl he met once, who was running away from someone and he took her in – his bird with a broken wing – and they spent three weeks together before she flew away.

'I knew about love and what it felt like to be in love before I met Brigitte. But the way in which we showed our love to each other, the way in which we were in love for many years, that was very special and I'd never known that before. I don't think I've ever known that same thing since, either. Not in that particular way.'

But then, strange ties bound Brigitte and Vadim.

One night, several years later, after they'd split up, he was in Torremolinos, hallucinating with a high fever, when he felt that feeling again – the same feeling he'd sensed on the train to Nice – and he phoned her in Paris. There was no answer, so he called her father.

'I know that twins can experience some sort of telepathic communication and I've had it happen several times, but only with Brigitte. That night, I asked Pilou to go over to her apartment. I don't know why. I just had this feeling. He said she'd been at his place for dinner and that she seemed fine. But I said no, he had to go over there right away. He did, and found her unconscious, having swallowed too many sleeping pills.'

Now living with Christian Marquand on the very fashionable Ile St Louis – in an eighth floor flat with a spectacular view – Vadim

40

was positively resolute about becoming a film director and, in his head, he'd set a goal to make it before the age of 35. In those days, the average age of film directors in France was somewhere between 50 and 65. There were young directors doing underground films, but it was unthinkable that anyone in his 20s would be permitted by a producer to direct a feature film.

Vadim, though, counted on his chances of breaking the mould. He told himself he had the drive and the talent. He knew he also had a sensational woman who loved him and he could plainly see how that sensational woman fitted perfectly into his plan for life.

So Vadim, who was on call to Marc Allégret whenever he needed an assistant, who was writing screenplays that he tried to get produced, and who was also working as a journalist for *Paris Match* – to pay the rent – now took on the task of turning Brigitte Bardot into Brigitte Bardot.

At his insistence, she went to acting school to study with René Simon, where young hopefuls spent as much time being seen as learning their craft. She and Simon didn't get along, and, despite Vava's assertion that Simon's school was one of those places actresses could get discovered, she dropped out after a few months. Before long, Hattemer and Boris Kniaseff also disappeared into her past.

In the meantime, as a couple, Pilou and Toty had an interesting cross-section of friends, including a number of people who were involved with the fashion business.

One of them was Marie Jeanne Hurst, who designed *haute couture* clothes for teenage girls at her boutique 'Virginie'. She hired Brigitte and Mijanou to model for her. Mijanou, then 13, would get very nervous and, although she continued to model every now and then, didn't like it at all. But Brigitte took to it and was very good at it.

Another family friend was André-Pierre Tarbes, who'd just created the perfume house Carven. One of his sideline businesses was to supply entertainment for French cruise ships – singers, magicians, masters-of-ceremonies and dancers – and, knowing that she was studying with Kniaseff, he offered Brigitte her first and only contract as a professional dancer.

Tarbes booked her for a 15-day cruise called 'Easter in the Sun' on the *Amiral de Grasse*. The ship left Le Havre on 5 April 1952 bound for the Atlantic Islands – Madeira, the Canaries and the Azores – with Brigitte considered a working member of the crew. She was paid 400,000 old francs ($112) for the trip, and shared a cabin with the famous Parisian model, Capucines, who'd been hired to do on-board fashion shows.

It was the first time her parents permitted her to spend time away from home without their direct supervision.

Because no one on board would otherwise know who she was, Tarbes invented a dance company – he called it 'Les Ballets de Paris' – and noted on the programme that Brigitte Bardot was their prima ballerina. Toty made her costumes – a series of colourful little tutus – and Brigitte herself worked out the routines, one of which included a tambourine tied to her waist that she played while she danced. She worked every night, even when the ship was rolling in the seas.

'She was naturally shy,' Tarbes says, 'a very timid girl who would get very nervous when she had to perform and needed to be reassured. She used to say, I can't dance. So we had to tell her, yes you can, you dance very well, everything will be all right, you're terrific. And even if she might have been slightly clumsy at times, the audience was charmed.'

Back in Paris, Tarbes hired her again on a few occasions to model for Carven. By that time Vadim had managed to get her work in a film. He'd shown her screen test to one of France's most prolific directors, Jean Boyer, who decided she was right for a part in a Bourvil comedy he was doing called *Le Trou Normand* ('The Norman Hole').

For Bardot, it was an inauspicious debut. She didn't like her role, didn't feel that she knew what she was doing and wasn't satisfied with her acting. Making matters worse, acting in a film didn't turn out to be as much fun as Vadim had led her to believe. It was too mechanical, too insipid and too exhausting. In short, it was too much like work.

No sooner was she finished with that one than Vadim struck again. Willy Rozier hired her to play the title role in *Manina – La Fille Sans Voile* ('The Lighthouse Keeper's Daughter').

Shot in the summer of 1952, she spent most of the time, true to the French title, unveiled. As she wasn't yet 18, Pilou had insisted there be a clause in her contract that nothing in the film would be an assault on her decency. Rozier had assured Bardot-père that Brigitte would never appear in anything less decent than a bathing costume. Somewhat naively, Pilou had assumed his daughter's virtues – at least her celluloid virtues – were safely intact. Instead, she spent much of the film pouring out of her bikini, which in 1952 was considered very risqué. There was also a nude scene, albeit very brief.

Pilou was scandalized. So was the Catholic Church. They branded the movie a menace to social and family values. Adding insult to injury, during the course of the filming, a number of photographers had been brought onto the set and a series of photographs had been taken. When they were published, Pilou hit the ceiling.

It's fair to say that, considering the era, the photos could reasonably have been considered provocative. Seen through the eyes of a protective, Victorian father, the photos of his teenage daughter were embarrassingly salacious. He now demanded that he and his lawyers be permitted to view the film with an eye towards cutting out any scene that offended him. Rozier wouldn't go for that but, as a compromise, he did agree to allow a judicial referee to see the film before it was officially released. In November 1952 – with Brigitte now two months past her 18th birthday – the referee ruled that the film was, in fact, decent and that it could be shown without any risk to her honour.

Pilou was placated, but only temporarily.

That Christmas, when the film opened in Morocco – then a

French colony – it was accompanied by huge posters showing a young girl completely nude and Brigitte's name was scrawled across the top.

It was more than a man like Pilou could be expected to take. On learning that the film was scheduled for general release in France in March 1953, he set about making certain that the offending poster was not going to be used. This time, instead of discussing the matter calmly with Rozier and the film's distributors, he sent his lawyers to court to obtain an injunction. He claimed the posters were a violation of a 1939 law that protected the sanctity of the family. He added that, as long as his daughter was never in the same state of undress that the poster suggested, 'except perhaps morally', all of this was not only misleading, it constituted fraudulent publicity. The courts agreed, and the publicity that followed the case – believed to have been largely instigated by Vadim, although he's always denied his hand in it – helped cement her image as a starlet.

The French National Film Promotion Office named her their 'Hope of today, star of tomorrow', but many critics weren't so sure. Even *Paris Match* – where Vadim had friends who were willing to help him in his quest to make Brigitte famous – found her acting poor, her diction affected and her widely praised beauty a debatable point.

But at least her career had begun.

Next on her agenda was marrying Vadim. She'd waited the required three years and reminded her parents that was long enough. Pilou now insisted that Vadim convert from Russian Orthodox to Roman Catholicism and when – probably to Pilou's surprise – Vadim happily consented, the last barrier was lifted. On 19 December – the day before their religious ceremony – Brigitte Bardot and Roger Vadim were married in a civil ceremony at the town hall that served the 16th arrondissement.

Later that night, Pilou set up a camp bed in his study for his son-in-law. Brigitte thought it was a joke. But her father reminded her that, in his eyes, they wouldn't be married until they were also married before God.

She couldn't believe he was serious and objected to having her husband sleeping in another room. Pilou was absolutely unmovable – little did he know – and his daughter would have to wait until she was married in church before she could sleep with her husband.

So, the woman who would in so many ways come to symbolize world-class raw sex spent her first night as Mme Roger Vadim Plemiannikov in bed alone.

The religious ceremony, which suddenly made everything all right, took place the following day at Notre Dame de Grace in Passy, with a reception at the apartment on the Rue de la Pompe.

*   *   *

After a brief honeymoon at Megève – Vadim has been an avid skier since the age of 14 – the couple returned to their own one-bedroom, third-floor walk-up flat, at 79 rue Chardon-Lagache, on the Auteuil side of the 16th arrondissement, a gift from Pilou and Toty.

They were also given Toty's old Citroën.

The two settled into a union that seemed filled with alternating hot-blooded love making and hot-blooded fights. One night, after an argument, Brigitte demurely asked Vava if he would take the garbage downstairs. He agreed and, the moment he left the apartment, she slammed and locked the door, leaving him outside in his pyjamas. After banging on the door to get back in – she refused to open it – he broke it down. Frightened, she started running around the apartment. He caught up with her and, he admits these days, thought about banging her head against the wall. Instead, he threw her to the floor, yanked the mattress off the bed, covered her with it, then started jumping up and down on top of the mattress. He has since excused such behaviour with the comment, 'A man has to be strong with Brigitte. And it's a fact that she hasn't had a strong man since me.'

During those first few years together, Brigitte and Vadim developed an extraordinary partnership. He formed her, shaped her, brainwashed her and brought out something in her that no one – least of all Brigitte – ever realized was there. He taught her slang. He taught her how to be sexy while eating with her fingers. He taught her how to put on that famous pout. He watched her all the time, the ultimate voyeur, and taught her how to be watched, how to become the ultimate exhibitionist. He taught her how to put her clothes on and how to take them off.

Eventually he even changed the colour of her hair, turning her into a blonde.

'Whenever I walked or undressed or ate breakfast,' she once noted, 'I always had the impression he was looking at me with someone else's eyes and with everyone's eyes. Yet, I knew he wasn't seeing me, but through me his dream. At that time I was enjoying myself, amused by what I thought were his innocent eccentricities. I didn't realize myself how much he was playing with fire and, even though he is cynical, he didn't either.'

Vadim taught Brigitte how to invent herself.

Once that happened, he was ready to invent the myth.

Some years before their wedding, he'd met an actor's agent named Olga Horstig-Primuz – her biggest star at the time was Michele Morgan – and he decided that she'd be perfect for Brigitte. He set up an appointment and, all these years later, Brigitte still calls her 'Mama Olga'.

'As soon as I met her,' Horstig-Primuz says, 'I didn't even have to think about it. I said right away that I would represent her. She was exquisite. She was irresistible. And I've always thought of her as my second daughter.'

So Mama Olga took on the task of trying to find work for Brigitte while Vadim remained executive director of marketing and public relations. Together they got her cast in a bunch of pictures in rapid succession. Their friend Daniel Gélin gave them both walk-on roles in *Les Dents Longues* ('The Long Teeth'), which starred his wife Daniele. Brigitte then made *Le Portrait de Son Père* ('The Image of His Father'), *Act of Love*, which starred Kirk Douglas and was directed by Anatole Litvak, and *Si Versailles m'Etait Conte* ('If Versailles Could Talk'), the cast of which included Sacha Guitry, Jean Marais, Claudette Colbert and, briefly, Orson Welles.

Vadim was still writing for *Paris Match* and hadn't yet started selling any of his scenarios. Brigitte was already earning more money than he was. But money has never impressed her, he says, so some of it got spent on him.

'She found out about this wonderful car that I'd fallen in love with. It was a 1939 BMW convertible. Someone had given it to Christian Marquand. Brigitte spent all the money she'd just earned on a film to buy it for me. She's always been capable of unbelievable generosity. Unfortunately, the car never worked. We drove it for two kilometres and then it stopped and I could never afford to have it repaired. But the gesture was there.'

Over the next couple of years Brigitte got roles in *Tradita* ('Hate, Love and Treachery'), *Helen of Troy*, which was directed by Robert Wise, *Le Fils de Caroline Cherie* ('The Son of Caroline Cherie') and *Futures Vedettes* ('Sweet Sixteen'), co-starring Jean Marais.

That particular film was a minor turning point in her career. Directed by Marc Allégret, with a script by Roger Vadim, it was the first time she worked with her husband. They collaborated on the scenario together, tailoring her lines to fit her.

Vadim now recognized that his wife could be herself in a film and that, by coming on straight, she could be a movie star.

In the meantime, she set the Cannes Film Festival on fire.

*   *   *

History will show that for Everyman, sex – the kind that has more to do with pleasure than with procreation – was invented on 19 September 1945, which was Shirley Temple's wedding night. After all, if little pig-tailed Shirley was doing it, then everybody could. Three years later, Dr Alfred Kinsey announced, officially, that just about everybody was.

In spring 1946, Christian Dior 'invented' the hour-glass look – soft shoulders, a narrow, well-defined waist and a bellowing skirt – creating a figure-eight shape, 'to liberate women'. Two months later, the Church of England warned of sexual temptations in the workplace. It claimed that young couples preparing for marriage were now up against 'the false romanticism' of the cinema and radio.

Sex was lurking at every turn.

It was on Broadway in Tennessee Williams' *A Streetcar Named Desire*. It was at Wimbledon, with Gussie Moran in lace panties under her tennis skirt, causing a near riot with court-side photographers. It was in the newspapers, reporting that Ingrid Bergman, who happened to be married at the time, was running off with Roberto Rossellini and planning to have a baby with him. It was in bookstores – and banned in bookstores – and later dramatized on television, when Grace Metalious invented a town called Peyton Place. It was on the railroad station newsstand, after Marilyn Monroe posed nude for a picture that later became the first *Playboy* magazine centrefold. It was in schools when sociologist Margaret Mead proclaimed marital infidelity to be an integral part of the modern, democratic culture, a manifestation of freedom of choice. It was freely available to anyone with a public library card when Simone de Beauvoir wrote *The Second Sex* – 'One is not born a woman, one becomes one' – and when J.D. Salinger wrote *Catcher in the Rye*. We were all Holden Caulfield.

By that time, Bardot had arrived at Cannes.

The *Festival International du Film*, which has always, to some degree, been about sex, went into business exactly one year and a day after Shirley Temple's wedding night. From then on –

indubitably so as not to confuse the two events – it was moved to April.

For the last two weeks of that month in 1953, everybody who was anybody in the film business came to the south of France. But nobody invited Brigitte. So Vadim invited the two of them.

He knew that the film world's entire publicity machine was geared up to looking for sexy stories and, to get his wife known, he decided to create a few. Of course, the beach was already crowded with stars – from Olivia de Havilland to Esther Williams to Yvonne de Carlo – but when one very long-legged, slim brunette showed up in a bathing suit and began strutting her stuff, Vadim's photographer friends took over. They shot pictures of her on the beach and in front of the Carlton. They also photographed her with her old pal from dancing class, Leslie Caron, who'd been nominated for the Best Actress Award as the star of *Lili. Paris Match* put the two former dancers together and published a photo introducing Brigitte as 'The new Leslie Caron'.

In those days, the United States Navy had their Mediterranean Fleet based in nearby Villefranche. Being a good neighbour, the Americans helped add to the festivities by anchoring the aircraft carrier *Midway* half a mile off shore. A photo opportunity was arranged for a group of stars who were ferried out to the ship. There was Edward G. Robinson, Kirk Douglas, Lana Turner, Olivia de Havilland, Anne Baxter, Mel Ferrer, Raf Vallone, Silvana Mangano, Vittorio De Sica and Gary Cooper.

There was also a young, long-legged, slim brunette in a raincoat.

The Navy warmly welcomed the stars, but when Brigitte got onto the flight deck and 3,500 sailors saw her raincoat slip off her shoulders to reveal her 5 foot 7 inch frame – which would measure 35–23–35 for the next 25 years – wrapped inside in a tiny dress, they went absolutely wild.

'I knew what would happen if she went to Cannes,' Vadim says. 'I got her to go because I knew it would catapult her career. What I didn't know was that someone had the idea to send her out to that aircraft carrier. I'm sorry to say that wasn't me.'

Over the years, thousands of starlets have tried to steal the limelight from the established stars at Cannes. But Bardot was the first to hijack the entire festival. No one since has ever managed it better or, thanks to the collusion of the United States Navy, with quite as much gusto.

*   *   *

In the autumn following the Cannes Film Festival, Brigitte Bardot hit the boards of a Parisian theatre for the first and only time, in Jean Anouilh's *L'Invitation au Chateau* ('Invitation to the Castle'). Anouilh had spotted her in a few films, had found her exciting and had approached Vadim to see if she would agree to play a supporting role.

Vadim passed the offer on to Brigitte and, immediately, she said no. She'd never done theatre, didn't think she could and wasn't going to risk failure by trying.

But Anouilh believed she could manage it and Vadim did too, so they got together to talk her into it.

'And she was terrific,' Vadim says. 'When you realize she'd just started making movies and had never been a formally trained actress, it was wonderful to see her hold her own. Anouilh was thrilled.'

Brigitte, however, was terrified by the very thought of it. Despite the proficient direction of André Barsacq and the constant encouragement she received from both Vadim and Anouilh, she not only doubted her own ability but, when she heard she had to stay in the play for three months, she complained that she couldn't possibly cope.

'Once she realized how good she was,' Vadim continues, 'she was very pleased with herself. It gave her the chance to show people who thought of her as nothing more than a flash in the pan starlet that she was capable of much more. But Brigitte is

50

Brigitte. The first week was okay. Then she started to grumble. She managed the entire run, but not without a lot of complaining because it very quickly became hard work.'

One night, towards the end of the run, she lost her place in a scene and blanked. She completely forgot her lines. There was an embarrassingly awkward pause before something flew into her head. Thinking that she'd refound her place, she began a speech. Much to the horror of the other actors, she'd inadvertently jumped an entire scene. Much to the horror of the stage manager, they automatically followed her into the final act. Eventually it dawned on her that something was wrong – she could see it on the faces of everyone else on stage – but didn't know what had happened until the play ended and the final curtain came down. With no options left to them, the cast took their bows and the house lights came up. The audience, most of whom thought there was supposed to have been an intermission at some point – and none of whom understood a thing about the storyline – went home an hour and a half earlier than scheduled.

She also, during these years, had a journalistic career, but that was even shorter lived than her stage career.

A mutual friend of Brigitte's and Vadim's was Philippe Letellier, then a photographer at *Paris Match*. One day he'd been sent to Lyons to photograph a fashion collection, which included some wedding dresses. He came back to Paris with his film, had the pictures developed but found himself, late in the evening, alone in the office, with no one to do captions for the layout. A deadline was staring him in the face when, around midnight, Brigitte showed up to meet Vadim.

Philippe told her that he had a real problem, that he had to get these photos in the magazine but didn't have anyone to help him do the layouts and the captions.

Not to worry, she said, grabbed a pencil, sat down, sorted through the photographs, chose the ones she liked best, put them in order and wrote all the captions.

So for two hours, at the age of 19, in the middle of the night, Brigitte Bardot was a journalist at *Paris Match*. Her text was published, word for word and, until now, no one besides Philippe Letellier and Brigitte Bardot knew that.

* * *

When Hugh Hefner got fired from his job at *Esquire* magazine, he withdrew what little money he had in the bank and in December 1953 came up with a magazine called *Playboy*. He was going to cater to the first generation of 20th-century males who were starting to live on their own as bachelors. He whetted their sexual taste buds with centrefold pictures of girls who were supposed to look as if they could be living next door. And although very few of his readers ever believed for a moment that the girl next door had staples in her navel, for the price of a magazine they could have a new girl next door every month.

Hefner was marketing a dream that was available.

Vadim, selling the world on the idea that 'Brigitte doesn't act, she exists', was marketing a dream that was unobtainable.

Hollywood picked up on his sales pitch that spring at Cannes and Brigitte was offered a contract at Universal. She even nearly accepted it. She was willing to meet producers in Los Angeles and actually got as far as the airport before she saw the plane, reminded herself that she hated flying and went home.

Horstig-Primuz also managed to get her an offer from Warner Brothers as a studio player, promising her $1,500 a week for the first year, $3,000 a week for the second year, and $5,000 a week for the third year, whether she worked or not. At first Brigitte said she'd take it – it was, after all, good money – then she thought about it and backed out.

'If I have to live there,' she said, 'I'll die.'

In fact, throughout her career, she steadfastly refused to make pictures in the States. The more she came to know the business, the more she was convinced that Hollywood would kill her.

'Stay away from there,' she'd warn fellow actors. 'Don't go there. Don't work there. Those people out there eat people like you and me alive.'

The British also tried to sign her. Producer Betty Box was making low-budget comedies in London and, as a rule, always tried to get a name from each market into her films because it helped sell the film in that country.

'I'd seen her early on, around the time of the Cannes Film Festival. She was obviously star material. She was very sweet, very voluptuous, very French. So I offered her a sexy role in a picture called A *Day to Remember*. But Brigitte, under the tutelage of Vadim, who knew that her English was limited, turned me down.'

Not one to give up easily, Box flew to Paris to meet with Bardot, Vadim and Horstig-Primuz, hoping to sign Brigitte for the role of the sexy young girl in the Dirk Bogarde comedy *Doctors at Sea*. Vadim set her fee at $2,100—which was not a lot of money considering the fact that Bogarde was making around $28,000. Still, it was three times what she'd earned for her first few pictures and a decent salary for a shortish schedule in a group film with a lot of other people. Box agreed and Brigitte came to London.

'Actually, her English in those days was quite amusing,' Box says. 'She made little mistakes, but that was one of the joys of working with her. I remember that when I picked her up at the airport I told her that Rank was having a preview that evening and if she wanted to come along she would be very welcome. She said she couldn't because she didn't bring a night dress.'

At a press conference for the film, Brigitte packed the ballroom at the Dorchester Hotel and mesmerized journalists with her doe-eyed one liners.

'Mademoiselle Bardot,' someone asked, 'what was the best day of your life?'

She came right out with, 'It was a night.'

'Who do you admire most?' someone else wanted to know.

'Sir Isaac Newton,' she answered, 'because he discovered bodies attract each other.'

When a reporter wanted to know why she wasn't wearing lipstick, she told him, 'I don't like lipstick. It makes troubles. I like to kiss. But if I kiss anyone when I am wearing lipstick, it makes troubles.'

Noted one reporter who covered that press conference, 'Normally intelligent, articulate men were struck dumb in her presence, or reduced to banality. One asked her what she thought of London policemen. Another, an influential editor, stared at her as though mesmerized and about to leap through her outsized hoop earrings. Then he swallowed and asked what perfume she was wearing.'

Vadim had coached her well.

If anyone remembers the film at all, it is for Brigitte's shower scene, which at the time was pretty hot stuff for the British cinema. It was even more memorable for the crew on the set because it was the first time on a major motion picture sound stage in the UK that anyone had done a genuine nude scene.

Box continues, 'The wardrobe people in British films in those days were so stupid. They used to stick bits of tape on top of a woman's nipples and give her flesh-coloured panties to wear. We did have a strict censor, that's true. But in this case, when she got into the shower and we set up the shot, you could see that she was dressed.'

The director, Ralph Thomas, worked with his camera man and his lighting man to find a way to shoot the scene so that the audience wouldn't see the tape and the panties. But, no matter how they lit it or which angle they used, it was obvious that Brigitte was wearing something.

'So Brigitte said, I know how to solve the problem.' Betty Box nods, as if the answer had been obvious right from the beginning. 'She said, you tell me when you wish me to be with nothing on and I will do it. She wasn't at all bothered. Although the crew wasn't quite as non-plussed about it. I remember there were a lot more people on the set that morning than usual.'

Dirk Bogarde found her to be 'a breath of fresh air', but the British press easily topped that. One journalist avowed, 'She's enough to make a bishop kick in a stained glass window.' And, by the time *Doctors at Sea* was released, Fleet Street had nicknamed her 'the sex kitten'.

With her international reputation growing, she returned to France, booked by Mama Olga to work with Michele Morgan and Gérard Philipe in *Les Grandes Manoeuvres* ('Summer Maneuvers').

Next, she was cast as the sexy temptress in *La Lumière d'en Face* (The Light across the Street'). For that, Vadim and Olga had worked out a multi-film deal with the producer Jacques Gauthier, but he died before the picture was finished. Needing someone to take his place, the company turned to a woman who'd been handling the production's administration, Christine Gouze-Renal. She wasn't sure she should take the job but, as the idea of a woman film producer in France was quite revolutionary, Brigitte encouraged her.

'We became friends during that film,' Gouze-Renal explains, 'although there was a 20-year difference in our age. What I saw in her was a girl who hadn't yet found her balance in life. Hadn't yet managed to find her footing. I also saw in her a girl who hated the film business, hated acting, hated being told what to do, and hated everything that surrounded the film business. Vadim had opened the door and she was certainly amused by it at the beginning. But once it became a job, once she was being told what to do, as soon as there were rules, the fun stopped. She thought the whole thing was awful.'

When *Lumière* was finished, Brigitte told Gouze-Renal, if you want to produce another film, I promise to sign a contract with you here and now. They didn't sign the papers that same day, but Bardot would make good on that pledge a few years later and – like her relationship with Mama Olga – she remains friends with the woman she calls 'Ma Cri-Cri' all these years later.

From there she went to work for director Michel Boisrond in a film scripted by Vadim called *Cette Sacrée Gamine* ('That Darned Kid'), then travelled to Italy where she made *Mio Figlio Nerone* ('Nero's Big Weekend') with Alberto Sordi, Vittorio de Sica and Gloria Swanson.

The only good thing to come out of that movie was the publicity she got for her milk bath scene.

Originally, the director had filled a pool with whitewash. Vadim, ever the opportunist, knew a good story when he heard one. What's more, he had the talent to embellish it enough to turn a good story into a great one. So he put out the tale that, when she saw the pool filled with whitewash, she said it didn't look right, and insisted on real milk. And not just any milk would do. He said she specified that it had to be asses' milk. The film was panned but the milk bath story ran in papers around the world.

Back in France, she was hired by Marc Allégret for another Vadim screenplay, *En Effeuillant La Marguerite*. Originally translated as 'Plucking the Daisies', the American distributor came up with the slightly obscure title, 'Please Mr Balzac'. But in England someone understood how to sell a Bardot film, and they called it 'Mam'zelle Striptease'. She got only second billing to Daniel Gélin, but there was no doubt in anyone's mind who was carrying the film.

Here was Vava undressing his wife for the world to see.

And here was Vava explaining to the world that, for Brigitte, 'Nudity was nothing more or less than a smile or the colour of a flower.' She has always claimed, 'I am very prudish, but I don't find that nudity is imprudish.' And, even today, Vadim maintains that was absolutely true. 'She never thought of nudity as a secret weapon that enabled women to seduce men. She was Eve before God lost his temper in the Garden of Eden.'

Best of all, here was Vava feeding an ever-increasingly hungry press with stories of Brigitte Bardot.

'She is more advanced than children of earlier generations,' he wrote about her in a handout. 'Along with this, she has blank spots. She knows Egyptian history down to the smallest detail, but I had to teach her that mice don't lay eggs and that the moon always presents the same side to the earth.'

He took every opportunity to talk about her and to build her image. 'She cannot fry an egg, but she covered the chairs and divans at home as well as a professional could. She drives her car in Paris with all the assurance of a taxi-driver, but she fears spirits that become invisible monsters. It is to protect her from these monsters when I am working that I bought her the cocker spaniel, Clown. Here, in order after Clown, is what Brigitte likes most in the world: other dogs, birds, the sun, money, the sea, flowers, period furniture, grass, kittens and mice. I did not dare ask her where she placed me, perhaps between the grass and the kittens.'

Being the Dark Ages, sex was not what it is today, and in order to be made proper – that is, taken away from the dirty raincoat crowd – it had to be disguised, turned into an intellectual exercise that could be dissected and discussed without disturbing God-fearing men and women, but especially men. So when an edition of *Elle* magazine – hardly the centre-fold type – wanted to describe Bardot's overt sensuality, they did it with a pedantic tone.

'Her perfect body seems to reinforce a purity that she no longer possesses but that is yet unchanged. With her inciting hip movements, she manages to create a poetry that is undeniable and deeply stirring.'

In other words, she moves like she knows how to have sex. This at a time when, 5,000 miles away in New York, no one dared to show anyone moving like that. When Elvis Presley – then commonly referred to as Elvis the Pelvis – was invited onto the Sunday night, cleared for family viewing Ed Sullivan Show, it was Sullivan himself who stipulated that the cameras had to stay in tight on the singer and could show him only from the waist up.

Owing largely to Vadim's well-honed marketing skills, the multi-film contract Brigitte had signed with Gauthier was bought by a young and ambitious producer named Raoul Levy. Six years Vadim's senior, Levy was an odd melange of wacky romantic and ageing hustler, who liked to brag that he'd been financially ruined five times before his 30th birthday. At the age of 44, he would kill himself over a woman.

Levy believed in Vadim and, through him, believed in Brigitte. He'd surmised that they were both ready for their breakthrough film. He could see that Vadim had put all the explosives in place. And he concluded that it was finally time to light the fuse.

Chapter Four

AND GOD CREATED WOMAN

Before World War I there was Pablo Picasso, Sergei Diaghilev, cubism and Montmartre. After it there was Ernest Hemingway, Scott Fitzgerald, Gertrude Stein, Gerald and Sara Murphy and Montparnasse. Artists and writers and intellectuals of all per-suasions flocked to Paris, installed themselves in warm, well-lit cafés, and held forth on life, most of them convinced that here they could reinvent their own moral codes.

In the wake of World War II, seeping out of the Left Bank *quartier* known as St Germain des Prés, came the first real French cultural movement since the 1920s. At the centre of it were Jean-Paul Sartre, Simone de Beauvoir and Juliette Greco. They threw off the shackles imposed by the Nazi occupation. They wrote of life and death and women in politics. They wrote of existentialism – man is the master of his own fate, and the universe is absurd and existence precedes essence – and they sang deep throaty songs in cellar *boîtes* about love and sex. They got drunk together, slept together, ripped down barriers that had long since separated the sexes, and for a brief time – from around 1947 to 1954 – fired the imagination of a younger generation who soon moved onto the stage to take up their cry. All of this long before the rest of the world ever heard of sexual equality and women's lib.

Françoise Sagan published *Bonjour Tristesse* and singers arrived like Edith Piaf, Yves Montand, Charles Aznavour and Gilbert Becaud. There were Georges Brassens and Jacques Brel, too. And film makers – who came to be known as 'the new wave' – such as Alain Resnais, Jean-Luc Godard and François Truffaut. They launched a frontal attack on the oppression of the film-making system in France and helped to shake out the old ways.

Looking back, Vadim, who was very much on the periphery of all this, recalls that there were so many interesting people who came out of that period and so many unknown people who stayed unknown, even though they might have made great contributions.

'It was an accident of history that was a period of great freedom. These days we speak of Juliette Greco and Jean-Paul Sartre, who wasn't really part of that circle because he didn't like it. But there was also Jean Cocteau and Jacques Prévert and Boris Vian, even though he wasn't so well known until later. There was a wonderful mixture in the *quartier* of bohemia, youth against all traditions, and a star system. Dali was there too. You could find just about everyone who was anyone in the arts and politics at "La Rose Rouge" or drinking coffee at "Le Flore" or just coming to see what existentialism was all about. It was a mixture of stars and unknowns where the real stars were the unknowns.'

Unfortunately, when word got out to the rest of the world, St Germain des Prés became a site for pilgrimages. 'It turned into a sort of false-Disneyland for Japanese tourists who were always looking for the table where Sartre sat. I remember one tourist asking me if everyone sitting at the café was an extra put there to make the place seem real.'

Vadim's own contribution to St Germain des Prés lives on. He maintains that it was during those years and in that *quartier* that he saw clubs where people played records so that other people could dance, and he somehow associated this with the museum in Munich, the Pinakothek. 'So I invented the word, discotheque.'

Even though Brigitte came out of the 16th arrondissement – a neighbourhood that represented everything the St Germain des Prés crowd undoubtedly found wrong with the world – she and women like Françoise Sagan played off of the spirit of liberalism emanating from St Germain des Prés to help break out of their parents' middle-class value system. Now in the 1950s, they openly lived less innocent lives than the children of the 1940s, and flaunted that in shocking new ways.

Suddenly youth and the power to shock became doctrine.

As soon as it did, the public was primed for something monumental to happen.

* * *

Gambling on the theory that she didn't have to act, that she merely had to exist, Vadim wrote a screenplay where she could be herself. He didn't write a role for her as much as he wrote her. But then, in his mind, he'd already invented Brigitte Bardot, long before he actually met her in *The Wise Sophie.*

Raoul Levy not only agreed to back the venture, he was willing to allow Vadim to direct. The project was never intended to be anything more than a group of friends making a low-budget black and white movie. But Levy approached Columbia Pictures and they expressed some interest, leading him believe they might be willing to put up enough money to make the picture in Eastman Color and in CinemaScope. The only problem was, Columbia Pictures didn't see Vadim as a director. He had no track record. Nor did they see Brigitte as a star. She was still considered a starlet. So they told Levy they wouldn't come up with any money unless he could put a bankable name above the titles.

Given the chance to turn the project into more than they ever imagined it could be, Vadim and Levy went looking for a star.

Enter here, Curt Jurgens.

Then in his mid-40s, he was a romantic lead who'd been big in his native Germany before the war. Imprisoned at the end of it – on the personal orders of Paul Josef Goebbels for expressing

61

anti-Nazi sentiments – he finally hit big outside Germany in 1955 with a film called, *The Devil's General.*

Suave and debonair – the sort of European actor that Americans used to describe as 'continental' – Vadim and Levy reckoned he'd be perfect, exactly the star Columbia would go for. There were only three things standing in their way: they didn't know him; they didn't have a part for him; and he wasn't available.

That, however, wasn't enough to stop two young schemers on the way up.

With what little money they had, they got on a train for Munich, where Jurgens was filming. Levy's original intention was to give Jurgens the part Vadim had promised to his pal Christian Marquand. When Vadim pointed out that not only would Jurgens be playing Antoine Tardieu as a St Tropez fisherman speaking with a German accent, he'd also be the same age as Madame Tardieu, his own character's mother. Understandably, Levy agreed to rethink his pitch to Jurgens.

The next best thing, they decided, was to write in a part for him.

Arriving in Munich, they installed themselves in the best hotel in town – they couldn't let Jurgens know they were nearly broke – and, as Vadim began scripting him into the movie, Levy began trying to talk him into the role. On their second day in Munich, Levy – who'd already stocked the room with caviar, smoked salmon and vodka – took pity on the overworked Vadim and hired a hooker for him. She came to the room but, instead of sleeping with her, he asked if she could type. When she said yes, he put her work.

Forty-eight hours later, Vadim had a rough draft of a screenplay, with a character outlined for Jurgens. He and Levy met with the German actor, gave him the storyline and, after hearing that he couldn't possibly make himself available under any circumstances for more than 15 days, they promised – rather rashly – they could shoot around his schedule.

Thanks entirely to Vadim's natural charm and Levy's talent as a conman – not to mention the prospect of an amusing few weeks in the south of France – Jurgens signed on.

'That', Vadim says, 'secured Columbia's participation. We were talking colour and CinemaScope and adding around $300,000 to the budget. It doesn't sound like a lot of money any more, but by today's standards it would put it in the category of, say, a $5 million picture.'

They called the movie *Et Dieu Créa la Femme* ('And God Created Woman') and shot it through May and June 1956, on location in St Tropez and at the Victorine Studios in Nice. Vadim worked quickly – he didn't have much choice, especially as Jurgens was available for less than a third of the ten-week schedule – and the entire film was in the can by 5 July.

It was a fairly lightweight story even when it was made, and all these years later it has not necessarily aged well. Arguably, had anyone else but Brigitte Bardot played the role of Juliette – the young woman shuttled back and forth between various men – the film would have been long since forgotten. But then, right from the beginning, it's evident that Vadim knew precisely what he was doing – that Juliette is Brigitte, that she's not acting, that she's coming on straight, that she's just being herself. And in the sexually repressive, cultural void that was the mid-1950s, this woman was something very new and very threatening – one of the world's most beautiful women stark naked. Or at least people thought she was.

The storyline is pretty basic.

Juliette has been taken in by an elderly couple. Lazy and somewhat rude, her most endearing quality is her pout. She walks through most of the film barefoot, not simply as a metaphor of Juliette's disdain for convention but because that's the way Bardot has spent much of her life.

First she falls for a handsome young man named Antoine – Christian Marquand – who is battling to keep his family's small shipyard from bankruptcy. At the same time, she's become the object of attention of a wealthy businessman named Eric – Curt Jurgens – who hopes she can rekindle his own youth. Then she marries Michel – played by a young, timid, good-looking, as yet unknown Jean-Louis Trintignant – who happens to be Antoine's younger brother.

When Michel goes on an overnight business trip to Marseilles, Juliette takes one of the family boats, which somehow catches fire.

She's rescued by Antoine, whom she thanks by making love to him on the beach. Michel returns and is told by his own mother that his wife has been unfaithful. First he fights with Antoine, then he goes to confront Juliette, who happens to be dancing wildly in front of Eric at a local nightclub. Michel produces a gun, apparently to shoot Juliette but wounds Eric instead. Antoine takes him to the hospital. Left alone, Michel now slaps Juliette to bring her to her senses. That's when she realizes he is, in fact, the man she's always needed and the two walk off into the Riviera night.

War and Peace this isn't.

'As a film,' one critic wrote, 'it veers between the commonplace of 19th century melodrama and the unbalanced structure of a sex film, where character, dialogue, and plot are simply ways of justifying, as speedily as possible, the next coupling.'

What no one realized at the time was that Vadim was taking sex out of back-alley art theatres and putting it into Main Street movie houses.

By today's standards, the acting is wooden, the plot tame – there's more gratuitous immorality in your average afternoon TV soap opera – and the dialogue pretty corny.

'She does whatever she wants,' Eric says of Juliette, 'whenever she wants.'

Riding her bike into town one morning, Juliette has a puncture. 'I'm flat,' she yells to a passing bus filled with men. One of them shouts back, 'Doesn't look that way to me.'

Later Michel asks her, 'What are you afraid of?' and she tells him, ominously, 'Myself.'

And when Michel says to her, 'You'd make a good wife,' Juliette responds, 'No, I like to have too much fun.'

But it wasn't the acting, the plot or the dialogue that earned *And God Created Woman* a place in movie history as one of the watershed films of the 1950s.

It was Brigitte Bardot.

Vadim had perfectly captured the woman–child who was his wife, and that character was unique. He'd touched enough raw nerves to make people uncomfortable with her blatant sexuality, at the same time that her sex appeal was enough to turn them on. And that outraged the censors.

Particularly infuriating, they decided, was the scene where Juliette comes home after her wedding. She goes to bed with her husband while her family is having a celebration dinner. In the middle of the meal, she comes downstairs, ignores them as she piles food on a plate, then heads back upstairs. When asked about her husband, she assures her family, 'I'm taking care of him.'

It was much too suggestive, the censors decided. But because everyone still had their clothes on and no one used language that could endanger public morals, there wasn't much they could do about it.

The scene where the French censor put his foot down, one scene that absolutely had to come out, was where Brigitte is in bed alone while her husband's youngest brother – who was supposed to be 14 or 15 – is watching from the doorway. Knowing he's standing there, she gets out from under the covers and walks, totally naked, past him.

'No, no, no.' The censor admonished Vadim, 'I cannot accept that and I require you to cut it out of the film.'

Vadim replied, 'I'd be happy to cut it out of the film, but first you have to find it.'

The censor didn't understand.

So Vadim explained, 'The scene doesn't exist. In bed, she's wearing a very long shirt that comes down almost to her knees. When she gets up, she's still wearing the shirt. That's what she's got on when she walks past the young boy.'

'No,' the censor said, 'that's not true,' and stuck to his version of the scene. 'She was naked. I saw it. Rerun the scene and I'll prove it to you.'

So Vadim reran it for him and there was Brigitte, as he promised she would be, wearing a long shirt. And still the censor didn't believe him. He now accused Vadim of shooting the scene twice, once for the cinemas and once for the censor.

Vadim swore he'd done nothing of the kind and took the censor to the laboratory where they were making copies from the negative. The censor verified the scene he'd watched against the negative – sure enough, there she was, wearing a shirt – and even then he remained utterly convinced Vadim had hidden the other version from him.

'That was one of the most amazing things about Brigitte's presence on film,' Vadim now says. 'People often thought she was naked when she wasn't. There is only one scene, at the beginning of the film, where she clearly doesn't have anything on, but she's hidden behind a sheet that's hanging on a clothes line. She's lying there talking to Curt Jurgens. You don't even see her breasts because she's lying on her stomach. There's nothing to see. Yet the censor and so many other people came away from that film thinking she was nude for most of it. It's an extraordinary phenomenon, totally unique to her.'

In the end, the French censor actually found very little he could take out of the film. At the last-minute, in a slightly feeble attempt to exert some authority, he objected to Juliette and Michel being nude in bed. Vadim reminded him that, except in wartime, very few married couples – presumably guardians of public morals have always been the exception – made love fully dressed.

66

Originally, only Jurgens' name was to appear above the title. But once the film was finished, it was unmistakable who the star was and Brigitte's name was moved above the title too.

*　　*　　*

One month before *Et Dieu Créa la Femme* opened in Paris – and several months before it would come to Britain – Brigitte Bardot checked into a fifth-floor suite at the Savoy Hotel in London, accompanied by Olga Horstig-Primuz, as the guest of the Cinematograph Trade Benevolent Fund. She arrived on Saturday 27 October, to spend the weekend, before attending a Monday night Royal film première at the Empire Theatre in Leicester Square.

The picture being touted was Michael Powell's *The Battle of the River Plate*. Starring John Gregson, Anthony Quayle and Peter Finch – and known in the States as *The Pursuit of the Graf Spee* – it was a war film, in English, in which she had no interest whatsoever.

Nobody these days seems to recall precisely why she'd been invited. Unlike some of the other guests – Victor Mature, Dana Andrews, Sylvia Sims and Anita Ekberg – Bardot wasn't working in London at the time.

However, *En Effeuillant La Marguerite* had opened just two weeks before in London, retitled *Mam'zelle Striptease* – itself, an unlikely candidate for a Royal film première – and *Cette Sacrée Gamine* was set to open as *Mam'zelle Pigalle* one week later. Also, *Les Grandes Manoeuvres*, now called *Summer Maneuvers*, was booked for a January release. So perhaps for the distributors it made sense to put her name on the list, as a foreign actress who might, if invited, show up.

For the organizers, she was just one of 20 performers to shake hands with the Queen. It wasn't as if they needed any more glamour; they already had Marilyn Monroe, who was in town with her husband, playwright Arthur Miller, working with Laurence Olivier in *The Prince and the Showgirl*.

67

Warned in advance to wear something respectable – so as not to offend Her Majesty's sensibilities or, presumably, to boggle Prince Philip's eyes – Brigitte showed up in a Balmain gown. Word obviously hadn't reached Marilyn, because she wore an extremely tight-fitting gold number, so décolletée that she didn't dare try a proper curtsey.

No one thought to introduce Brigitte and Marilyn. And when *The Times* reported on the event in the following morning's edition, the only star named was Monroe. There is no mention of Brigitte at all. Nor would it have dawned on Marilyn to say hello to a young French starlet when she herself was the Queen of the Cinema, at the peak of fame.

So when they met – late that Monday night, in a dressing room backstage that had been transformed into a 'ladies' convenience' – it was almost by accident. Brigitte had gone there to touch up her eye-liner. Marilyn walked in to powder her nose.

According to Brigitte, 'It was very brief.'

So brief, that not a word was spoken.

Both of them were nervous about meeting the Queen and Brigitte thought to herself, Marilyn is very beautiful.

For one instant, the two women looked at each other.

And from the look in Marilyn's eyes, Brigitte says she knew that Marilyn knew that they were in the same boat.

*   *   *

Vadim brought the picture in for somewhere around $600,000. Various reports claim that it cost only 140 million old francs ($400,000). But he says, no, it was more than that. The problem was that it grossed less than 50 million old francs ($145,000) when it opened in France.

What's more, when it opened – with a Champs-Elysées première on 28 November 1956 – it got horrible reviews. Most of the criticism was aimed at Brigitte. The papers said things like, 'the best thing about this film is that it will forever end the career of

68

that annoying little starlet'. They said things like, 'what a terrible image this film will give of France as portrayed by the vulgarity of Mlle Bardot'.

Unquestionably, she troubled the critics because this was not just sex, this was dangerous sex. And not everyone involved with the cinema believed the cinema was ready for it.

François Truffaut, for instance, labelled the film 'amoral'. Writing in *Arts* magazine he noted, 'She undresses in front of the window, facing the light as it shines through her nylon shirt. In bed, instead of joining her sick husband, she taunts him. The next morning, she bathes nude and we don't know what we see. Like when she jumps on the back of a motorcycle and shows her legs. On a chair, to hook up I don't know what, she lets us see her legs. We have the right to speak here of pornography and to wonder about the connivance of the censor.'

Many French people agreed with him, and their indignation was reinforced when, just after the film's release, three young hoodlums murdered an old man while he slept on a train near Angers. A public outcry went up, some of it aimed at her for having perverted local youngsters.

A critic in *Le Figaro* did not hide his own prudishness when he asked, 'What does a husband think when he shows, with such complacency, the naked body of his wife?'

A reviewer for *Radio-Cinéma* magazine conceded that *Et Dieu Créa la Femme* was an interesting sociological document, 'in spite of Brigitte Bardot's lack of talent, in spite of the absence of Roger Vadim's scruples, whose talent as a pushy guy is in inverse proportion to his talent of expression, in spite of an attempt at cerebral eroticism, in spite of some pornography.'

While Jacques Doniol-Valcroze defended Bardot in the *France-Observateur*. 'Thank goodness there is Brigitte Bardot. And here France is the winner on every level. I'm not joking. No other country can brag about possessing such a pretty girl, as graciously provocative, with the silhouette of Auguste Renoir's young girls, a dancer's walk, a mane of sea-weed and wild pony, and an exquisite roundness that would have pleased Maillol.'

At first glance, the film looked as if it was going to sink without a trace in France. And it nearly did. Had that happened, the course of Bardot's life would, certainly, have been radically changed. Her career might have ended. Or, at best, she might have turned out to be little more than a local phenomenon.

However, in the eyes of people outside France – which included the whole of the rest of the planet – this film was something special.

It opened in London on 13 March 1957 and attendance was so strong that it quickly went out on general release throughout the UK. In a futile attempt to pacify the religious lobby, the British distributor had changed the title – no sense blaming God for this – calling the film *And Woman . . . Was Created*. It would be another ten years before the original title was restored.

Not surprisingly, the British censor, like his French counterpart, went crazy when he saw the film. The very thought of this young woman doing everything she did on screen so upset him that, at first, he refused to give the picture a rating, which was tantamount to banning it. So Vadim was forced to agree to certain cuts. But they weren't enough to damage the film seriously and, once it was released, the critics acknowledged that Bardot was unique.

'BB on screen is not simply a selfish delinquent,' read the *Observer*'s review. 'She has freshness and charm and a touch of mischievousness. She is irresponsible and immoral but not deliberately cruel. She does not fit into any of the previously accepted categories of film personality – the sweet, pure, clinging type (Phyllis Calvert, Grace Kelly), the *femme fatale* (Marlene Dietrich, Greta Garbo), the full-blown pin up (Jayne Mansfield, Jane Russell), or the bright-eyed adolescent (Audrey Hepburn, Leslie Caron).'

70

In the States, where the film didn't première until November 1957, Americans couldn't believe what they were seeing. For the very first time, they could watch a real nude scene, in big screen colour. And some movie houses that booked the film for two weeks were still showing it a year later.

'I play myself,' she told the press. 'I'm not good enough to play somebody else. That's why I like simple, wild, sexy parts.'

She might as well have declared war.

'Now anything goes,' barked one of the Hollywood trade papers, pointing out that Elia Kazan's 1956 *Baby Doll*, starring a sultry Carol Baker, had been denied a Production Code Administration seal of approval and condemned by the Legion of Decency. 'Compared to "And God Created Woman," it seems downright tame.'

Unknowingly, Brigitte had thrown open the floodgates. Elizabeth Taylor would soon play a call-girl in *Butterfield 8*, Shirley Jones a woman of easy virtue in *Elmer Gantry*, Melina Mercouri a prostitute in *Never on Sunday* and Nancy Kwan a prostitute in *Flower Drum Song*. Vladimir Nabokov's *Lolita* would hit the best-seller lists. So would the Grove Press edition of D.H. Lawrence's *Lady Chatterley's Lover*. Furthermore, there's little doubt that Bardot's nudity helped to break the ice for Marilyn Monroe's famous 1960 nude scene in *Let's Make Love*, because by then it was okay to do that. Sure, Hedy Lamarr had taken her clothes off in *Ecstasy*. She was nude for almost 10 minutes, riding on a horse. But the film was made in Czechoslovakia in 1933, it was in black and white and, even if she was billed as 'the world's most beautiful woman', the camera was pretty far away.

Just as significantly, *And God Created Woman* reminded Americans of *Rebel Without A Cause*, the 1955 film that brought James Dean to stardom. They saw this as the French variation on the rebellious youth theme, at a time when American youth was beginning to be rebellious.

Look magazine went so far as to call her, 'the female James

Dean'. Years later, a writer would turn that around to read, 'She's James Dean in bra and panties, more usually without.'

Life magazine bragged, 'Since the Statue of Liberty, no French girl has ever shone quite as much light on the United States.'

Newsweek labelled her 'the symbol of temptation. She possesses the kind of personal chemistry that forces the viewer to find deep inside himself everything he either would like to forget or habitually denies.'

Simone de Beauvoir, writing in *Esquire* magazine, informed America that Bardot was disliked in her own country. 'Not a week goes by without articles in the press telling all about her recent moods and love affairs, or offering a new interpretation of her personality, but half of these articles and gossip items seethe with spite.'

She said Brigitte was receiving 300 letters a day – the actual number was soon closer to three times as many – and that among them were letters from indignant mothers accusing her of corrupting their sons, and from grown men offering their services to satisfy her most wanton sexual desires.

'Her eroticism is not magical, but aggressive. In the game of love she is as much the hunter as she is the prey. The male is an object to her just as she is to him. In her role of confused female, of homeless little slut, BB seems to be available to everyone. And yet, paradoxically, she is intimidating. Nothing can be read into Bardot's face. It is what it is. It has the forthright presence of reality. It is a stumbling block to lewd fantasies and ethereal dreams alike.'

Describing Brigitte as 'temperamental, changeable and unpredictable', de Beauvoir recognized that in life, as on the screen, she did little more than follow her own inclinations. 'She eats when she's hungry and makes love with the same unceremonious simplicity. Desire and pleasure seem to her more convincing than precepts and conventions.'

Subjected as she was to every sort of praise and, at the same time, every sort of abuse imaginable, de Beauvoir felt that Bardot had only Vadim and herself to blame for it. 'He invented a resolutely modern version of the eternal female and thereby launched a new type of eroticism. It is this novelty that entices some people and shocks others.'

With the benefit of hindsight, actress Jeanne Moreau would proclaim, 'Brigitte was the real modern revolutionary character for women and Vadim, as a man and a lover and a director, felt that. Suddenly what was important was vitality, eroticism, energy, love and passion. One had to remember it was Vadim who started everything with Bardot.'

The Catholic Church in America had its own opinions and immediately banned the film. When a small-town movie house in upstate New York scheduled it, a local priest tried to buy all the tickets so that no one could see it. The cinema manager refused to sell his entire booking to the priest, so the priest declared that movie house an official no-go area and threatened excommunication to any Catholics found there. Within hours, he was joined by another local clergyman, who called the film 'an assault on each and every woman of our community and nation, living or dead, our mothers, sisters, wives and daughters'.

The bandwagon gathered speed, across the nation, with demands that the film be banned. In Dallas, Texas, the local police chief forbade Blacks from seeing it on the theory that they would become overly excited by it and possibly create public disorder. The Watchtower Bible and Tract Society – Jehovah's Witnesses – condemned her to eternal damnation. In Philadelphia, detectives raided movie houses and confiscated copies of the film. In Memphis, the film was not simply banned, but a powerful local women's group warned Bardot that she would never be welcome there. 'Her film is rude, lewd and immoral.'

One American critic hoped to turn off the curious by denouncing Bardot as 'the symbol of the loneliness and insecurity of modern youth'.

Apparently Gary Cooper was so shocked when he viewed the

film, he said he'd pay anything for a bag to put over his head so no one could see that he was there.

Yet all the arguments in the midst of all the tumult failed to deal with one, now undeniable, truth: audiences wanted more skin with their entertainment and they were willing to pay for it.

In the first nine weeks that the film was shown in the States, it out-grossed the movie's entire run in Paris. It became the first French film ever to out-sell an American home-grown epic when it topped the charts, ahead of big Hollywood films like *The Ten Commandments*. In some cities, Bardot's receipts were more than double those of the very popular *Around the World in 80 Days*. But then, never before had Americans seen anything the likes of Brigitte Bardot.

'There lies Brigitte,' *Time* magazine pointed out, 'stretched from end to end of the CinemaScope screen, bottoms up and bare as a censor's eyeball.'

'And God Created Woman,' the publicity hawked, 'but the Devil created Brigitte Bardot.'

The *New York Times* asserted, 'Brigitte conquered New York in three weeks. Marilyn can go back to posing for calendars.'

The *Saturday Evening Post* brought out a special 'BB' – the initials were everywhere – subtitled 'The bad little girl'.

In the Bible belt of America's South, school-organized parents' and teachers' associations considered 'BB' a walking danger to men.

On the other hand, a group of students at Princeton University unofficially awarded her a Doctor of Philosophy and Masters in Physical Education.

This was eroticism in a way Hollywood had not yet dared. Suddenly, every distributor in America wanted Bardot's earlier films – even those that were less than wonderful, like *The Light across the Street*, *Please Mr Balzac* and *The Bride Is Much Too Beautiful*.

The studios wanted her too, and offers in excess of $250,000

74

per picture poured in from Hollywood. In those days that was a staggering sum, worth roughly 10–12 times as much today.

As the film's takings topped $4 million in the US alone, a French paper calculated it was 'as much as the export sale of 2,500 Dauphine cars'. That, in turn, prompted a French government official to note, 'Mlle Bardot is making an important contribution to France's balance of payments.'

The pandemonium caused outside France gave Levy the ammunition he needed to go back to the French distributors to argue for a second release. It was a very rare event, indeed, that a movie should reappear a year after it was first shown. But the distributors knew a money-maker when they saw it. All the more so when they had their noses rubbed in it. Based entirely on the unbelievable response to the film throughout the rest of the world, it was re-released and became a huge success in France, too.

One French paper wrote, 'Since Garbo and Marlene – and here, since Danielle Darrieux – we haven't seen anything like this phenomenon of collective reverence. The greatest directors want to work with her. The greatest actors want to work with her. They all feel if they don't they'll be judged as nobodies. And yet when she's alone in her apartment, before going to the studio to start work on 'La Femme et le Pantin,' BB, triumphant and vulnerable, continues to doubt herself, looking in the mirror and repeating, "I'm bored."'

Nothing, not even Vadim's wildest dreams, could have prepared either of them for what was about to besiege her. While working on the picture, neither of them imagined that they were creating a monster. No one did. That Vadim was an untried, under-age director making a feature film with a substantial budget was already pretty radical. But it was still only ever intended to be an adventure shared by friends and lovers with the enthusiasm of youth.

Vadim shrugs, 'It's so difficult to say afterwards what you were feeling before. But I do recall at the time that I was looking to make a film that could change things. So I wasn't surprised that the film did change things. What shocked me was how the film almost disappeared in France. And also the scandal that surrounded the film's eroticism. You have to understand the mentality of the era in order to understand the extent to which we were still living in the time of dinosaurs. Society was stuck in the Stone Age. It was a major surprise that we were still so far away from any modern view of eroticism, sexuality, women's lib. Funny, but even today I meet people who were then between 17 and 25, and they say that film really did change something for them, like the way they were thinking about women. I couldn't possible have envisioned that at the time.'

·   ·   ·

Given the mythical status that both the film and its star have achieved, all sorts of stories have grown up around it.

While filming interiors at the Victorine Studios that June, Raoul Levy spotted Winston Churchill being given a tour. He rushed up to the man, with Brigitte in tow.

'Allow me,' he said, 'to introduce to you the star of the French cinema, Brigitte Bardot.'

'Decidedly,' the old man said, giving her a good look, 'French cinema is charming.'

Later, Field Marshal Bernard Montgomery was asked what he thought of Brigitte Bardot. His answer was, 'Never set eyes on her, at the cinema or in the newspapers. But I'm meeting Marlene whatever-her-name-is at lunch tomorrow.'

Even though he had his hands full directing, Vadim made certain that a regular flow of copy was coming out of the film's production offices, aimed at the press. For instance, he leaked word that the love scenes Brigitte was doing were the most realistic ever filmed and that the actors were getting so carried away that

76

they continued after the cameras stopped. Reprinted thousands of times, the story has since become part of the film's legend. That Vadim was looking to make headlines has little to do with how true the story was.

Sadly, the film is difficult to watch today. The colour has faded and it all looks very dated. Because it was shot in CinemaScope, when you watch it on television sometimes all you see is Brigitte's nose talking to someone else's nose. Still, it has by now grossed something in the region of £40 million.

For her efforts, Levy paid Brigitte four million old francs ($11,400).

All Vadim ever saw was one million old francs ($2,850). 'That was for 18 months of work. I even calculated that, based on the time I spent writing the script, shooting the film and working on post production, I got less money than a maid would have made during the same time.'

When he first began putting the script together, Vadim had a letter from Raoul Levy promising him 'three points'. Even if that meant three per cent of the net profit, it would have been worth a lot of money. But one day Levy went to Vadim and told him Columbia needed that letter because they had to make some changes. It was a business matter. So Vadim gave him the letter.

He never got it back.

*   *   *

A few years after she made *Et Dieu Créa la Femme*, Brigitte told a journalist how Vadim had promised her within weeks after they'd met that he would make her a star. 'He taught me everything. He made me out to be free with my love. It's part of the legend he built up around me. It's what he has made the public think.'

Yet Vadim gallantly acknowledges that there is a great deal more to her phenomenal success than simply his own Machiavellian genius for publicity.

'It's true that I had friends in the press, had worked as a journalist and that I was always fairly relaxed when it came to the media. So it's easy to confuse the name Vadim with provocation or scandal. I certainly knew how to handle publicity and the press and how to get the media interested in her. But I never pushed Brigitte. I counselled her and made sure that she didn't get involved in dangerous publicity. That's all I had to do with her. She did all the rest by having that wonderful spontaneity when she spoke. It all came from her.'

She was, he asserts, unique enough to become a star simply by playing herself.

'It is precisely because she was not the product of anyone's imagination that Brigitte was able to shock, seduce, create a new style and explode in the world as a sex symbol. She was born with a very personal and imaginative sense of dialogue. She was born with the remarkable ability to arrive somewhere and turn the atmosphere electric. I repeat, she comes from another dimension. I've seen her walk into a restaurant, and this is long before she was known, and watched people who were sitting with their back to the door turn around to see her. And once people spotted her, they couldn't take their eyes off her. That's down to her presence, which comes from outer space somewhere. And it also comes from her *joie de vivre* which, when she isn't trying to kill herself, is enormous.'

Her extraordinary presence is something that has astonished almost everyone who has ever spent time with her.

'She has always had an unbelievable electricity surrounding her,' notes an old friend, photographer Philippe d'Exea. 'I once walked into Regine's nightclub with her. And even in a place like Regine's, where they're more than jaded about famous faces, the instant she came in, everything stopped.'

At the end of Brigitte's career, it was equally evident to her last director, Nina Companeez. 'Call it charisma or magnetism or just the magic spell she could cast. Whatever, it was truly incredible. There was something so obviously unique about her. Of course, she had perfect posture and the most beautiful walk. But it was much more than just that. She'd step into a crowded room and the entire room would stop. I saw it happen all the time, especially in restaurants, where people who were just about to put a fork into their mouth would, literally, freeze right where they were, as if she sent out signals, and they instinctively knew she was there.'

Given such stunning power, Vadim goes on, it's easy to understand how Brigitte could automatically make journalists go 'tilt'.

'The danger was to let her do too much. My role was not to present her to the world but to keep her from over-exposing herself in the media. I was a guide rather than a promoter. I'd tell her watch out for this and watch out for that and, because she used to hate interviews and publicity anyway, it wasn't difficult talking her out of them.'

Publicity might have helped to make her a movie star. But to become an international social phenomenon – to have influenced a generation in the way she did – every element in a very long and complicated formula had to be just right. To understand her, Vadim says, there are several things you need to know.

First: 'Brigitte was a very conventional bourgeois girl. Catholic. Sixteenth arrondissement. You couldn't have found a more establishment upbringing. But the family was nevertheless very interesting, in spite of the fact that the mother and father raised their children following every rule set down by that society. Where she came from, where her manner of speech came from, where her attitude to life came from, it certainly wasn't a part of her upbringing. She didn't go to see underground films. She didn't befriend men on the street. Her early boyfriends all came from the same milieu. She was entirely immersed in this bourgeois, strict society. There's no rational explanation how, in her head, she was Brigitte Bardot.'

Second: 'She had only one real passion and that was dance. No one could know that better than me. People sometimes confuse being a dancer and being an actress and think it's the same thing.

79

It's not at all. For her, dance was a genuine passion. She had a talent for it and she worked at it. Which she never did as an actress.'

Third: 'She met, totally by chance, a young man with whom she fell in love. It was entirely due to sentimental reasons, out of affection for him, out of love – the most grotesque and at the same time beautiful love possible – that she gave up her career as a dancer, abandoned any hope of ever becoming a prima ballerina with an opera company, to follow the man she loved into the movies.'

He emphasizes that no one should believe for an instant that she was in any way prepared for what was to come, to cope with being thrown quite so suddenly into quite such an extraordinary world.

'It's like Dorothy in the *Wizard of Oz*. Brigitte was living with her rabbit on a farm in the middle of nowhere, going to school every day, and suddenly she was swept up by a tornado and taken somewhere else. She had no idea where she was going or what would happen. Except in her case it wasn't a tornado, she was swept up by love.'

*　　*　　*

While filming *Et Dieu Créa la Femme*, she'd fallen for Jean-Louis Trintignant.

At first it seemed to be nothing more than an attempt to make Vadim jealous. When he didn't get jealous – and she would complain about that for years – her fling with Trintignant turned into something a lot more serious.

Vadim had seen the end coming. 'I'd liberated Brigitte and shown her how to be truly herself. That was the beginning of the end of our marriage. From that moment, our marriage went downhill.'

In fact, he says, he'd been preparing himself for it for over a year.

'Brigitte needs such intense passion every moment of her life and I just couldn't fulfil that any longer. I actually found it tender and loving that we ended our marriage in such a way. So many relationships end sadly. People destroy each other. Even if people don't part as enemies, there is always a moment or two when things degrade. But that's not how it ended with us. We ended our marriage with a work of art, a film, we made together, even if we never had any idea what the impact of that film would be. It was a positive, romantic and optimistic way to end a marriage.'

But in his wildest dreams he'd never expected that it would be Trintignant who'd lead Brigitte away from him.

'The first time she met him she said to me, "You're not going to oblige me to work with him. He's got such tiny legs. I couldn't pretend to be in love with him." So, in the beginning, I certainly didn't have the impression that I was throwing Brigitte into the arms of anyone who was going to seduce her. Even though I knew something was going to happen, I didn't have Trintignant in mind.'

According to Vadim, she never said it was because of him that she was so deeply unhappy at times. But while they were living together she would say that he was not giving her what she needed to be happy.

'Later on, after we split, she discovered that she was like that and it never changed. And therefore she couldn't blame it on me. But when we split, it was obsessive in her, that I give her what she wanted. We had some extraordinary moments. I made some mistakes, we were both young, and so was she.'

With Vadim, she was constantly going out, meeting people, going to dinners, the two of them working hard at getting connected in the world of French cinema. With Jean-Lou – that's what she called him – she found a calm, quiet young man who read poetry. She found someone who was almost the exact opposite of Vadim.

She even told her secretary, Alain Carré, 'He is soft and fresh and calm and sincere. Like me, he prefers calm and quiet to the

81

crazy life of studios and cocktail parties. He has a very warm heart and we never argue. With Vadim, we were always arguing and I hated that.'

With Trintignant she'd found what the French call *'l'amour en pantoufles'* – love in bedroom slippers – an easy, relaxed, stay-at-home kind of love. The only problem was that Jean-Louis was married to a young actress called Stéphane Audran.

'I love my husband,' Brigitte said as soon as *Et Dieu Créa la Femme* was finished, 'but I love Jean-Lou more.'

Her separation from Vadim was a genteel affair. 'I've never seen any divorce go as smoothly,' he says. Like the old pals they were, they discussed how they wanted to proceed. 'I asked a friend of mine to be her lawyer and I hired a lawyer who was a friend of hers.'

A little over a year later, in December 1957 – just as *Et Dieu Créa la Femme* was turning her into a household name across the United States – a judge ruled that they were no longer man and wife.

'We divorced in a very civilized and friendly manner,' he smiles, in a gentle, nostalgic way. 'Although there was a sad moment or two. After it was over, she and I found ourselves alone in the hallway of the courthouse. I took her in my arms and we kissed each other.'

Chapter Five

CHARRIER

Once Brigitte and Vadim had officially announced that they were ending their marriage – she explained, 'People blame me for leaving Vadim, saying that I owe everything to him. Maybe I have hurt him. But maybe I was not completely in the wrong' – it seemed only right, in her mind at least, that Trintignant would leave his wife. But that wasn't to be. First the army got in the way. Then Stéphane Audran refused to grant him a divorce.

One month after she finished work on *Et Dieu Créa la Femme*, Brigitte made good on an earlier promise and starred in the Christine Gouze-Renal production of *La Mariée Est Trop Belle* ('The Bride Is Much Too Beautiful') with Louis Jordan. When that was finished, two weeks after her 22nd birthday, she began looking for somewhere new to live with Jean-Lou. She'd decided the Chardon-Lagache flat was too depressing, so she bought herself a new place at 71 Avenue Paul Doumer. It wasn't far from where her parents were living and, by coincidence, it was just around the corner from the main offices of Bardot & Company.

A small maisonette on the seventh and eighth floors, it cost her a then impressive 11 million old francs ($31,500). To the left of the entrance hallway, there was a tiny corner that served as her secretary's office. Her bedroom, on the same floor, was off a small balcony. The living room was upstairs, bright and open, with a fireplace at one end and a dining area next to the kitchen.

Brigitte and Jean-Lou moved in just after New Year's.

Now she went to work for Michel Boisrond filming *La Parisienne* ('Parisienne'), in which Charles Boyer appeared, then started on *Les Bijoutiers du Clair de Lune* ('Heaven Fell That Night'), as part of her multi-film deal with Raoul Levy. To direct, Levy had signed Roger Vadim.

Trintignant's original posting as a conscripted soldier was in Paris, so he left the flat every morning, came back for lunch, left for the afternoon and was home in time for dinner. That worked fine, as long as she was filming in Paris. But in June, when she went to Spain to work with Vadim, it was less than fine. She didn't always get along with Vadim's new wife, Annette Stroyberg, she found the shooting difficult and she hated working on location. To be with Trintignant at weekends, she'd fly back to Paris, which was a considerable strain for someone who detests flying.

In the film, there is a donkey. Having graduated from those youthful days when she owned one cat or one rabbit or one dog to beginning a small menagerie by picking up strays along the way – and given Brigitte's life-long penchant for making friends with every animal within 100 miles of every film set – it's hardly surprising that she would have adopted the donkey. She named him Chorro and, when the hotel where she was staying refused to allow her to keep it in their garage, she brought it up to— her room.

But not all of the animals on the set fared as well. There was a cow in the picture and, to sedate it, a Spanish vet gave it a dose of anaesthesia. The animal reacted to it and there was nothing anyone could do. It died with Brigitte kneeling next to it. Ever since she has actively campaigned against the use of animals in spectacles.

The cow's death depressed her enormously and held up shooting. Combined with her fatigue, it made her ill.

She was also bored. To kill time she began seeing a local

actor named Gustavo Rojo. Word of that got back to Trintignant after Rojo – rather prematurely and without mentioning anything of the kind to Brigitte – announced their wedding plans. Needless to say, Jean-Lou was less than thrilled. By the time the picture was finished and Trintignant might have had a chance to patch things up with her, he was transferred to an army post at Trier, Germany.

By Christmas the romance was over.

'She wears people out,' declares Alain Carré, who lived through this period as her secretary and chief confidant. 'She is impulsive. She has also always been someone who can easily hurt people when she's angry. Jean-Louis was charming but too weak to take her in hand. He wasn't man enough to control her.'

For a time she continued spending weekends with Trintignant – taking the train to Germany on Friday nights, returning to Paris on Sunday nights, faithfully accompanied by Carré. But it wasn't long before the best thing she could say about those weekends was that, at least she didn't have to fly there.

'She's never been one to love from afar,' Carré goes on. 'A man can never leave her on her own. Brigitte needs someone with her day and night.'

Trintignant's absence was filled briefly by a young French composer–singer named Gilbert Becaud. Trintignant found out about that too and, rather than risk a scandal, Becaud – who was married at the time – tried to back off.

As Brigitte herself used to relate the story, Becaud was working in Geneva and she was determined to see him. One day she simply showed up unexpectedly. Because he didn't want people to know she was there with him, he suggested that, before the end of his show, she should sneak into his dressing room and hide in the toilet. He said that, after everyone was gone, they could then go out for dinner.

So while he was on stage, she snuck into his dressing room and hid in the toilet. But before long she fell asleep.

When she woke up, well after midnight, the theatre was empty and Becaud was not there waiting for her.

Drunk with rage, she found his car outside a restaurant, got into it, stuck her foot on the horn and blasted it, non-stop. She woke the entire neighbourhood and caused such a rumpus that Becaud had to tell reporters that Brigitte was making a nuisance of herself.

As a result, she took ill, leaving Carré to tell the press that food poisoning due to some bad mussels was not, as they were speculating, another suicide attempt.

*   *   *

Her career was reaching full speed. And, although she didn't know it, her career would stay at full speed for nearly ten more years.

When Otto Preminger bought the screen rights to Françoise Sagan's *Bonjour Tristesse*, he thought about hiring Bardot to play Cecile – a spoiled little girl who gets herself involved with her father's love triangle. Vadim talked Bardot out of accepting the part. Preminger employed Jean Seberg instead and the film failed.

Around the same time, Vadim and Levy got it into their heads that a perfect on-screen match would be Brigitte with Frank Sinatra. Vadim did an outline of a story and met with Sinatra in Las Vegas. Sinatra seemed interested, so they got into some serious discussion. They even reached the point where Levy was willing to offer both of them $200,000 plus a cut of the profits. But Brigitte refused to do the film in the States and Sinatra refused to come to Paris, and the deal fizzled out. 'It doesn't matter,' Sinatra remarked. 'People would have been sick of her before our picture was even made.'

Bob Hope wanted her too.

His television production staff proposed to pay her $25,000 for a ten-minute appearance. Olga assured Hope's people that Brigitte wouldn't do it, but passed along the request anyway.

86

True to form, Brigitte said no because she'd planned to go to Meribel to ski. Hope tried to persuade her, saying they'd come to Paris for her. He said, all you have to do is show up at a studio, stand around with me for ten minutes and then going skiing. But Brigitte said, no, I'm going skiing, turned her back on Hope's $25,000 and left, on schedule, for Meribel.

Unable to sign Sinatra, Raoul Levy cast her alongside France's biggest male lead, Jean Gabin, in a drama based on a novel by Georges Simenon, called *En Cas de Malheur* ('Love Is My Profession').

When Gabin was told that she was his co-star, he was genuinely shocked. 'What? That thing that goes around naked?' He soon found her to be both a lot more professional and a lot more fragile than he'd imagined. He was soon describing her as someone who obviously needed a lot of affection.

Exhausted after that film, she and Mijanou left Paris for a brief skiing holiday at Cortina d'Ampezzo in Italy. But there was no taking time off from the press.

'There were so many paparazzi chasing after her,' Mijanou says, 'following her everywhere, always taking pictures, never letting up for even a few seconds, that she wound up spending three days hiding in her room. She wouldn't come out. There were journalists actually standing in front of the door, trying to listen to what we were saying inside.'

Always willing to protect her big sister, Mijanou tried to fight them off. But she was out-gunned and out-manoeuvred at every turn. And occasionally, Mijanou says, her efforts to defend Brigitte backfired.

'Going out with Brigitte one night, she whispered to me, "Watch out, there are photographers just over there." I was so angry at the way they kept stalking her, at the way they were so obsessed with her and at the way they were ruining her life, that I took off my shoe and threatened them with it. I screamed at the top of my voice, "Leave us alone. Go away." Brigitte thought it was hilarious and the next morning there was the photo in the papers, of a crazy younger sister waving her shoe and, behind her, Brigitte with an angelic smile.'

For her next movie, she went back to sex and striptease in *La Femme et le Pantin* ('A Woman Like Satan'), the third time she'd worked for Christine Gouze-Renal.

Although this was her 22nd film in only six years, she was now almost exactly half way through her acting career.

An early hint that all was not well with her life came in an aside she made to someone on the set of that picture. She mused, 'I feel I've missed out in life. I should never have made movies. But now I'm caught up in the rat race. Perhaps at 18 I should have married someone stable, a real companion. Perhaps I should have had children, a villa at Arcachon, and a lot of togetherness without all the dramatics.'

She wasn't yet 24.

At the end of that year, *Cinémonde* magazine voted Bardot and Gabin their number one stars. But the French were not the only ones. Bardot was beginning to top all the popular lists as everyone's favourite actress, easily beating off any competition in Europe from Michele Morgan or Gina Lollobrigida, and in the States from Elizabeth Taylor or Marilyn Monroe.

Word came from the USSR that Russian fans, who'd only heard about her and had never seen one of her pictures, were paying a week's wages for a black-market photo of her. While Germans fans started fighting if they had to queue too long to get into one of her films.

In Britain, the head of a chain of cinemas that specialized in sex films commissioned a local artist to produce a near-nude, life-size plastic model of Bardot, which he then placed in the lobby of the movie house showing her latest picture. First, the model was stolen. It turned up only several days later in the lost property office at Euston Station. When the film had run its course, the model was put up for sale. One woman wanted it to give to her son for his 21st birthday. Another wanted it for her fiancé. An artist wanted it because, where he lived, in the north of England, he couldn't get nude models. Offers also came in from the crew of a Royal Navy ship, and from the sailors who worked in the engine room of the ocean liner the *Queen Elizabeth*. It was eventually sold to someone in Manchester who wanted it, just because he wanted it.

By this point, there couldn't be anyone in the world who doubted that the camera loved her. Some women can be very beautiful in person and for some reason that beauty doesn't translate onto the big screen. But Bardot had everything and, when she was photographed, it was amazing. She was acclaimed as the most beautiful woman in the world. Some people also saw her as the most dangerous woman in the world. Others felt she was the most liberated. Brigitte Bardot was inexorably trapped inside the myth that was coming to be known as 'BB'.

'For a while,' she's said, 'my initials protected me. I could hide behind them. People would speak about "BB" and I would think they were talking about someone I didn't know. They would say, BB is this or that, right or wrong, without knowing anything about the real Bardot.'

As for who first named her that, she has a typically cynical response. 'Considering that Brigitte and Bardot both start with the same letter, it was obviously a very erudite person.'

The fun had long since worn off. She simply wasn't interested in show business. Explains Olga Horstig-Primuz, 'She used to get so nervous making films that she'd break out in spots.'

Brigitte saw herself trapped, and years later admitted, 'I never found any real pleasure in acting. It was never the basis of my existence.' She saw it as nothing more than a job. When she went to the studio, she would tell herself, 'I'm going to the office.' The only reason she was willing to work at her job was because it was a way of earning a lot of money. But she knew by now that she didn't want all the things that came along with immense fame. Unfortunately for her, it would take another 15 years before she would begin to extricate herself from it.

Generally punctual and better prepared with her lines than

many stars, Brigitte went to the studio because she had to, because that was the office and offices are where people go to work. Her father had set that example for her. The only benefit of being on location was that, at least while she was working, she could also look at the mountains or the beach. In that sense, she showed a certain discipline. It's just that, because she didn't really care about the cinema, she had a unique method when it came to choosing films.

'She didn't decide to do a film because she loved the script,' Gouze-Renal says frankly, 'she chose her films for the director, or the other actors, or, in my case, because of the producer. Someone would come to her and say let's make this movie and she would like them enough to say okay. Whether the script was wonderful or awful didn't come into it. And in many cases she chose her films badly. Some of them are downright awful.'

It wasn't that she didn't know how to read a script – which is one of the crafts that any actor must learn – it was rather that she didn't pay much attention to the script.

'If it sounded cute,' Vadim says, 'she'd do it. That was the basis of her decision. She'd say, "*Oh, c'est mignon*" – it's cute – and sign on. Of course, that's no criterion for a serious actress. But for her, the easier it was, the lighter weight it was, the more *mignon* she found it. And when she got into an important drama, something heavyweight, she'd hate it and would walk around saying, "Why have I started this?" And, "What kind of hell have I put myself into?" No, she never found any real pleasures in being an actress and her criteria for doing a film were very peculiar.'

Ironically, she might have found herself in better films – maybe even have had a much more rewarding career – had she been less beautiful. But because she was so frighteningly beautiful, everyone was always telling her that – she heard that all day, every day. After a while she couldn't help but believe it. The roles she was offered were almost always for very beautiful women and didn't stretch her acting ability.

Vadim agrees. 'It's true that in the choice of her scenarios she lacked the necessary discipline to find the best films. But again, that was because she didn't like making movies. She wasn't interested. She did it superficially. Although there's another way of looking at it too. If she lacked the desire, it might have stemmed from a keen sense of lucidity, where she knew enough to be afraid of certain roles in advance. Those roles might have been more interesting but they were too far afield from the personality of Brigitte Bardot. Roles where she'd have to play someone else besides herself. So in the end she always came back to the easy roles, where she could be Bardot.'

Jacques Charrier's opinion coincides with Vadim's. 'She could have had a very different career, a huge career as an actress, but she didn't want it. She never really wanted to expand her talents, to go to the limits, and beyond. More importantly, she was never able to distance herself from her career. It haunted her entire life.'

*   *   *

Within a year of purchasing the apartment on the Avenue Paul Doumer, she bought La Madrague and began spending what time off she had in St Tropez.

That's where she met Sacha Distel.

The nephew of a well-known French bandleader, Ray Ventura, Distel had been on the periphery of stardom for a few years. He was young, quite handsome and obviously ambitious. He started the school of music that came to be known in France as 'Scoubidou' – an early version of French rock and roll and part of what would come to be known throughout the world, thanks to the Beatles, as 'The Yeah Yeah Yeah' vogue.

It was the summer of 1958, a few months after her divorce from Vadim was finalized. She was not yet 24. He was just 25.

Hanging out in a small rented flat in St Tropez, he bumped into a young woman he knew named Irène Dervize, a journalist with *Paris Match*, in town to write a piece about Bardot.

The way he tells the story, Bardot was proving difficult and was refusing to see Dervize. 'Brigitte was terrified by her new-found fame and literally under siege by journalists from all over the world.'

He says she was trying to protect herself by hiding at La Madrague and Dervize was just about to head back to Paris. As a last resort, she implored Distel to go with her to La Madrague. The idea was they'd bang on the door and see what happened. Distel insists that he wasn't too sure how good an idea this was, didn't particularly want to impose and, anyway, wasn't by any means certain that Brigitte would open the door for him either. But Dervize was persistent and so the two set off. To the surprise of them both, according to Distel, Bardot not only opened the door but seemed genuinely glad to see them – especially Distel.

Irène Dervize – who is these days Irène Bolling, wife of one of Europe's foremost jazz men, Claude Bolling – is adamant that it didn't happen that way. She claims that, when she told Distel she was going to La Madrague, he invited himself along.

In any case, that meeting turned into an article for Irène Dervize and a dinner invitation for Sacha Distel.

As there wasn't much in the fridge – again, that's Distel's version, and he later incurred Bardot's wrath by explaining that there was hardly ever anything in her fridge because she was too stingy to put anything in the fridge – they went to a restaurant. Afterwards they made their way to a club called L'Esquinade. The cha-cha was in vogue, so they cha-cha'd for much of the night. Then came a few slow songs, and Distel found Bardot in his arms. He went back to La Madrague with her that night.

It turned into a full-blown summer romance.

Young and beautiful, they made a splendid couple. Within three days, they were front-page news, hounded and followed wherever they went. Photographers followed them from St Tropez to Paris. Mob scenes greeted them in Italy in September 1958 when they arrived at the Venice Film Festival together. It took a force of 4,000 policemen to protect them from the crowds.

None of it particularly pleased Bardot, who was all too familiar with this sort of thing. At the same time, none of it particularly hurt Distel's budding career. The story that now circulates among those journalists who recall those heady days of the Bardot–Distel romance has Distel himself tipping off the journalists to their whereabouts. At one point, so they say, certain journalists actually told him, if you ring us again, we'll never mention you in our papers for as long as you live.

For a while there was some serious talk of marriage. The press reported that when Distel introduced Brigitte to his parents, his mother gave Brigitte her own engagement ring – a star-shaped sapphire encircled with diamonds. Today, Brigitte says that's not true. Although, she confirms that when she introduced Distel to Pilou and Toty, they were less enthusiastic about this possible match than his parents were.

But the burden of being engaged to her proved too difficult even for him to bear. More than 30 years later he labelled his affair with her 'a full-time job. She needed the man she was in love with to be with her constantly, to do the things she wanted to do, and to take second place.' In the end, he says, 'I didn't want to be Monsieur Bardot.'

That said, being referred to as the future Mr Bardot didn't stop him at the time from launching his singing career.

In those days, the actor André Pousse was one of France's leading impresarios, booking acts for many night clubs and also representing several American variety shows, including Ed Sullivan. One day, Sullivan rang Pousse to say, 'I want Bardot.'

Knowing he didn't even have to ask Brigitte, he told Sullivan, 'Forget it. She won't go to America. She hates to fly.'

Sullivan urged Pousse, 'Offer her as much as $50,000 for three minutes.'

In an era when many people weren't earning one-fifth of that for a year's work, it was a colossal amount of money. And, with a ten per cent fee earmarked for Pousse simply for arranging the deal, he promised Sullivan to do his best. But he cautioned, 'Don't get your hopes up because it won't work.'

93

True to his word, Pousse rang Bardot and passed along Sullivan's offer. And true to his intuition, she turned him down flat.

Trying to keep Sullivan happy – and still thinking about his commission – Pousse rang the television host with a counter-proposal. 'I can get you Brigitte Bardot's fiancé.'

Realizing how any use of Bardot's name could draw an audience, Sullivan quickly agreed to pay Distel a $6,000 appearance fee. Once that was settled, Pousse gave him the bad news. 'Brigitte's name cannot be mentioned.'

'No matter,' Sullivan said, and a few Sunday nights later he introduced Distel to America as 'the man who every man in the world envies and wishes he'd been engaged to this man's fiancée.'

Such was Bardot's fame that no names had to be mentioned. No one in the States had yet heard of Distel, but they knew immediately who his fiancée was.

Their torrid summer faded into a chilly autumn, as she prepared for work on a Raoul Levy comedy set in World War II, *Babette s'en Va-t-en Guerre* ('Babette Goes to War').

Distel faded into the background. She left him with a budding career. But he too left her with more than just memories. He left her with a life-long passion for the guitar. As she says, 'He brought music into my life.'

Rather ironically, some time after Distel broke up with Vadim's first wife, he found himself involved with Annette Stroyberg, Vadim's second wife.

Remarks Vadim, 'Sacha seemed to display a marked penchant for my women. It was a tribute to my good taste that I would have willingly done without.'

·   ·   ·

Her new co-star was born in Metz, France, in 1936.

His father, Joseph Charrier, was a colonel in the French artillery, so the boy grew up as an army kid, moving from post to post, living in different places, including Africa. But, unlike his brothers, who opted for military careers, he studied at the Ecole des Beaux Arts and, with his heart-throb good looks, drifted from painting, ceramics, interior architecture, into acting. After training at the Centre d'Art Dramatique in Paris, he began appearing on stage, including the French production of *The Diary of Anne Frank*.

From there he got his first film, *Les Tricheurs* ('The Cheaters').

Levy had seen Jacques Charrier on stage – Brigitte had as well – and decided he was promotable enough, both for his talent and for his looks. So Levy was willing to consider him as his second choice for the male lead in *Babette*. Charrier got the role after David Niven said no.

During shooting in Paris and London, she quickly fell for Charrier.

When the two of them came to England together, she announced that she wouldn't be staying at the Savoy, where a suite was booked for her, but was moving into Jacques' hotel, the Mount Royal at Marble Arch.

Typical of the frenzy her presence inspired, the manager of the Mount Royal ordered his biggest suite to be completely redecorated for her. And at the Royal Air Force base at Abingdon where she was scheduled to spend a Saturday and Sunday filming, the commander announced that, for the first time in his military career, most of his personnel had refused weekend passes.

Falling in love with Charrier brought with it a familiar dose of indecision. Back in Paris she realized the Distel connection hadn't been cleanly severed and that he was still a part of her life.

Nor did Distel make it easier for her. In a last-ditch effort to keep from losing her, he tried to recruit help from Alain Carré. He wanted Carré to convince Brigitte to go to St Tropez – to get her away from Charrier for a while – so that she could consider the future. He believed that, given time, she'd come to her senses, realize that her future lay with him, and happily put everything back together.

Carré broached the subject and, at first, Brigitte agreed.

An hour later she changed her mind. She said, since she and Carré were going to St Tropez, they might as well invite Charrier along. So she told Carré, get on the phone and extend the invitation to Jacques. But Charrier was not to be found and the best Carré could do was to leave messages all over town for him.

Now Distel phoned again and, after a long heart-to-heart with Brigitte, she announced to Carré that, instead of going to St Tropez with Charrier, she was staying in Paris to be with Sacha.

At that point, Charrier rang to say he'd got a message that Brigitte was looking for him. Carré put her on the phone. A few minutes later she told him, you, Alain and I are going to St Tropez on the Blue Train tonight. Don't be late. She then left it to Carré to tell Distel that she was, in fact, going to St Tropez as originally planned.

Well, sort of as originally planned.

When Brigitte and Carré arrived at the Gare de Lyon, Charrier was waiting for them. She and Jacques spent four days together at La Madrague, before he had to return to Paris. No sooner was he gone than Brigitte phoned Distel and asked him to come to St Tropez.

Driving a fancy little sports car, Distel rushed south, only to have an accident outside Aix-en-Provence. He wasn't injured, but the car was ruined. Convinced he had to get to her as soon as possible, he arrived at La Madrague after a 120-kilometre journey in a taxi. But he didn't stay long. They both realized it wasn't working and that same night he was on a train for Paris.

Any torch Distel might have carried for her after that was thoroughly doused when, at the end of April 1959, she went off to Chamonix-les-Houches with Charrier. Staying together in a chalet, completely isolated by a late spring snowstorm, Brigitte got pregnant.

Charrier had wanted this to happen. She'd done her best to

prevent it. But in those pre-pill days, they both knew how easily accidents could happen. As soon as she found out that she was pregnant, even before she told Charrier, she phoned Vadim. She said she absolutely needed to see him but wouldn't say why. He offered to call in. She said no, that Jacques was very jealous. She said it was his nature to be very tough with her – that was, decidedly, a new experience for her – and she didn't want him to find out that she'd called.

Vadim promised to pick her up in his latest blue hardtop Daytona Ferrari on a street corner at the Port de la Mouette. She was there anxiously waiting for him. She jumped into the car, they started driving around and that's when she told him, 'I'm pregnant. What do I do now?'

She'd been pregnant before, by him, and together they'd dealt with one of those pregnancies in Switzerland. He knew she didn't like children. And if having a child upset her to the point that she might do something stupid – such as get depressed and try to commit suicide – it would be wrong to insist she have it. He knew it would be easy for her to go back to Switzerland and handle it that way.

But then he thought to himself, when a woman has a child there is a metabolic and a psychological change that takes place and maybe this will change her feelings towards children. He wondered, how will she ever know if she really dislikes children unless she has one. He also worried that if she had any doubts, if she thought she might want this child, it would be wrong to insist she have an abortion.

'Intellectually,' he says, 'had I followed my own instincts, I would have suggested she have the abortion. But given the circumstances and all the emotion that surrounds the miracle of birth, even if the odds were one in ten thousand that she would love this child, I urged her to have it. We drove around for an hour and a half. I argued that if she didn't have this child, she'd go to the end of her life never know-ing if she could love a child. I think it's that discussion she

97

and I had in my car that helped her decide to have the child.'

Vadim's wasn't the only counsel Brigitte sought. In the midst of such a major dilemma, she also turned to Christine Gouze-Renal.

The two women talked about it – Gouze-Renal also knew that Brigitte didn't like children – so she offered to help her get an abortion. It wasn't yet legal in France – that wouldn't happen for another ten years – but abortions were readily accessible to anyone with enough money to pay for one.

However, when Gouze-Renal and Brigitte contacted the most famous gynaecologist in France – who would normally have performed the operation – he refused to do it for medical reasons and the clinic in Switzerland refused on the grounds that Bardot was now too famous.

Gouze-Renal explains, 'There was no way Brigitte could sneak into a clinic without everyone for miles around knowing about it. And no one in that business wanted to make headlines.'

*   *   *

Brigitte announced the news to Charrier and he insisted she have the baby. He also said they would get married.

Unsure of herself, afraid of what motherhood would be like, worried about how she could ever cope with a child, Brigitte nevertheless agreed. Anyway, by that time, word was already starting to spread through the media that she was expecting. Terminating her pregnancy was, at this stage, just about impossible.

Not surprisingly, given the problems the media had already caused her, she and Charrier wanted to keep their wedding plans a secret. They were both apprehensive that fans and the press would ruin what they hoped could be a small family wedding. And their fears were well founded.

Unable to get married in church – as far as the Vatican

was concerned, Brigitte was still married to Vadim – the civil ceremony was set for 18 June, at the town hall in Louveciennes, where the Norwegian chalet was.

With only one week to go, Bardot and Charrier showed up in St Tropez, both wearing wedding rings, telling the reporters who tracked them wherever they went that they were already married. The idea was to put them off the scent of the actual ceremony. On Wednesday 17 June – the day Bardot and Charrier returned to Paris – Toty confirmed in St Tropez that the couple had married ten days before. She did not say where the wedding had taken place, simply that the knot had already been tied.

That ruse failed.

So did the one worked out by Alain Carré and Bardot's stand-in, Maguy Mortini.

Newspaper and magazine editors were sure something was about to happen so they posted photographers on 24-hour sentry duty outside the flat on Avenue Paul Doumer. To mislead them, Carré and Mortini pretended to be Jacques and Brigitte. They kept the lights on in the apartment until late at night, frequently appearing at the window, giving the photographers brief glimpses of the happy couple. By then, Charrier and Bardot had long since made their way to Louveciennes.

Unfortunately, someone at the town hall had leaked the truth – that the ceremony was on for Thursday – and, when the two families arrived for the secret wedding, *Paris Match* was waiting for them.

Included among the 10–12 member crew was Brigitte's friend, photographer Philippe Letellier. 'A wedding in France must be held in public. That's the law. So we felt perfectly entitled to go into the room with them.'

Curiously, overseeing every marriage in the country is a bust of Marianne, the symbol of France. Little did Bardot know, as Mayor Fernand Guillaume invited the two families to take their places in the *Salle de Mariage* – where Marianne stared down at them – that one day her face would adorn the bust of Marianne.

That one day she would be chosen by popular ballot to be the symbol of France. And that for many years to come, literally millions of young couples would gaze back at Brigitte Bardot bearing witness to their wedding.

Suddenly, there were flashbulbs going off everywhere.

Startled that the photographers had followed them into the room, Brigitte burst into tears. 'I don't want my picture taken.'

Charrier screamed, 'This is impossible. It could only happen in France.'

Pilou turned on the Guillaume, and blamed him. 'I come to you and this is how you receive me?'

The mayor retorted that he had nothing to do with it. Bizarrely he claimed, 'I can't, after all, disguise myself as a boxer to marry them.'

Pilou told him, 'Monsieur, you're ruining everything.'

Guillaume took offence, 'Monsieur, you're annoying me.'

The local police chief arrived just in time to demand of Pilou, 'How dare you speak to the mayor like that.'

To which Pilou answered, 'For God's sake, I'm the father!'

Now Colonel Charrier tried to intervene, only to be told by the police chief that, had he been warned this might happen, he could have provided additional officers to keep the peace.

Bardot-père insisted something be done.

The mayor indicated that the wedding party – and only the wedding party – should follow him into his office. Everyone reassembled there, but again, in keeping with French law, Guillaume ordered that the door to his office remain open. The police chief posted a few men to keep the photographers out. Indignant that they were being denied their livelihood, the photographers started fighting, first with the police, then with each other, pushing and shoving to get a better position in the open doorway.

In the middle of this clamour, the ceremony lasted seven minutes.

The groom kissed the bride, the in-laws shook hands, everyone apologized to the mayor and the mayor apologized to everyone. Brigitte Bardot was officially Mme Jacques Charrier.

Next came the task of getting out of the town hall. There was only one exit, so, putting on a brave face, the Charriers and the Bardots fought their way through the camera-clicking mob, got into their cars and retreated to behind the high wall at the Bardot family villa.

After a private luncheon there, Carré and Mortini resumed their disguises. And this time they pulled off the trick pretty well. Shielding their faces to make the photographers think it was Bardot and Charrier in the rear seat of a car, they raced the paparazzi back to Paris. Once inside the apartment, they locked the door and refused to come out. The photographers took up their vigil and the stand-off began.

As soon as the coast was clear back in Louveciennes, Bardot and Charrier left unnoticed for the Gare de Lyons where they caught the Blue Train for Ste Maxime. From there, they drove to La Madrague and spent nearly 10 days of peace and quiet.

But the marriage seemed jinxed.

Charrier suffered an attack of appendicitis and was forced into hospital. Before he was fully recovered, Brigitte had to move to Nice to start work on *Voulez Vous Dancer Avec Moi* ('Come Dance With Me'), her third outing with director Michel Boisrond. And already the press was pondering her future with Charrier.

Bardot responded with characteristic candour. 'Each time I've had a new love,' she said, 'I haven't made it a mystery. I spoke about him, I showed him off. It is precisely my frankness that scandalizes people. I swear to you that if I didn't love Jacques Charrier, my husband, any more, I would say so. If there was ever someone else, I would say so as well. It's not because I am, now again, a married woman, that I am going to change.'

A few days out of the hospital, as Charrier was recuperating in Nice, word came from the army that he would have to report for his military service in November. The obligation in those days was two years. And, even though he came from a military family,

Charrier could tell this wasn't going to be easy. He arrived at the embarkation centre on time and was sent to a post in Orange, leaving her to live alone.

It was history repeating itself – shades of Trintignant.

But Charrier was less able to cope with army life than Jean-Lou. He was constantly taunted by the men in his barracks. Sexy photos of Brigitte turned up everywhere. They joked and teased him and, because he was Bardot's husband, the press was never far away. There was no way he was going to be treated like any other soldier by the other soldiers. He tried to get out, but the army turned him down.

When word arrived that his wife needed him – she was now eight months pregnant – Charrier was granted a three-day pass. They'd been apart only four or five weeks, but when he walked in the door she hardly recognized him. He'd lost nearly 20 pounds and was stuttering badly. Two days later, at the thought of having to return to camp, Charrier broke down. He was taken to the Val de Grâce hospital where he was put through an intensive sleep cure. While under observation there, Charrier tried to slit his wrists. As a result, with his health in tatters and the birth of his baby imminent, he was granted compassionate leave of absence for one year.

The state of her husband's health, together with the press barrage that they were both subjected to, took their toll on her. She now told close friends that Charrier had forced her to have this baby and that pregnancy was God's punishment.

It seemed as if the whole world was against her. And wherever she turned, those feelings were reinforced. One day, after visiting Charrier in the clinic, Brigitte went for a walk with her father. They hadn't gone a block when a man came up to her and started insulting her. 'You little slut. It didn't take long to find another man.'

By the time Charrier returned to the apartment, the paparazzi were lining up along the Avenue Paul Doumer waiting for the birth of the baby. Brigitte had purchased the two-room flat next door to use as a nursery. But at this point she still intended to have her baby in a hospital.

As soon as the name of her doctors got out, journalists tried to bribe them into sneaking cameras into the delivery room and taking photographs of the new-born baby. Whenever a possible clinic was mentioned for the birth, reporters took up positions there, waiting for her, bribing nurses to get pictures.

Whoever managed to come up with those first photos of Brigitte Bardot's baby could name their price – suddenly they were, without a doubt, the hottest commodity in Europe.

The press kept phoning her, slipping questionnaires under her door, then knocking on her door hoping she'd be the one to answer it. They blocked the street and rented flats across from hers, setting up their cameras to get pictures of her at home.

With a month to go, Brigitte found herself trapped in her own apartment, forced to live there with the curtains shut to protect herself from long-lensed intrusions.

Her sister Mijanou remembers, 'Brigitte's marriage with Jacques was already extremely difficult for her. She's always needed a lot of affection and Charrier never gave her much of that. There is this very immature side of her, where she needs to be treated like a little doll. Charrier wasn't capable of doing that. But when the press turned her pregnancy into a major news story and she found herself trapped inside her apartment, like a hostage, that was inhumane. She spent the last month of her pregnancy imprisoned in her apartment because there were so many journalists downstairs waiting for her, and photographers across the street, her life became a living hell.'

In an attempt to secure a bit of privacy, Charrier hired bodyguards. He put two of them at their front door with orders to keep the press away. A third was stationed downstairs, at the entrance of the building. But the crowds outside were so big and, at times, so unruly – shoving matches broke out every time anyone tried to get through the crowd – that the police were forced to station officers there for crowd control. Even then, Pilou and Toty were pushed and shoved when they came to visit, as were any delivery men. When one showed up with a crib and another followed shortly afterwards with a cot, the rumour spread that she was expecting twins.

Exasperated, Bardot signed a letter written by Charrier and addressed to the editors of all the newspapers and news agencies in Paris. 'Please stop this harassment, which is so especially difficult to stand for a woman about to give birth.' In exchange for some peace and quiet, she wrote, she would meet with reporters after her child was born.

Apparently, it didn't have any effect.

With no news to report, stories broke that Bardot had been insured for five million francs ($1 million) should anything go wrong during the birth.

Hoping to extract a truce by answering a few questions, she agreed to respond to a list put to her in writing by the newspaper *L'Aurore*. They asked the usual, silly questions. Her answers showed, however, that she was still, somehow, trying keep her sense of humour.

Q: Do you want a boy or a girl?

A: A boy. There are already too many girls in my family.

Q: If it's a boy, what will his name be?

A: I don't know.

Q: And if it's a girl?

A: It will be a boy.

Q: Have you gone to childbirth classes or read anything about childbirth?

A: No. I'm looking for subjects for my next film.

Q: Will being a mother change your style of acting?

A: Why?

Q: Will you take the baby yourself for walks in the street?

A: You'd like that a lot.

Q: Will you show him your films? And if so, which ones.

A: He'll have to wait until he's 16.

Not content with that, reporters clamoured for more stories. When a rumour spread she'd somehow snuck out – which was virtually impossible, as all the doors were well covered – reporters raced to the four nearest hospitals, where they claimed beds had been reserved for her at each one.

No sooner had they staked out the clinics than another rumour spread – this one that she'd somehow made her way to Le Bourget airport and had hopped a flight to Holland where she was going to have her baby at a well-guarded, secret location. The airport was abruptly inundated with journalists who refused to believe the staff that no one named Bardot or Charrier had recently flown out from there to anywhere.

Not yet convinced that their readers were satiated with Bardot stories, *L'Aurore* published the Le Bourget flight to Holland rumour under the slightly misleading banner headline, 'Brigitte Bardot a Disparu'. In the literal sense it translates directly to, 'Brigitte Bardot Has Disappeared'. While that's what the rumour was – and even though a rumour should never be a valid excuse for running any story – that's also the phrasing French newspapers use to announce prominent deaths.

Back along the Avenue Paul Doumer, confusion reigned to the point that the local police sent a senior officer and eight more men to maintain public order. Acting on complaints by her neighbours, a police search of the neighbourhood found reporters and photographers hiding everywhere – including inside her building and on all the nearby roofs. Two fellows who showed up claiming to be TV repairmen – complete with overalls, toolbox and ladders – attempted to climb up to the roof but were immediately uncovered as photographers. When the police began to clear the area, fights broke out and arrests were made.

On the Saturday before the birth, another pair of photographers got into the building and onto the back stairs. Dressed as nuns, they claimed to be collecting money for their church. Their intention was to knock on her door, get sight of her and shoot a fast picture. But they were stopped in the hallway by Charrier.

The incident so upset Brigitte – in the midst of all this constant commotion – that one of her doctors put his foot down and said he wanted her transported immediately to a clinic where she could be better looked after and better protected.

But it was now virtually impossible for her to leave the apartment.

As if that wasn't enough, she'd been suffering for some months from a recurring urinary infection that, in her ninth month, had brought on a minor complication that caused a lot of pain in her kidneys. She hated what she looked like, hated what this baby inside her was doing to her body, hated the way the world had closed in on her, hated the fact that she was a prisoner in her own home and was in constant pain.

'It was inhuman what the press put me through,' she explained to a French television audience 20 years later. 'I couldn't take a walk. I couldn't go out. I couldn't go to see my doctor. I couldn't even have my baby in a hospital. I was encircled by the press from all over the world. Journalists rented maids' rooms across the street, for fabulous sums, so they could peek into my living room. For three months, with curtains drawn and shutters closed, I lived buried, without moving. I couldn't even go to have X-rays, which I needed.'

Her doctors finally ordered that a birthing room be set up in the apartment. And on Monday 11 January 1960, a little after 2:30 in the morning, Nicolas Charrier was born.

An hour later, the weary new father went downstairs to announce his son's birth to the 300-strong crowd of photographers and reporters camped outside. He informed them that Brigitte had been in labour for four hours, that the baby weighed just over six pounds and that when his wife was told she had a boy, her response was, '*Chic alors*' – 'How neat!'

He then invited everyone into the café on the corner for a glass of champagne, to toast the baby's health.

Shortly thereafter, *Cinémonde* magazine estimated that there had been more than one million lines written about her in French

106

daily newspapers, to this point, and twice as much in the weeklies. They also surmised that almost 30,000 photographs of her had been published worldwide. Another survey showed that Brigitte Bardot was the main topic of conversation in 47 per cent of all French homes.

Two decades later, having been retired for ten years, *Le Journal du Dimanche* conducted a survey called 'Women and French Political Life'. When they asked 18–24 year olds which woman they thought had accomplished the most for the image of France, Brigitte Bardot was the clear winner.

That same year, the readers of *Paris Match* magazine voted her the most admired woman in France.

Chapter Six

BIRTHDAY BLUES

A French film crew was shooting a now long-forgotten picture in the Arizona desert. And in the midst of such heat, the director sent someone out to buy sodas. The hapless messenger drove for a dozen miles before he came to a tiny general store and petrol station in the middle of absolutely nowhere. He went inside, gathered up all the drinks he could find, put them on the counter and reached for his wallet. That's when he discovered, to his chagrin, he didn't have any American money.

Reluctant to return empty handed, he offered the man behind the counter the only thing he had – a 100 franc note.

The petrol station owner took it, stared at it for a long time, then wondered, 'What the hell is this?'

The messenger put on a brave face. 'It's French money,' he said, as if he always paid for everything in America this way.

The petrol station owner grunted, checked both sides of the banknote, then pointed to the picture on the front. 'This guy here, this De Gaulle?'

'Ah . . .' the Frenchman said, 'No.'

The petrol station owner turned the bill over. 'This here Brigitte Bardot?'

'Ah . . .' the Frenchman had to admit, 'No, no, it's not.'

The American shook his head, 'Not De Gaulle? Not Brigitte Bardot?' He returned it, 'No good.'

*   *   *

On the morning of her 26th birthday – by then she was one of the most famous women in the world – Brigitte Bardot had convinced herself that fame was the source of her unhappiness.

The incessant clash between her private life and her public persona had become unbearable.

She didn't feel capable of looking after Nicolas – 'How could you expect me to raise a child when I still needed my mother?' – and her marriage with Charrier was on the rocks. Everything she did and everything she said and everything she wore was reported in the press. But now, having tracked her, haunted her, photographed her, scrutinized her, analysed her and invented stories about her, they were criticizing her. They were insisting she wasn't real, that she was merely the embodiment of male fantasy, that she was nothing more than a dream of conquest without consequence. Death seemed like an easy way out.

*   *   *

As soon as she was capable of returning to work, six weeks after the birth of her son, Brigitte made a brief, uncredited appearance in *L'Affair d'Une Nuit* ('It Happened at Night'), which Christine Gouze-Renal was producing for her actor husband, Roger Hanin. She's on camera for only a few seconds, sitting at a table in a restaurant with Charrier and Gouze-Renal.

From there, Brigitte found herself catapulted head first into Henri-Georges Clouzot's *La Verite* ('The Truth'). Cast as Dominique, she played a young girl from the provinces who comes to Paris only to get caught up in the dangers of a bohemian lifestyle. In a fit of passion, she kills her lover. Facing a conviction for murder, and incapable of making anyone understand the demons that drive her, the film ends, prophetically, with Dominique slashing her wrists.

110

Birthday Blues

Looking for a suitable co-star, Clouzot elected to audition possible leading men in a bed scene with Brigitte. Jean-Louis Trintignant was on the list, but he'd broken his leg in a skiing accident and was ruled out. The other candidates were Jean-Paul Belmondo and Laurent Terzieff – both of whom had made their debuts two years before with Jacques Charrier in *Les Tricheurs* – Jean-Pierre Cassells and a handsome 23-year-old known named Sami Frey.

So Bardot – chastely wearing jeans and a t-shirt – got under the covers with this queue of young men.

Charrier was anything but pleased. First, he objected that Trintignant might star with her. Then he objected to the screen tests. After visiting the set, watching her pretend to make love to four different men, he asked her to quit films. She refused. When the press picked up on that – adding to the incessant speculation that their marriage was finally over – the two of them left town to hide in the Alps for a while, hoping the papers would soon find someone else to haunt.

It wasn't to be.

Clouzot's final choice was Frey, and Charrier didn't much like that either. Almost as soon as Brigitte started filming with Frey, Raoul Levy declared that he'd had enough of her husband and banned him from the set. In the end it was all too much for Charrier's nerves. He suffered another breakdown and, for the second time in his life, tried to commit suicide. He was taken to a clinic in Meudon and subjected to another extensive sleep cure.

And all this time, the pressures of coping with reality continued to build up inside Brigitte.

Finding her especially highly strung and even more on edge than usual – 'She is very childish,' Clouzot complained – the director decided that to get any sort of decent performance out of her he needed to calm her down. So he prepared her for certain scenes by doping her with tranquillizers and the occasional shot or two of whisky. The result, he later rationalized, was excellent for the characterization he was seeking.

111

The film was an important financial success – years later she would claim it was her favourite film – but Clouzot's methods didn't produce quite the same triumph for her nerves. Already frayed, the mixture of sedatives and alcohol merely pushed her closer to the edge. Furthermore, unlike any of her previous directors, Clouzot was not just a taskmaster, he was a genuine tyrant. A practitioner of the totalitarian school of film making, at one point while trying to motivate her for a scene, he grabbed her by the shoulders and kept shaking her. 'I don't need amateurs in my films. I want an actress.'

She reacted by slapping him twice, shouting back, 'And I need a director, not a psychopath,' then storming off the set.

The press couldn't get enough of her battles with Clouzot, but soon turned the story upside down, claiming they'd become lovers, adding that she'd already traded in Charrier for Clouzot, whose Brazilian-born wife happened to be dying in a hospital. They even went as far as to insinuate that the Charrier suicide attempt had been concocted specifically so that both Bardot and Clouzot would soon be free to marry. Naturally, the more Bardot and Clouzot objected to this harassment, complaining that there was no truth in any of it, the more the papers decided it must be true. It ended only when someone working on the picture leaked word to the media that her new love wasn't in fact Clouzot, but Frey.

Now the papers had a new story to run with and, this time, it was true.

What no one seemed to care about was just how thoroughly confused Bardot was, trying to juggle the dying days of her marriage with Charrier, the dawning days of her affair with Frey, while also suffering the dictatorship of Clouzot. By the time the picture was finished, she'd reached the end of her tether. Sensing the need for a shoulder to cry on, she confessed to Vadim, 'If only men were like the sun. I could spend the rest of my life stretched out, sunbathing in peace. But with men I have to keep moving on.'

In the middle of this, Charrier began talking about his return to the army. He told friends he intended to join the paratroopers, fight in Algeria and become a martyr by getting himself killed there.

Thinking he might find some inner peace if he started painting again, Brigitte went looking for a studio retreat and wound up buying an old barn with a thatched roof in the village of Bazoches, not far from Montfort-l'Amaury, some 25 miles outside Paris. It was in a pretty terrible state, but fixing it up would be fun and it perfectly suited her rustic taste. She also loved the fact that there was a lot of land where animals could roam freely. It cost her 250,000 new francs ($50,000).

It might have been a place to save her marriage, except that she and Charrier didn't get the chance. One of the explanations Bardot usually offered for splitting up with Vadim was that he never got jealous. Now, one of the reasons she was tiring of Charrier was that he did. Years later, he would deny that he ever got as jealous as the papers made him out to be. 'All her films are love films, love stories, and have love scenes in them. So how could I object to her shooting love scenes?'

But the situation had long since got out of hand. The turbulence that haunted her private life would not abate. And she'd been rudely reminded of it in a series of ten newspaper articles by her former secretary, Alain Carré, published that June.

Among other things, he'd revealed how she could turn her temper on and off, like a tap.

One night, he wrote, Brigitte's chum Jicky Dussart rang to remind her that he and his wife Anne had a dinner date with her and Jean-Louis. Bardot wasn't in, so Carré innocently enough suggested they come by around 7.30. When she returned to the apartment, he told her about it. But she flew into a rage, screaming at him, 'How dare you make arrangements for me without asking? I don't want to see anyone. I didn't invite anyone.'

Carré went to the phone, and frantically tried to reach the Dussarts to head them off. When he couldn't find them, he said, Brigitte forced him to hand-write a note, which he had to hang on the door, apologizing that he'd forgotten Monsieur and Madame had a previous engagement in town. The Dussarts showed up, rang the bell for the longest time, obviously suspecting that Brigitte was home. They eventually forgave Brigitte but it was a long time before they'd speak to Carré.

He'd also illustrated how, when she had an idea in her head, she wouldn't let anything stand in her way.

She found a toothbrush one day in a sink at the studio, liked the blue of the handle, brought it home and announced to Carré that was the colour she wanted her bathroom. The painters tried to mix their paint to match the shade but couldn't manage it. She refused to let them off the hook and they wound up painting the bathroom five times before she finally admitted defeat.

What's more, he still maintains, 'People always reacted strangely when they were around her. There was always a lot of tension because, as soon as other people got near her, they were never themselves.'

He recalled in his articles how she had dinner at Sacha Distel's apartment one night and Sacha served a Beaujolais that she'd enjoyed. The next morning she asked Carré to ring Distel's wine merchant and order a case of it for her. But, she warned, make certain it's the same. Carré arranged it and a few days later a case of wine was delivered. When she saw it, Brigitte threw a tantrum, accusing the wine merchant of trying to rip her off, and accusing Carré of being totally incompetent.

He said that she grabbed the phone herself, got the wine merchant on the line and berated him for not sending her the wine she'd ordered. 'It took quite a while before she calmed down long enough to hear the wine merchant explain that it was the very same wine. But he didn't think the label on the bottle was pretty enough to send to Brigitte Bardot, so he removed the label from every bottle in the case, and replaced it with a prettier one.'

Carré, who didn't mince his words in the articles, described her as stingy. He noted that, some time around 1959–1960, a French financial journalist calculated that, based on the export revenue from her films, Brigitte Bardot was, in fact, France's second largest

114

source of foreign income, after Dassault Aviation. But, instead of being flattered, she went into a frenzy. She complained that she was paying too much tax every year and that the government should do something for her. By her calculations, they were taking away the equivalent of her income from one out of every three films. She said it was disgusting and threatened to write to Général de Gaulle and the minister of finance to tell them that if they didn't lower her taxes she'd stop making films and the government would lose all that money.

Carré wrote then, 'She is economical, has simple tastes, the mind of a businesswomen and refuses ostentation.' Today he refines that to, 'She can have love in her heart and innocence in her eyes but in her head she's got a calculator.'

Needless to say, none of Carré's revelations – however true they may or may not have been – pleased her.

According to him, 'She was okay in the beginning about the articles I wrote, but then she changed her mind. She tried to stop publication but failed. I saw the series as a way of setting the record straight. At one point she even told me she would write a preface. Of course that never happened. I wanted people to know what she was like. I was on call seven days a week. It was a type of slavery. But this wasn't about hurting her. I had a great deal of affection for her and at times she treated me like a brother. I wanted people to know that she's very capricious.'

Capriciousness seems to be a recurring theme in her life. For instance, one afternoon at La Madrague, she was taking the sun on a beach mat when lunch was announced. She got up, and looked around for a few minutes for the top of her suntan lotion. She asked, 'Where is it?' and 'Have you seen it?' and recruited everyone to help her look for it. An hour later, when it wasn't found, she stormed off to her room and no one got lunch.

Now, confused and angry, unable to seize control of her life, she confessed to the entire nation in a television interview, 'I must kill the monster that is in me. I must chase away from my halls the intruder who has the name of BB. I want to be able to say BB is no more, long live Brigitte!'

It came to a head early that autumn. Charrier was expecting her at La Madrague. He waited there for the first week of September and when she still hadn't arrived by Thursday the eighth, he got into his car and drove to Paris. On Friday afternoon, she agreed to meet him later that night outside of the Rhumerie Martiniquaise, a cafe in the middle of St Germain des Prés.

She showed up with Sami Frey.

It was more than Charrier could handle. He lost his temper, challenged Frey and punches were thrown. A photographer who'd been stalking Brigitte managed to get some pictures. But when Brigitte, Charrier and Frey fled from his camera by jumping into a car together and speeding off, the photographer reported that the whole thing was very suspicious. The newspapers now speculated that the fist fight had been nothing but a publicity stunt.

* * *

To escape this madness, Bardot left Nicolas with his nurse at Bazoches, left Charrier to brood with friends in Biarritz, left Frey to brood with friends in Paris and, on 19 September, flew to Nice — so anxious to get away that she would even take a plane. But she didn't go to St Tropez, where she could be guaranteed that the press would continue to hound her. She was met at the airport by her friend – and now co-conspirator – Mercedes Zavka, a woman her own age from Milan who'd been dating one of Vadim's pals in Paris.

Some weeks before, Zavka had decided she needed a rest and borrowed a friend's villa in the hamlet of Les Cabrolles. On a slope near the tiny village of Ste Agnes, not far from the border with Italy, five kilometres into the hills above Menton, there were only five houses in Les Cabrolles – population 15 – including one small pink provençal house with a large garden. It was a perfect rural hideaway.

In mid-September, almost out of the blue, Brigitte's mother

(photo Louis Féraud)

Father Pilou   Mother Toty

Sister Mijanou

With fiancé Vadim (private photos)

Young Brigitte
(private photos)

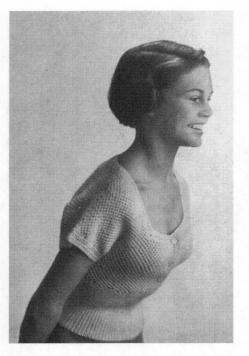

Cover girl, May 1949
(*Elle Magazine*)

Brigitte's first published photos, March 1949
(*Jardin des Modes*)

At the
Cannes Film Festival 1953
(Popper)

Vadim the director
(Popper)

With Jean-Louis Trintignant on the set of
And God Created Woman (Kobal)

Constantly surrounded by crowds (Popper)

Above: (l) with Sacha Distel (Popper)
and (r) with second husband
Jacques Charrier (Popper)

With Christine Gouze-Renal
(private photo)

Above: First photos with baby Nicolas (Popper)
Right: Leaving hospital with producer Francis
Cosne after her suicide attempt in 1960 (Popper)
Below right: Disguised with Sami Frey
(Associated Press)
Below: With chum André Pousse (private photo)

(photo Louis Féraud)

phoned Mercedes at the villa to tell her how bad things were in Paris for Brigitte. Toty wanted to know if Brigitte could come to stay with her.

'It wasn't my place,' Mercedes Zavka explains, 'so before I could tell Toty yes or no, I had to ring those friends from whom I'd borrowed the house. I asked them if they'd mind if I had someone staying with me. I didn't tell them it was Brigitte Bardot. But I felt I had to ask, because I knew Brigitte was always a problem to have around. If for no other reason, the press was always hounding her. They said they didn't mind, so I called Brigitte in Paris to say it was okay.'

So Zavka picked Bardot up at Nice Airport and took her back to Les Cabrolles.

'She's always been a lonely girl. She can be witty and fun, but when I saw the state of mind she was in, having just finished the picture with Clouzot, which had been very difficult, and being in love with Sami Frey and being still married to Jacques, I knew it was really bad time for her.'

For the next nine days, the two women lived like a pair of recluses. They saw almost no one. On the rare occasion when someone in Les Cabrolles asked, Mercedes said that her companion was called Zozo Souana. That was the name Brigitte invented for herself, using the first letters of Mercedes' family name, much the same way she invented the nickname Vava for Vadim.

Although Zavka went to play tennis every morning, whenever they left the villa together, to walk in the hills or to go into town, they wore headscarves and sunglasses and somehow – miraculously – avoided being recognized.

At first, the press reported Brigitte was at Bazoches. When they discovered she wasn't, they said she was ensconced at the home of the actress Daniele Delorme in Rambouillet. When it turned out that she wasn't there either, they were convinced she'd gone to the mountains with Sami Frey. Eventually they decided she must be somewhere on the Riviera. It was obvious she wasn't in St Tropez – everyone always knew when she was in residence, as if she flew a flag on the roof of La Madrague the way the Queen does at Buckingham Palace – so they scoured the coast.

On Tuesday 27 September, Brigitte and Mercedes drove to St Paul de Vence, to the Colombe d'Or where they lunched with Clouzot.

And that's where the photographers spotted her.

Word went out that Bardot had been found, and the wolf pack moved in on her.

Clouzot later reported that Brigitte said to him over dessert, 'I have no private life any more. I have no life to speak of at all. I am a hunted woman. I can't take a step without being surrounded and questioned. I am being tortured.'

The paparazzi raced them back to Les Cabrolles and set up their stake-out on the road leading up to the villa.

The next day, Brigitte's birthday, she and Mercedes had lunch at La Mère Jeannine, a beachside restaurant they frequented at the very end of Cap Martin. A large wooden house painted red and screened against the wind that came off the sea, it was private enough that the two women could spend afternoons there, eating freshly grilled fish, napping on chaises longues and swimming in the tiny cove off the rocks. Only the owner, his family and the waitress knew who Zozo really was. It was a good place to keep the paparazzi at bay. But that afternoon, sitting at the table they claimed as theirs – the one right next to the open barbecue – following a lunch of grilled sardines, fresh fruit and a bottle of wine, a fan approached, asking to take a photo. Suddenly Brigitte snapped, 'I beg you to leave me alone, monsieur. Leave me alone or I am going to die.'

It was the final straw. At 26, constantly stalked, never left alone, Brigitte Bardot was exhausted, world weary and, finally, unable to cope.

The two women left La Mère Jeannine at around 4 pm. Shortly after they got back to the villa, a local florist arrived with a bouquet of 40 roses for Mme Souana. It was a birthday gift from producer Francis Cosne, with whom she was scheduled to do her next picture, *La Bride sur le Cou* ('Please Not Now').

A couple of hours later, their housekeeper, Baptistine, was preparing a lobster dinner and had baked a cherry pie, which was to serve as a birthday cake, when Brigitte told Mercedes, 'I'm going for a walk.'

It was already dark outside and dinner was almost ready, but Mercedes didn't think anything of it.

Half an hour later, when Brigitte hadn't returned, Mercedes asked Baptistine to see if she could find her. 'I didn't want to go outside because the press were outside and I didn't want them to think anything was wrong. But when someone tells you she's going for a walk and it's already dark and she doesn't come back when she knows it's dinner time, you begin to wonder where she is. I told the housekeeper not to make any noise or attract any attention.'

Baptistine returned to say that Mme Zozo was nowhere to be seen, so Mercedes hurried next door and explained to the man living there – his name was Jean Valetta – that her friend was missing.

Valetta hurried to find some flashlights and suggested they go looking for her.

Baptistine was in the midst of explaining the situation to her daughter, son-in-law and 13-year-old grandson – his name was Jean Louis Bousnous – when Mercedes came into the house to tell them, 'I've lost Zozo.'

Valetta handed out the flashlights and the adults went in search of Brigitte.

'They left me on my own when they went to find Zozo,' Jean Louis recounts, 'and I was a bit afraid. I wanted to pretend to be looking for her too, so I took a flashlight and walked down the hill to the stable where there were some sheep. I stood there for a while, then turned around with my flashlight, completely by accident, and saw her.'

Bardot was sitting next to the well at the bottom of the garden,

119

with her knees pulled up to her chest, her arms wrapped around her legs and her head on her knees.

The boy screamed for help and the adults came running.

Valetta got to her first, touched her hands, felt how cold they were and immediately thought she was dead.

Her clothes were covered in blood.

She'd slashed her wrists with a razor blade.

Baptistine's son ran to call for a doctor while Valetta and Mercedes carried her up to the villa. No one knew how long she'd been in a coma. It turned out to be nearly 45 minutes. The doctor arrived quickly, saw her wrist wounds were not serious and, realizing that she'd also swallowed a large dose of barbiturates, pumped her stomach. Once she was revived, he decided she needed to be transported to the Saint Francois Neurological Clinic, 18 miles away in Nice. He called for an ambulance and rode with her.

The paparazzi, their vigilance rewarded, chased after what could have turned out to be the biggest story of the year.

The following morning, doctors at the clinic issued a statement that she was out of danger, although, they added, she was suffering from acute nervous depression. They also acknowledged she'd come within minutes of dying.

Back at the villa, once Brigitte was on her way to Nice, Mercedes became worried that there might be something that the press, or the police, could use to publicize the attempted suicide.

'I took what few papers there were, just in case she left anything, and destroyed them. I didn't want the press to find anything they could publish.'

The news must have got out on radio pretty quickly, because Clouzot showed up at the villa, accompanied by Raoul Levy.

'None of us wanted any publicity,' Zavka goes on, 'but we were all in such a state. I left as soon as I could for Cannes. I didn't want to be there when the press came back or when the police came around. I wanted to get away from there so that my name would never get mixed up in this. I slept that night at the Carlton and visited her the next day at the clinic, taking her some make-up.'

Later the press would report that a suicide note was found. And the text of it would be printed time and time again in accounts of the incident. It's not true. There was no suicide note. Nor was there anything in the papers Mercedes Zavka destroyed that in any way indicated Brigitte was thinking of killing herself.

Later the press would also report that Brigitte had bought the sleeping pills she'd used from a pharmacist in Menton. That too would be repeated in all the printed accounts of this story. And that too is not true. Brigitte already had the pills with her when she arrived from Paris.

One newspaper even went so far as to name a pharmacist who'd sold her the pills. They interviewed him and, even though they clearly had the wrong man, his comment is significant. First, they asked him if he'd recognized his client as Brigitte Bardot and he said he hadn't. Which is true because she wasn't his client. Next, they asked him how he could possibly not have recognized Brigitte Bardot. And he answered, revealingly, 'I serve a hundred Brigitte Bardots every day.'

Pilou and Toty were told of the suicide attempt at 11 that evening, and they made plans to go to Nice the next day. But when they got Brigitte's doctor on the phone, he warned that they wouldn't be able to see her for a few days. Charrier was also told that night. And although he originally announced he'd drive to Nice in the morning, he wound up staying with friends along the French–Spanish border.

A gathering crowd in front of the private clinic, in the fashionable Cimiez quarter of Nice, became a worry for Brigitte's doctors and the hospital administrator ordered the clinic's front door to be locked. Police were dispatched to guard it. Three teenage girls showed up, stationed themselves near the front gate and announced they intended to stay there, day and night, until they saw Jacques Charrier. The clinic's switchboard was perpetually lit up, with total strangers ringing from as far away as South Africa and Australia, simply to ask, 'How's Brigitte?' By mid-morning of 29 September, flowers began arriving, non-stop. The only people allowed in to see her were Mercedes Zavka and Christine Gouze-Renal.

Back at Les Cabrolles, French teenagers congregated at the well where Brigitte had been found. They left flowers and some of them even prayed. The local priest became concerned and accused them of idolatry. He noted that they were coming from as far away as Lyons to turn the well into a shrine. 'These young people are giving to a woman the adoration they should be reserving for Our Lady. The next thing, I suppose, is that miracles will be worked at the well.'

Pilou and Toty arrived on Saturday, met by an army of journalists.

They visited Brigitte for brief periods over the next few days. Then Toty met the press. Facing journalists three rows deep in the bar at the Negresco Hotel, she made a tearful plea, begging them to forget Brigitte Bardot. 'If you continue to stalk her, she'll do it again. Please leave her alone. I want to keep my daughter.'

Toty won several friends for her cause, but she couldn't convince everyone. As Brigitte recuperated at the clinic, mail poured in for her. In addition to hundreds of get-well wishes, one woman wrote, 'Next time you want to die, throw yourself off the Eiffel Tower, that way you'll be sure not to fail and there'll be one less bitch on the earth.'

With nothing new to report, the press wondered if this suicide attempt was just a publicity stunt to put a head of steam on *La Verité's* box office takings. After all, instead of reading about it in the papers, fans could watch Bardot slit her wrists on screen.

'It's odd,' one London daily professed, 'that in her latest film now being given the publicity treatment, Bardot attempted suicide. The method – by cutting her wrists and taking drugs.'

A French daily hinted that, because *La Verité* had gone over budget, the film's backers had cooked up the stunt believing that

Bardot's name on the theatre canopy was not in and of itself enough to get them a return on their money.

Clouzot, who'd once accused her of being very childish, now tried to make people believe that 'her force as a film star of talent is just beginning'.

But the press remained sceptical. While photographers climbed trees outside her hospital room to get photos, French tabloids, such as *France Dimanche*, joined more up-market magazines like *Paris Match*, claiming that this was a familiar type of publicity stunt, that they'd seen it all before.

One of the few voices of sympathy came from the *Daily Express* in London. They called her 'a doom-laden Peter Pan trapped in an adult world which she hasn't yet learned to live with'.

Christine Gouze-Renal was also quick to defend her friend. She said at the time, 'Suicides do not happen in 24 hours. They are a culmination of the way we are forced to live. People everywhere in the world have an ambivalent attitude towards Brigitte. They hate her and love her at the same time. She felt she was going mad.'

Looking back, all these years later, Gouze-Renal knows very well it was anything but a publicity stunt. 'This time she really wanted to die. The problem with her has always been that she never saw herself the way other people did. She went from being a child to being an old lady. She was never anything in between. She was never an adult.'

Vadim agrees. 'This was no publicity stunt. It happened on her birthday, which for her is already a bad date, and she only survived because that young kid found her. Nor was it just a cry for help. There were other times when she did that, five or six other times, when she left the door open so that someone could get to her in time. No, this time she was convinced she was going to die.'

Many people suggest that her problems have always stemmed from fame, but Vadim is not one of them. He believes that most people who have known great success – politicians, painters, actors, directors, musicians, writers – those people who get to the point in their career where others say, he or she is a star, get to that point because they are, eight or nine times out of ten, very egotistical.

And people who are egotistical are people who are totally alone.

'Fame raised the stakes for her and added to her solitude. But it is her nature to be lonely.'

As long as they're alone, he says, they receive information, because they aren't cut off from the world, but they don't waste any time in returning it. They keep everything. Their egoism allows them to maintain the fantastic internal energy that is necessary for stardom. And even if they don't realize it, they're always thinking one thing – me, me, me. He likens it to the principle of phosphorus. It absorbs light but never gives any off.

'Brigitte was such an egoist that she didn't even know she was an egoist. No one else existed except her. The result is a profound solitude. Great loneliness. And that explains why, in spite of her extraordinary pleasure for life, her joy, her enormous charm, in spite of how adorable she can be when she spends the evening with friends playing the guitar and singing and dancing, she's funny, she laughs, she's great company, in spite of all of that, there is still, at the very bottom of her soul, a colossal loneliness that is the result of a colossal ego.'

It becomes painful for her, he argues, because she's intelligent enough to know this.

'Which is why she cracks, why she suffers enormous depression. It's her awareness of her own loneliness. And it's almost always set off by something beyond her control. When her birthday comes around she's more fragile than at other times. When she has sentimental problems, like a silly dispute with a lover, she finds herself faced with her solitude and that's when she tries to take her own life. That's the only solution someone can think of, when they're totally alone, to try to find another world. When she believes that she can't communicate with anyone else in this world, because of that egoism, she tells herself that death erases everything. That's why she's tried it so often.'

Over the years, Vadim has often wondered how he could help her but concedes he's never found a way because, in the end, he believes, there isn't any way.

'She was born with that. The same way she was born with that beauty of hers. No one can change that. It's not something that happened because of her parents or society. If she'd been born 200 years before or 600 years later, she would have been like that. It's also totally logical from her point of view, for someone who so desperately needs to be loved and can't find it with the human race, to look for it with her animals. They compensate her for that. Everything she does is intuitive. She's never thought it out. But if you look closely at her desire to save animals, to cater to them, to surround herself with them, I think it's fair to say you'll see a frightening degree of loneliness, and that stems directly from her egoism.'

Brigitte left the clinic in Nice on 2 October and went straight to La Madrague. The press followed her. She emerged from the house a few weeks later, and before long she was going into the village to shop, as if everything was back to normal.

Except now Vadim was on her arm.

Rumours spread of their re-marriage. Both of them denied it, which only convinced more people that it was about to happen.

'This is all so stupid,' she barked at reporters who were again pestering her non-stop. 'Vadim is my best friend. In fact, I like him better now than when he was my husband.'

But it took a real investigative whiz-kid to come up with the scoop of the affair. He revealed in his paper that, even in her so-called seclusion, for Bardot it had been 'business as usual'.

The genius in question – who had somehow confused journalism with fiction – claimed that anonymous sources had disclosed to him that when Bardot left Paris she was accompanied by her press attaché. That during eight days in Menton, she was in non-stop meetings with two producers, one impresario, three studio publicity agents and two public relations people. And that, when she finally decided to end her days, it was simply because, 'She hadn't seen a journalist all week'.

Chapter Seven

TRYING TO KEEP CONTROL

During the summer of 1960 – while she was still working on *La Verité* – Bardot got it into her head that she wanted to quit making movies.

She started telling friends, 'I'm fed up living the way I now live.' She cancelled a picture in which she'd been scheduled to star with Jacques Charrier – as much because of her failing marriage as for anything else – and said she'd fulfil any other obligations she had and would then retire. Her last film, already contracted for, would be *Le Repos du Guerrier* ('Warrior's Rest'), which Vadim would direct. And she liked the thought that the man who'd helped make her a star would then help her exit the stage.

'It will take me another 10 or 11 months. After that, it's curtains. After that, I'm free.' Finding a second career, she said, would not be difficult. There was one in particular she thought she might enjoy, and that was becoming an antiques dealer. But there would be time for a decision like that later on. For now, she emphasized, 'My decision is irrevocable. I'm going to live the way I want to live. I don't care about money. I don't need mink coats or jewels. I can live with very little. I'm 25 years old. In ten years, it's goodbye to my youth. So I'm going to take advantage of what's left and say goodbye to the movies.'

It didn't happen.

Within three months of her attempted suicide, she was back at work.

The first of these films, *La Bride sur le Cou* was supposed to be a slapstick comedy. But it didn't start out very funny because she didn't like the director – a young fellow named Jean Aurel – and by this time she had enough weight to see him fired. She complained about him to Francis Cosne and in Aurel's place, Cosne hired someone whose screen credit for this film would read 'Artistic Direction' – Roger Vadim.

'We've known each other so long,' Vadim said as he stepped into the picture, 'that I'm the only person who can tell her anything. She has to be surrounded by people who treat her like a queen, which I don't.'

In response, Brigitte was willing to concede, 'He knows how to handle me in front of the cameras better than anyone. He understands me very well.'

No sooner had she finished that then Michel Boisrond partnered her with Alain Delon in a film that was a series of sketches called *Les Amours Célèbres* ('Famous Loves').

Christine Gouze-Renal now came back into Brigitte's professional life for the fourth and final time. She'd got it into her head to star Bardot in the film version of Noel Coward's *Private Lives* and convinced Louis Malle to direct. As soon as he said yes, Gouze-Renal went to see Joe Fogal at MGM in New York – they owned the screen rights – and he thought the idea of putting Bardot into a Noel Coward piece was terrific. But for whatever reason – Gouze-Renal never found out why – MGM couldn't release the rights to her, or wouldn't release the rights to her, and Fogal had to say sorry.

Returning home to Paris, Gouze-Renal decided she could still use the title anyway – *'Vie Privée'* in French – and told Malle they were going to make a picture about the private life of a movie star.

Knowing what they both did about Brigitte, there was no doubt whose life this was going to be based on.

When Gouze-Renal originally mentioned the idea to her, Brigitte smiled. As the project developed, however, Brigitte grew to hate it.

'She didn't want to do the picture,' Gouze-Renal says. 'But I knew her and one of the ways I talked her into it was by promising to rent a house for her and me on Lake Geneva. I installed my housekeeper Gaby, whom Brigitte liked, so we'd have someone to cook for us, and it was just us girls. I was with Brigitte all day on the set, and then with her at home at night. We'd sit up in bed and giggle and laugh. We were just like schoolgirls. She was wonderful.'

It didn't last long.

To begin with, Louis Malle fell in love with her and the simple, happy atmosphere Gouze-Renal had hoped to create rapidly deteriorated. Brigitte's life became extremely complicated yet again.

Then, crowds pursued her everywhere. They hung around the set, followed her on shopping trips and refused to give her any privacy. One afternoon 500 people surrounded her, pushing and shoving and closing in on her. She felt as if she was suffocating – suddenly she couldn't breathe – and she passed out. It took several policemen to fight their way through the crowd, to clear people away from her, to give her some air, before they could revive her and get her to safety. There was also that night when a woman, a total stranger, walked up to her and spat at her.

Adding to those difficulties, by the time they got to Spoletto, Brigitte didn't like her co-star, Marcello Mastroianni, and he couldn't stand her.

'It turned into a circus,' Gouze-Renal continues. 'When Marcello first arrived on the set, it was almost as if he was an unknown. The crowds and the press and the paparazzi were everywhere and they were all focused on Brigitte. It continued, non-stop, throughout the film. They hardly cared about him, hardly paid any attention to him. It wasn't that he took it very badly, or behaved badly, but it did irritate him. After all, he was a star too. Unfortunately for him, without doing anything more than being there, with just her presence, Brigitte had unknowingly reduced him to second-rate status. And that's not something that people with egos, the way most movie stars have egos, can easily accept.'

As if all that wasn't enough, what finally made this picture truly excruciating for Brigitte was the script.

'It was too close to who I was,' she told friends when it was over. 'A certain prudishness held me back. And at the same time it showed the hell that was my life in those days.'

Malle merely rewrote incidents out of her life, which meant that for Brigitte, playing each scene was like reliving old nightmares. In one scene, for example, her character – Jill – comes home after a long night, at five or six in the morning, and gets into the lift to go upstairs to her apartment. A cleaning woman gets in the lift with her and, as the lift climbs, all you hear is the cleaning woman insulting Jill.

That was Malle's version of a true incident where Brigitte had been visiting a friend in a hospital and got stuck in an elevator with a nurse who was carrying a food tray. Unprovoked and without any warning, the nurse suddenly took a fork off the tray and stabbed Brigitte several times. The nurse kept screaming that her son was in the army, fighting in North Africa, while Brigitte was at home, making millions for stripping. Bardot was, understandably, terrified. And she still has small scars on her arm from that day.

'Many people found the film exaggerated,' Malle says. 'They thought we made the story up. They couldn't believe these things actually happened. But most of them did. Most of it was right out of Brigitte's life. We didn't have to exaggerate. That's what happened to her all the time.'

Writing in the London *Evening Standard*, Alexander Walker was savvy enough about movie stars' lives to point out, 'The aim is to show what stardom is like and the answer is, sheer hell.'

But that's just about the best thing anyone had to say about the film.

Working with Brigitte for the first time, Malle says he was surprised to discover that she was lazy. 'She didn't like having to do the work. She didn't like rehearsals. The simple fact is, she didn't like acting. But she was talented. She was wonderfully photogenic and had magnificent presence. If certain things didn't work, maybe it's because Brigitte and Mastroianni were supposed to be lovers in the film but they wouldn't speak to each other off the set.'

When finally pinned down about it, Mastroianni confided, 'There are two Brigittes, the sex symbol which the world thinks it knows, the girl who eats up men for breakfast every day, and there is Brigitte, the simple, ordinary girl. The only trouble is, Bardot sometimes doesn't herself know the difference between the two.'

Right or wrong, he blamed it on Vadim. 'When he created her, he set out to make an impossible dream for all men. Unhappily for Brigitte, he almost succeeded. Now she can't be a real person unless she gives up acting for good. She can only be something for people to giggle at and gossip about. She has become the object of scandal and of prying eyes, and of finger-pointing. She hates to be lonely, but now that is what she has to be most of the time.'

A few years later, in an American interview, Mastroianni showed a particularly nasty streak. 'She's not too bright as far as men are concerned. She's a victim of the men who fall in love with her who all became famous through her. They live on her name, and basically they're all the same type. Youngsters, nobodies, who got themselves known and reach an unwholesome conclusion with their nervous breakdowns and their inability to complete military service. It's fortunate she doesn't make too many pictures or France wouldn't have an army.'

Hoping to put a different spin on what she knew had been a painful experience for Brigitte, Gouze-Renal arranged a big gala opening in Paris. Brigitte promised to attend, so 'Le Tout Paris' was invited.

The afternoon of the opening, Gouze-Renal herself decorated the box where Brigitte would sit, filled it with flowers and went

131

over every detail to make certain that everything would be perfect when Brigitte arrived.

At seven that evening, Brigitte rang to say she wasn't coming.

Gouze-Renal was horrified. She pleaded with Brigitte, 'You can't do this to me. It's awful to change your mind like this.'

Brigitte said, 'But this film is about my life.'

Gouze-Renal argued, 'Everyone is going to be there and you promised you'd come.'

Brigitte confessed, 'But if I come, because everyone knows this is about me, I will feel totally nude, totally naked.'

That was all she had to say. Christine Gouze-Renal understood exactly what her friend was trying to tell her. 'It was one thing for her to show the world her body. It was much more difficult to expose her soul. What could I do? I told her, I understand, because I did understand. And the gala was held without her.'

* * *

To finalize their divorce in 1962, Jacques Charrier hired a young lawyer named Gilles Dreyfus. In an uncontested plea, Charrier was awarded custody of Nicolas. Neither Brigitte nor Charrier had gone to court. He was in Italy making a film. She was skiing at Meribel with Sami Frey.

She wouldn't spend any quality time with Nicolas, out of her own volition, for another five years.

The Bardot–Vadim team got together, as planned, to make *Le Repos du Guerrier*, and when that was finished she announced her retirement for the second time.

'In life,' she said, 'it's sometimes good to step back. I've been filming for ten years without a pause. I need to get my bearings.'

Vadim could only wonder, 'What else can she do, be an interior decorator?'

Within the next 12 months, she'd made four more films.

She found it too difficult to turn down Jean-Luc Godard when he offered her the lead in a film he was doing based on an Alberto

132

Moravia novel. The book was called *Il Disprezzo* (*A Ghost at Noon*) but the film version was *Le Mepris* ('Contempt'). The supporting cast included Jack Palance and Michel Piccoli, with appearances by director Fritz Lang and even Godard himself. Producers Joseph E. Lévine and Carlo Ponti paid her 2.5 million fancs ($510,000) for her work – the largest fee she'd commanded to date – and, when Brigitte saw there was a nude scene, she got Olga Horstig-Primuz to extract another 100,000 francs ($20,300) from them before she would do it.

Her character in this picture was called Camille Javal, and years later cinema historians would decide that was, in fact, her real name. They would write that Brigitte Bardot was just a stage name and that she'd been born Camille Javal. It is clearly untrue. But even reputable histories of the cinema repeat this basic error of fact.

While Godard filmed *Le Mepris* in Italy, Jacques Rozier took one look at all the photographers hanging around the set, chasing after Brigitte, and turned a camera on them, filming a documentary simply called *Paparazzi*.

Being Italy, the crowds and the photographers and the excitement created by her presence were infernal.

'Each time I say something in front of a journalist,' she remarked in utter disgust at being constantly hounded, 'I earn him 500 francs. The same goes for the photographers.'

To get even with them – or at least to try – she decided to bring her own photographer along with her wherever she went. The job fell to a man who's been her chum for more than 40 years, Jicky Dussart.

'She's a child–woman who personified female freedom,' he says. 'The last of the stars. That said, she can be very difficult to photograph. First of all, contrary to what many people imagine, she never liked to pose nude. She's very prudish. So whenever I photographed her nude, she was always a bit uncomfortable. She was always aware of never showing too much. And then, after an hour or so, she'd get bored. I'd shoot maybe 50 pictures of her in an hour and she'd get bored and say, that's enough. Even in her movies, she never liked to show her ass.'

More important than having been her personal photographer, the two are soul mates. They met in 1953 when Brigitte and Vadim were living on the rue Chardon-Lagache. Today she considers Jicky to be the older brother she never had – she even describes herself as 'an insufferable sister' – and he lives in a house on her property at La Garrigue in St Tropez. Their life-long friendship comes from sharing a sense of humour. And the two are forever making each other laugh.

While filming *Le Mepris*, Brigitte was sitting off to the side of the set all by herself, peeling an orange, when Dussart happened by and mumbled, 'What an epicure!'

She didn't know the word. 'What do you mean?'

'An epicure,' he repeated. 'You know, being epicurean. Someone who likes the finer things in life. Someone who has luxurious tastes.'

'Oh.' She shrugged it off and continued with her orange. Several months later, at a press conference, Dussart was standing behind her when a reporter started annoying her. Miffed, she turned to Dussart and asked, 'What do you call those guys who eat oranges?'

The two broke up.

'At another press conference,' he says, 'it must have been in New York because everyone was speaking English, a reporter decided to try out his French. He asked her, "What was your first *cachet*?" using the word to mean contract. Quick as a flash she told him, "*Un cachet d'aspirin*", which means an aspirin tablet.'

Again, the two went into hysterics.

Then there was day at La Madrague when he'd gone snorkelling and she was watching him from the window. A dozen young girls arrived on her beach hoping to see Brigitte.

Spotting Dussart, they shouted at him, 'Can we see her? Can we see her?' Except in French, '*On peux la voir?*' can also mean 'Can we see it?'

At first he tried to ignore them, but they kept asking that same question, so he stood up, started to walk ashore and shouted to Brigitte, 'Should I show them?'

She understood immediately and called back, 'Show them, show them.'

So Dussart dropped his bathing suit. The girls ran off shrieking. And with Jicky standing at the water's edge, his shorts around his ankles, Bardot literally fell onto the floor, hysterical.

Now in Italy, Jicky and his then wife Anne became Brigitte's constant companions.

She was living in a wonderful old **Palazzo** – someone tried to make her believe it had once been a whore house – that had a huge terrace. Unfortunately, she couldn't use it because several dozen photographers were manning the balconies just across the street. She felt trapped there, and quickly grew to hate it.

The only thing she really wanted to do while she was in Rome, she announced to Jicky and Anne, was go to the Vatican. She'd been raised Catholic and, even if she wasn't necessarily the most exemplary, practising Catholic in the world, there has always been a deeply spiritual side to her. But with the photographers on sentry duty, there was no chance of that. And she resented it enormously.

Immediately Jicky said, I can get you out of here and into the Vatican without anyone knowing. She said I'll bet you can't. He said I'll bet I can. And the wager was on.

First, he insisted, all three of them had to dress alike. So Brigitte, Jicky and Anne all put on clothes that made them look similar, like your average French tourist in Rome. No expensive scarves, no designer clothes. Nothing to make anyone think she was a movie star trying to disguise herself.

Then, he snuck her out of the building and, instead of a limo, they went by taxi to the Vatican. Once there – with Jicky on one side of her and Anne on the other – they manoeuvred themselves into the middle of a crowd of tourists so that nobody could spot them from afar. Protected, they simply moved with the crowds through St Peters and, later, through the Sistine Chapel.

'Not one single person recognized her,' Anne Dussart says. 'Not one single person came up to her. Not one single photographer followed her. It was one of those rare moments in her life when she felt perfectly anonymous, perfectly safe, perfectly happy.'

When her work on the picture ended, Sami Frey showed up and the four of them took a short holiday together, driving around Italy.

Or, at least, they tried to.

Anne Dussart continues, 'There we weren't so lucky. We spent some time in Capri and then took the boat back to Amalfi, because she wanted to see Mount Vesuvius and Pompeii. But, on the boat from Capri, Sami disguised himself like a peasant with a ridiculous hat and she tried to disguise herself like a charwoman. However, she looked too much like a movie star, with her dark glasses and her scarf tied around her head exactly the same way Brigitte Bardot always tied a scarf around her head. When she got off the boat and headed straight for a waiting car parked at the port, even if she'd been carrying a broom, she couldn't have fooled anybody.'

Fans closed in on her and the photographers descended. In Naples the four of them spent all their time walking backwards to get away from the crowds. Brigitte never got to Vesuvius.

Now the four of them theorized that the only way they could possibly have a decent vacation was to stay away from big towns, and that the thing to do was to seek out tiny little villages and stay in tiny old hotels where nobody could find them.

That plan didn't work either.

One night they heard about a tiny little hotel on the top of a hill and, convinced that nobody would find them there, they drove all the way up the mountain, only to discover there was a business seminar at the hotel and absolutely everyone recognized her.

Another night, in southern Italy, on their way to see the ruins at Paestum, they checked into a small hotel, which

Anne Dussart recalls as having been an absolutely horrible place. Still, they could have managed in awful rooms with sagging beds for that one night if it hadn't been for someone there knowing who she was and sending out the signal. The crowds and the photographers arrived and she was back on the run.

'That's the thing about hanging out with Brigitte,' Anne Dussart sighs. 'We were always on the run.'

*   *   *

Once Jacques Rozier had finished his 22-minute documentary *Paparazzi*, Italian director Oswoldo Civirani began shooting another documentary about Brigitte's life as a movie star, this one called *Tentazioni Proibite* ('Forbidden Temptation').

She then had the misfortune of making a film called *Une Ravissante Idiote* – which was called in English, at varying times, 'A Ravishing Idiot', 'Adorable Idiot', and 'Bewitching Scatterbrain'. Co-starring Anthony Perkins, the main problem with this film – besides the fact that it wasn't funny – was the title. Bardot is anything but an idiot. Yet that role, and similar roles, typed her. People believed she was the same in real life as she was on the screen. And that only added to the general mayhem that surrounded her off-screen life.

After an uncredited walk-on part in *Marie Soleil* – which featured Jacques Charrier and which she agreed to do as a favour to Antoine Bourseiller, who was making his directing debut – she had a credited minor role in *Dear Brigitte*.

It was the story of an eight-year-old boy who is obsessed with Brigitte Bardot and becomes her pen pal. When his father, played by James Stewart, takes him to Paris, they meet. She was paid nearly $20,000 for her three-minute scene – which, of course, took the day to shoot – but her salary was the least expensive part of the deal.

Because she wouldn't go to Hollywood, there was nothing for Hollywood to do but to come to her. The total cost to the producers for that one day shoot was a staggering $140,000. Then again, it is the only three minutes in Brigitte Bardot's entire film career when she worked with a veritable Hollywood legend.

* * *

Ten years after her 1953 success at the Cannes Film Festival, she returned. This time, instead of meeting the US Navy, she met a handsome young Frenchman named Robert Zagury.

She told friends, 'My heart turned over.'

A soft-spoken, gentle businessman born in Casablanca, Morocco, of a Brazilian father and French mother, he and Bardot might well have been one of the world's most beautiful couples. But he too discovered, the hard way, just how awful it was to live under the constant pressures that Brigitte was always being subjected to.

As soon as they met, the press latched onto them – it was front-page news every time there was a new man in her life – and from that point they were never left alone. Tourists were also always following them, coming up to them, bothering them.

'This was an era,' Zagury says, 'when movie stars were the most important of the stars. There weren't many internationally known athletes in those days. Television, at least in Europe, was still a young medium and hadn't created many stars. Nor had the music industry. There was Elvis, but he was unique. The Beatles and the Rolling Stones were only just beginning to emerge internationally. So movie stars were the top and she was at the top of that heap. As a couple, we were forever going in and out of back doors. It was impossible to live a normal life. If we wanted to see friends, those friends had to come to us.'

Their first year together was the usual mixture of passion and confusion. It took her some time to move Sami Frey aside.

Until then, Frey had been for Brigitte 'the only man who can make me vibrate like a woman'.

Once Zagury was permanently installed in her life, he began trying to extract her from the turmoil that was engulfing her. Up to that point, Brigitte hadn't travelled much. With the exception of sojourns in Italy and England, she hadn't been outside France very often. Zagury knew she hated flying, but he'd lived in Rio for many years, spoke the language and was convinced that she'd adore Brazil.

During the summer of 1964, Louis Malle signed her for his new picture, *Viva Maria*, in which she would co-star with Jeanne Moreau. Principal photography was set to begin in Mexico the following January, so Zagury persuaded her that, since she had to fly all that way in any case, they might as well stop in Brazil because it was, sort of, on the way.

Brigitte and Zagury flew out of Paris that autumn in search of solitude. They landed in South America to an unexpected and unnervingly tumultuous welcome.

When their Panair Do Brazil flight taxied to a stop in Rio, hordes of journalists ran out onto the tarmac and crowded around the gangplank to get to her. It was such a mob scene, she was afraid to get off the plane. Zagury tried to negotiate a truce, but the reporters and photographers wanted Brigitte and nothing short of getting to her would do. She stayed on the plane until he was able to signal to a friend to get his car and bring it up to the foot of the gangplank.

Once the car had navigated through the crowds and was in position, Brigitte and Zagury made a dash out of the plane, down the steps and into the rear seat.

Journalists swarmed the car and photographers rammed their cameras flush against the windows to get pictures of her. Flashbulbs were popping in their faces, people were screaming questions, he was angry and she was crying.

Trying to cheer her up, Zagury joked that, in all the confusion, they'd forgotten to go through customs and immigration.

She wasn't amused.

They somehow got out of the airport and onto the road leading into Rio – a road now lined with hundreds of people waving to her and hoping to get a glimpse of her, as if she was an arriving monarch. Chasing right behind them were carloads of journalists and photographers, some of them actually leaning out of their car windows, desperate to get more pictures.

The race ended at the Copacabana Palace where Zagury had reserved the penthouse suite.

Ten floors below, 300 journalists and photographers – plus a large herd of fans and curious onlookers – now gathered on the beach.

They wanted Brigitte Bardot but she didn't want anything to do with them.

It turned into the Brazilian version of a Mexican standoff.

The crowds refused to go away until she came out and, as long as they were there, she refused to go out. Four days later, trapped inside the apartment, with Brigitte growing more upset each day, Zagury was finally able to work out a cease-fire. He said that Brigitte would appear at a press conference, that she'd make herself available for their questions and do a photo session. But then they would have to leave her alone.

No deal, the journalists said. As long as she was in Brazil, she was fair game, and the photographers held their ground too, saying they wanted to keep taking pictures of her. Now Zagury asked, if he arranged to have his own photographer provide the press and the various agencies with photos during their entire stay in South America, would they then leave her alone for the duration of her trip?

Everyone eventually accepted Zagury's compromise and Brigitte came out of her fortress. She did the press conference and she did the photo session and Zagury saw to it that the agencies were kept stocked with photos. True to their word, the press backed off – it was a unique occurrence – giving the two of them nearly four months alone, the first four consecutive months of peace and quiet Bardot had known since becoming a major star.

But then, Zagury knew the perfect hideaway.

He took her to a tiny fishing village 200 kilometres up the coast, called Buzios. Just past Cabo Frio, it was in those days a difficult five-hour drive from Rio. There were no roads. There were no phones. There were no hotels. There was no running water. There was nothing but one small shop, a church, and some fishermen's cottages. They did have electricity in the village, but only just – it was shut off every night and didn't come on again until after dawn – so Brigitte and Bob lived most evenings by candlelight.

The fishermen called her 'Dona Brigitte' and, without television, none of them knew who this blonde woman was. When she sunbathed nude on the empty white sand beaches, no one bothered her.

It was much like what St Tropez must have been 50 years before she arrived there. Today, Buzios is much like what St Tropez is now. There are 10,000 homes, dozens of restaurants and hundreds of boutiques. There are hotels by the score and souvenir shops and wind-surfing rental stands, all catering to the hundreds of thousands of tourists who flock to the beaches there each year to show off their suntans or just to hang out at the sidewalk cafés waiting to be seen.

It all happened because she'd been there.

Buzios became famous as the place where Brigitte Bardot once lived. Such was the power of her name. Unwittingly, she'd transform a remote fishing village in the middle of nowhere, on the other side of the Atlantic, into a major tourist attraction simply by showing up. Without ever intending anything of the kind, she turned Buzios into the St Tropez of South America. And they've never forgotten her. She doesn't know it, but the local newspaper – whose title translates as 'The Wet Turkey' – still lists Brigitte Bardot as an honorary director on its editorial board.

•   •   •

Next stop was Mexico.

Arriving there with Zagury, her plane was blocked by several hundred journalists and photographers, anxious to get at her.

It was Rio all over again.

The police couldn't disperse the crowd and after 20 minutes, with Bardot and Zagury stuck inside, the customs and immigration formalities had to be done on the plane. It was then a car to Cuernavaca, with Bardot and Zagury in one car and hoards of journalists and photographers following them for the entire 50-mile trip.

A popular genre in those days was the 'buddy' film, and *Viva Maria* was Malle's parody of that. As he explains, 'I'd just made a very depressing film called *Feu Follet*. It was about the final 24 hours of a man about to commit suicide. He wanted to kill himself and, after the film, just about everyone in the audience did too. So I decided that my next film had to be fun, an adventure, a comedy. I also decided because the last one was about men, this one should be about women.'

When Malle originally approached his two stars with the project, each said they were thrilled with the idea of working in that type of a comedy. Then he sent a first draft of the script to their agents.

'I knew exactly what would happen. In fact, I won a bet on it. Jeanne's agent complained that Brigitte's role was more important and Brigitte's agent complained that Jeanne's role was too important. It was a sign of things to come. They were ferociously competitive and it became a very difficult film to make.'

Moreau and Malle had already made three films together. They'd also been lovers. And when Malle first called her about this film, she says, he told her the Americans wanted to cast her with Shirley Maclaine. Brigitte's name wasn't mentioned at that time. Anyway, she and Bardot had only vaguely met socially and didn't really know each other.

Once the two women settled down to work, Moreau says she found a woman who was, surprisingly, very unsure of herself.

'Being an actress was never Brigitte's dream. Because she was always praised for her beauty, I felt she didn't have enough self-esteem. No one ever told her how good she was as an actress. And I thought she was very good. But she didn't rely enough on herself. She always thought she was just a sexpot because that's the way it started.'

Everything might have been okay between the two women, Moreau says, except for the fact that Brigitte had an entourage of hangers on, and they tended to get in the way.

'I didn't like them. It's not always very pleasant to see people acting like slaves. I find it's embarrassing. It didn't bring out the best in her. She was a charming, funny and talented young woman. I preferred her alone. And I liked her very much when we were alone. But her entourage wasn't of a very high quality. She was different when they were around. Somebody who needs an entourage is somebody who's frightened. So it made her arrogant. And she didn't need to be that way. She was so beautiful, so extraordinary.

Louis Malle adds that there were further problems with his stars' health and, as usual, the press.

To begin with, Malle remembers, Jeanne found out she was allergic to pineapples. Moreau says, sarcastically, 'I was suddenly allergic to lots of things.'

Malle indicates, 'One of them would fall ill, we'd have to wait and then when she was better the other would fall ill. We ran something like two months over time.'

Further complicating everyone's life, he says, there were hundreds of journalists hanging around. 'The first day of shooting there were something like 130 journalists trying to get on the set. Brigitte refused to come out of her trailer. Jeanne had to show up and make a little speech to appease them before we could get them off the set. Then the journalists started writing stories about how angry Jeanne was with Brigitte and how angry Brigitte was with Jeanne, when none of it was the case. But when Brigitte and Jeanne saw those stories, they started getting angry

Bardot — An Intimate Portrait

at each other, which is a perfect example of how journalists can create news.'

Moreau confirms, 'It was not a very happy set. In fact, I think you can accurately say that it was a very tense set. There was a huge crew and there were a lot of journalists always hanging around. It put a great strain on us. At lunchtime, we had huge tables for the crew and the actors and then there was a huge table, not far away, for the journalists and the photographers. They were always waiting for Brigitte and me to get into a fight. Also the weather conditions were difficult. While we were in Cuernavaca it was perfect, but when we shot in Vera Cruz and Guanajuarto, the climate was quite painful.'

Faced with these difficulties, Brigitte started arriving late.

When Moreau questioned her about it, Brigitte said she just couldn't wake up. 'It got to be such a mess. At one point I called her and said, "Listen Brigitte, everybody needs sleep. So when you know you're not coming to work, please tell me and I'll stay in bed as long as you and then we can arrive at the same time." It was nerve wracking for everyone. Louis started getting upset. Everybody got upset. It all got so out of hand. I wish somebody had calmed it down. I couldn't understand how we'd turned such a beautiful situation – with a lot of money, a good script, good people, a fun film – and transformed it into a nightmare. I was glad when it was over. It was very tiring, very exhausting, very demanding, and there was too much fuss around it.'

Brigitte later said she felt as if she and Moreau had lived together like two comrades in the army who'd fought a war. And to that Moreau says, 'It felt exactly like war.'

Not surprisingly, what friendship they'd managed to have on the set did not continue after the film. 'No, but that happens many times.'

Some 15 or 20 years later, on a trip to St Tropez, Jeanne Moreau did try to ring Bardot at La Madrague, but says she never got through. The truth of the matter is that Brigitte wouldn't take the call. And while some people would be insulted – many of

Brigitte's old friends and old acquaintances who have suffered a similar fate have taken it as a personal affront – Moreau displays some compassion for her former co-star. 'I understand that I come from her cinematic past and that she leads a totally different life now. I hope she's happy with it. She once had a strong sense of friendship, but those friends, like me, belong to her other life. I didn't take that as a rejection.'

No, it was definitely not, Bob Zagury remembers, a very happy movie. Although there were some cheerful times, almost all of them away from the set.

While he and Brigitte were living in a big rented house at Cuernavaca, someone in the crew, who knew she loved animals, gave Brigitte a rabbit, which she took into her bed. The rabbit slept with her and Zagury and, in the morning, had breakfast with them.

The nicest thing Zagury can say about the rabbit, even now, is that it was especially fond of Brigitte's orange juice.

Someone else on the film presented her with two duck chicks, which couldn't have been more than a couple of days old. The next day, a crew member brought her a stray puppy that been found wandering around the neighbourhood. Unfortunately, the dog killed one of the ducks, sending Brigitte into a fit of tears.

The dog must have sensed something was wrong, because he ran away.

Normally she would have gone looking for it but, because she was so upset, she let the dog go. In the meantime, the remaining duck began following her around wherever she went. She'd walk somewhere in the house, and the duck would be a few steps behind her.

When Zagury remarked that the duck was shadowing her, Bardot's comment was, 'He thinks I'm his mother because we walk the same way.'

*   *   *

To publicize the film, Bardot agreed to go to the United States for the very first time.

She and her entourage assembled at Paris's Orly Airport at noon on Thursday 16 December 1965. Police had set up barricades so that the fleet of cars bringing her party and their luggage – dozens of suitcases for a total weight of 600 kilos – could be whisked through a special check-in. Crowds had gathered early that morning, and so had reporters, and before she could get onto the plane the journalists wanted to hear from her.

After all, this wasn't just any excursion, this was Brigitte Bardot's very first expedition to the United States.

'It's a queen who is departing,' one Parisian newspaper wrote, 'a queen with her retinue. A numerous retinue, surrounding her, to stave off the vertigo that comes with skyscrapers.' Among those included, the paper noted, was 'her knight' Bob Zagury, her hairdresser, her press agent and her impresario. 'It is a genuine commando force.'

This was at a time when she was still wearing fur and the papers revealed that she'd taken six different fur coats for her eight-day trip, but not one single mink. 'It's too common,' one of the dailies explained. 'Everyone in America has mink.'

An Air France spokesman – who proudly pointed out that the plane she would be flying on had been renamed 'Viva Maria' – also told the press that they hadn't put on any special cabin staff in the first-class section to cater to her, although they had brought on extra lobster, just in case she wanted seconds at lunch.

On board, the lunacy continued.

Film-maker François Rauchenbach was there with a crew to play fly-on-the-wall, recording for posterity's sake each minute of her American adventure, while those reporters who had been able to get on the flight noted her every move during the Atlantic crossing. They also conducted in-depth interviews with people in the tourist-class section, to see what they thought about sharing this historic moment with Brigitte Bardot.

146

An American GI, who gave his name as US Army Specialist Norman Shaffer from Pottstown, Pennsylvania, summed up the tourist-class section's reaction to this momentous, trailblazing occasion when he told reporters, 'They don't make them like that in Pottstown!'

Arriving at Kennedy Airport around three that afternoon, the Bardot party was met by Louis Malle and a frenzied press corps.

Whisked off the plane and hustled directly into a special room at the arrivals hall, her first sight of the New World was of 50 photographers, 100 journalists, a forest of microphones and eight TV cameras.

'What do you think about the war in Vietnam?' came the opening question.

'Did you vote for Charles de Gaulle?' someone else shouted.

Slightly confused, she reminded them, 'I'm here to talk about Brigitte Bardot.'

So now they went in search of more relevant information, such as, 'How old are you?'

On firmer ground, she looked at the reporter, 'Thirty-one. And you?'

Everyone laughed.

Someone else wanted to know, 'What do you think about being called a sex-kitten?'

'It's all right', she said, 'if you've got the right figure for it.'

The same reporter asked, 'Do you feel like a sex symbol?'

'I am myself,' she said.

'Well, then, who are you?'

She told the man, 'Look for yourself,' stepped off the platform and paraded in front of the table, like a model on a catwalk.

The room burst out in applause.

Someone wanted to know, 'Will you still be like this at 60?'

She responded, 'I'll never be 60 because, between then and now, I'm certain science will make a lot of progress.'

A female reporter tried to find out, 'Do you think a woman has to have children in order to be fulfilled?'

147

Brigitte told her, 'You should try anything once.'

A male reporter dared, 'So what do you think about free love?'

And she happily replied, 'I don't think when I make love.'

It was a ten-car police-escorted motorcade that took Bardot and her entourage into Manhattan, where they took over a good part of the Plaza Hotel. And, because the American press couldn't get enough of her, she did a second press conference the following day.

The same woman who'd quizzed her about children asked, 'How do you reconcile your ideas on marriage and free love?'

Brigitte recognized her immediately. 'Have you tried it since yesterday?'

The woman replied, 'Yes. But, what do I do now?'

Brigitte shrugged, as if it should be obvious. 'Keep trying.'

Her reviews for the press conferences far outshone the reviews she got for the film.

The *New York Telegram* noted that she genuinely impressed a crowd who are not otherwise easily impressed. At the airport and again at the hotel, 'Miss Bardot and the audience both enjoyed the performance and shared a kind of private joke about the whole thing.'

Bosley Crowther in the *New York Times* was only slightly amused by the film – his lukewarm review didn't do much to help ticket sales – while Pauline Kael, writing in the *New Yorker* found most of the comedy to be quite unfunny. That was the general opinion in Britain too, where Kenneth Tynan in the *Observer* decided the whole thing was pretty contrived and failed to justify the basic gimmick of pairing Bardot with Moreau.

With hindsight, Louis Malle isn't so sure that it was a total failure. 'The thing about *Viva Maria* is that Brigitte triumphed. The film worked well in Europe but flopped in the States, even though it was launched over there like a major US picture. The problem, I think, was that they dubbed it badly into English. Especially Brigitte's voice. They got that all wrong. It was terrible.'

148

Trying to Keep Control

Despite the film, its première – a full-scale blow-out on Saturday night at the Astor Theatre on Times Square – was nothing short of total mayhem. A crowd of 5,000 people descended on the corner of 44th and Broadway to get a sight of her. The New York City Police Department assigned 75 officers to crowd control, assisted by nearly 30 security guards, privately hired by the theatre management. It got to the point of being a near-riot and ambulances had to be called because there were seven injuries.

There was such confusion in front of the Astor that, when Louis Malle arrived with his date – a then unknown English actress named Julie Christie – and the crowds saw a blonde on his arm, they thought it was Brigitte and mobbed her too.

'It was', Malle says without any hesitation, 'absolutely terrifying.'

The crowd was totally out of control by the time Bardot showed up.

While being escorted through the mass of people who now blocked the pavement, as police officers tried to get her from her car into the theatre, she was hit by one person and had a camera shoved in her face by another. The camera's flash bulb went off right next to her eye and the following morning a doctor had to be called to treat the burn.

On Sunday, Zagury managed to sneak her out of the hotel for a few hours. Not only had fans been camped out in front of the Plaza since the day she arrived, there were people hanging around in the hallway outside their room. With the help of hotel security, they got away undetected by going through a service door at the back of the hotel. Free from the press, they strolled around Midtown until lunchtime. Coming across a restaurant that seemed okay, they decided to have something to eat. But Bardot was wearing slacks and the manager wouldn't let her in.

'It's not that she didn't like the States,' Zagury says. 'She simply never got to see it. People never left us alone in New York. We were prisoners there. It was only slighter better in Los Angeles.'

149

Unbeknownst to Brigitte, the press and the fans weren't the only ones showing a vigorous interest in her. The director of the Federal Bureau of Investigation, J. Edgar Hoover, was also concerned. Personally offended by *And God Created Woman*, he'd categorized Bardot as someone who was subverting the nation's morals with her lascivious antics on and off camera and had directed that a file be opened on her. The United States Department of Justice now admits that reports were sent to the director from FBI agents working in France – who routinely compiled a non-priority investigation into her background – and from field agents in New York and Los Angeles, who casually noted her movements and the contacts she made while in the country. The file is still active.

How reassuring it is to know that, in those dangerous Cold War days of 1965, the man who'd brought John Dillinger to task, who'd rounded up Nazi spies and – as it would be revealed 25 year later – who was prone to wearing simple, stylish little black dresses, dutifully spent the taxpayers' money to protect the nation from the likes of a five foot seven inch bleach blonde from Paris.

For Act II of her America tour, Bardot and company flew to California on Monday night, where press relations – both for the film and for her – were handled by Pierre Salinger, who'd been John Kennedy's White House press secretary. Under his guidance, things went a bit more smoothly. They didn't have the riotous crowds, but there were still a few hundred fans waiting for her at the airport, mixed into a mass of reporters, photographers and television camera crews.

As soon as she stepped off the plane, she was led to a podium where she opened the festivities by peering out over the bank of microphones, and asking, 'Well, what do we do now?'

A reporter asked, 'Who is Brigitte Bardot and how do you view her?'

She preened, 'Here she is. Are you disappointed?'

'How come,' the question was thrown at her, 'you've waited so long to make your first trip to Hollywood?'

She confessed, 'I don't like to fly, and it's too far to walk.'

'We've been told your luggage weighs nearly 1,500 pounds,' a reporter said. 'Why did you bring so many clothes with you?'

She shrugged, 'I'm asking myself the same question.'

'Are you wearing a wig?' another reporter enquired.

She tugged at her hair. 'It seems to be staying on. Surely it must be mine.'

Someone else wanted to know, 'Tell us, exactly, what kind of woman are you?'

Ever the flirt, she asked, 'Do you want to live for a week with me to find out?'

Playing along with her, the reporter said, 'I'd have to ask my wife.'

'But of course,' she nodded. 'That's what I mean. You and me and your wife!'

After the film's LA première, she agreed that this trip had taught her a serious lesson. 'In the future, I want to live a quiet life.'

With that she hurried back to Paris – 'They considered me like a toy doll in America, who'd been manufactured by all the publicity, so in my press conferences I wanted to show them I could say more than just "mama"' – and promptly went to bed, exhausted from trying to pretend that she cared about any of this.

*　　*　　*

Unlike several previous live-in lovers, Zagury never worked with Bardot when they were together. That came later, just after they'd split up, when he produced a TV special with her that was a first in many ways.

To begin with, this wasn't Brigitte Bardot the actress, this was Brigitte Bardot the singer.

Then, he thinks, it was the first time – at least since she'd become a star – that she truly enjoyed working.

Knowing her as well as he did, Zagury made certain that the project didn't take three or four months, the way a movie does. He says they put it together at a more leisurely, less stressful pace. Nor did he hire a huge crew, the way movie sets are filled with technicians. He did it with just four people, and all of them were friends.

'We'd work for part of the morning, filming her singing, and if she said she wanted to take the afternoon off to go shopping, then we'd quit for the day and go shopping. We wound up with a total of about 15 minutes while we were in St Tropez. And when she saw how good it looked, that she looked good and was good, then we went to Paris and put together the rest of it, which turned it into a one-hour show.'

He'd managed to fire her imagination, and along with that came her enthusiasm. She was filled with ideas and whenever one flew into her head, he pursued it with her. She decided, for instance, that she wanted to do something with a motorcycle, so she and Zagury asked the incomparable Serge Gainsbourg to write a song for her. He penned one called 'Harley Davidson' that same night and they shot the clip two days later. When she told Zagury she'd once seen a set that she now wanted to use, and that it happened to be an exhibit in the Musee d'Art Moderne in Paris, they took Gainsbourg there, showed him the set and two days later he gave her the song 'Contact'.

The result was a series of 17 clips – each one featuring a song wrapped around a little story – which became the very first prime-time American network TV special to feature a French singer.

In those days, all groups and singers put their music on film, but none of them had ever used film like this. None of them had ever shot sequences on location with playback. And, while

152

neither Bardot nor Zagury realized it at the time, history will show that they had inadvertently invented what is today called the music video clip.

Chapter Eight

SACHS

There is a channel running just in front of the beach at La Madrague, about nine or ten feet wide and about five feet deep. Beyond that, there's a large shelf of extremely thick algae – the locals call it *mat* – which lies just beneath the surface of the water, stretching into the bay. The water there is less than a foot deep, much too shallow for most boats to come directly into the beach.

Of course, Bardot knows about the narrow channel, and she knows too of the dangers posed by the algae shelf. But many journalists, paparazzi and nosy tourists don't.

Countless times – literally thousands of times over the past 35 years – she's been on the beach, or has been taking the sun on the pier in front of La Madrague, when she's heard an approaching speedboat. The instant she sits up, the people in the boat spot her, and when they do they aim their boat directly for her.

All she has to do is stay where she is, watching them race towards her.

And right on cue they hit the algae bed.

Hundreds of boats have capsized. Most of the time they just dig themselves into the *mat* so deeply that they can't get out. It's worse than mud because it glues them in tight.

And, when that happens, she lets a triumphant smile cross her

155

lips and goes straight back to sunbathing, undisturbed, at least until the next time.

In the days when she was still spending a good part of each summer at La Madrague, she liked to go around the cape to meet friends for lunch at beaches like Club 55. Naturally, the paparazzi would follow her, lying in wait off-shore to get more photos of her. After lunch, they'd race her back to La Madrague.

Here she always held the advantage.

Turning sharply around the cape, where the Opel family property sits, she'd swing a sharp left into the channel that would bring her safely home. The paparazzi, instead, would always turn wide, hoping to cut her off. And sure enough, as soon as she got to her dock, they'd hit the algae shelf.

She'd go home laughing while they'd have to sit there until help arrived to tow them back into deep water.

Needless to say, Brigitte never felt the urge to ring someone for them.

.   .   .

Before going to the States on the *Viva Maria* press tour, she took another one of those walk-on roles in a Jean-Luc Godard film called *Masculin-Feminin*. She played a woman rehearsing a play. The actor with her was the young director for whom she did a previous walk-on, Antoine Bourseiller.

Back from the States and still involved with Zagury – although the relationship was winding down – she had a minor fling with her then dentist, Paul Albou, whom she bumped into at the Parisian nightclub, Castels. They danced for a while, then disappeared for a week.

Because of the press, Albou says he romanced her with walkie-talkies. 'To avoid the photographers, I bought us a pair of walkie-talkies so that we could warn each other when they were on the prowl. She was petrified of them, of the way they never stopped hounding her. She lived in constant fear of invasion. I remember, one night at La Madrague, there was a streak of lightning that lit up the room and she nearly panicked. She thought it was a flashbulb.'

The media's presence and her constant fear of invasion created an enormous amount of pressure which, Albou points out, had to take its toll on every relationship she had.

'There was always so much tension surrounding her. I think it's true to say that some men got off on that. They found it thrilling to be constantly on call. But men always had to enter her life. Gunter Sachs was the only one who brought her into his.'

●   ●   ●

At the turn of the century, somewhere in the part of southern Germany that used to be known as the Habsburg Empire, an engineer named Ernst Sachs invented the freewheel hub, which would allow bicycles to go downhill without being pedalled. It was the beginning of a minor Bavarian industrial dynasty.

His son, Willy, inherited that business and over the years built up the firm of Fichtel & Sachs, expanding out of bicycle hubs to ball bearings, motor bikes, car engines and automobile accessories. He married Eleonore von Opel – whose own father, Adam, had founded the German automotive manufacturing company that bore his name – and together they had two sons, Ernst Wilhelm and Fritz Gunter.

In 1935, Willy and Eleonore separated. Ernst Wilhelm stayed with his father, while three-year-old Fritz Gunter went to live with his mother in Switzerland. There it was customary for offspring to tag a mother's maiden name onto their father's family name. So as he was growing up – mainly in the canton of Grisons – he was called Gunter Sachs von Opel. Years later, the French press would look at that name, learn that he'd been born in Maimberg Castle near Schweinfurt-am-Main – it's true, but it wasn't the old family *schloss*, his father bought it because living in a castle was a pretty fancy thing to do – assume there must have been nobility in his lineage and would simply bestow on him the title Count.

'The closest I ever legitimately came to using the title', he says, 'was when I named my boat the Count von Dracula. I also sometimes wore a black cape and signed my letters Count Gunter von Dracula.'

He studied mathematics at university in Lausanne and in 1955 married a young French woman named Anne-Marie Faure who was born in Algiers – a *pied noir*, as the French who were raised in colonial North Africa are called. Gunter went to work for his father and Anne-Marie gave him a son named Rolf. The future seemed assured until 1958, when tragedy struck.

The same year that Gunter won the European bobsleigh championship, his father passed away. Then, in June, after a car accident, when Anne-Marie's doctor diagnosed a slight back problem and recommended surgery, something went wrong with her anaesthesia and she died on the operating table.

At 26, Gunter was a widower with a young son.

Having inherited something in the range of $80–115 million – it's difficult to be more precise because his father's businesses were private and the true value of the assets wasn't easy to estimate – he tried to bury his grief in the non-stop party life of an international playboy. Or, at least that's what it looked like on the surface. In reality he says, his party days were generally restricted to holidays.

'Unlike a lot of my friends, I didn't play all year long. I couldn't. I travelled a lot and I worked very hard. I had a business to run.'

In early June 1966, Sachs was staying at one of several homes he's got in St Tropez and invited two of his best friends out to dinner. He took Serge Marquand and Gerard LeClery to the Vieille Fontaine restaurant in nearby Gassin, intending to spend the evening talking about a sailing adventure they'd planned.

But Serge, who is the younger brother of Vadim's pal Christian Marquand, and LeClery, who is the son of the French industrialist founder of the André shoe store chain, always made Gunter laugh and that night was no exception.

Marquand remembers, 'We were laughing like crazies. We were having a very good time. Brigitte was a few tables away, eating dinner with some friends. She saw us, frankly she couldn't have missed us, and because she and I have known each other since she was 14 years old, she came over to say hello. She vaguely knew Gunter, at least she knew who he was. So we talked for a while and then arranged to meet after dinner at Papagayo.'

While they were still in the restaurant, Gunter says, Brigitte kept looking over at his table. 'I had met her, briefly, on one or two previous occasions. Two times, I think. But only to say hello and shake hands. We didn't know each other. But this time there was a lot of eye contact. It was very exciting.'

At Papagayo, Brigitte and Gunter danced for a long time and before the night was out he'd split her away from the rest of the group and taken her back to his estate, La Capilla. They stayed there together for two days.

On the afternoon of the third day, she told him she had to get back to La Madrague to take care of some papers. That was the exact expression she used – '*Pour faire les papiers*' – which Gunter took to mean, she needed to go through mail or deal with her accounts or go over contracts. In fact, he didn't give it a second thought, until Serge wondered where Brigitte was. Gunter explained that she'd gone to do her paperwork, and Marquand burst out laughing. Gunter didn't get the joke, so Serge told him that 'paperwork' was Brigitte's code for another date. In other words, she'd left him to see someone else.

That didn't particularly bother Gunter – after all, at this point they certainly didn't have any sort of commitment to each other – but Serge thought Gunter should go to rescue her. 'Go be a knight on a white charger and save the damsel in distress.'

Gunter wasn't so sure. He reckoned that if she wanted to spend time with someone else, that was her business. Anyway, she didn't strike him as being someone who was in much distress.

But Serge wouldn't let up and finally Gunter agreed. 'Okay, I'll drive over there.'

'No,' Serge said, 'you can't just drive up to her front door. You've got to do something much more romantic.'

'All right,' Gunter said, 'I'll get my motorcycle.'

'Still not romantic enough,' Serge argued. 'Why not arrive by boat?'

Gunter was all for being romantic, but he knew about the *mat* that guarded the entrance to her beach from the sea and he reminded Serge, 'It's pitch black out there at night. It's dangerous.'

'No problem,' Serge said. 'It's true that if you're not careful you'll wind up in the seaweed. But I have a plan.'

Gunter had heard that before from his pal, and thought to himself, 'I should know better by now.' Still, he let Serge talk him into it.

Later that night, at 'Zero Hour', Gunter – wrapped in a long black Count Dracula cape – got into his Riva and sailed it from his house, making his way carefully to the cape, to his cousin Christina von Opel's house.

As promised, Marquand was there on the shore, dressed in a wetsuit, sitting on his motorcycle.

When Serge heard the approaching Riva, he turned his headlight towards it and flashed several times. The code was one flash, turn left. Two flashes, turn right. As long as the light stays on, keep going straight. So with Serge guiding the Riva through the pitch black night, Gunter made his way slowly down that narrow channel.

They'd agreed that Gunter couldn't just tie up at Bardot's dock and nonchalantly walk into her house. It wasn't anywhere near dramatic enough. So, according to Serge's plan, when they got close enough, Marquand climbed off the motorbike and jumped into the water. Once he was in place, hiding under her dock, Gunter revved the boat's engines and, now able to see La Madrague, came racing in.

With water splashing everywhere and the engines making a racket, he jammed on the brakes, leapt out of the boat – leaving his frogman cohort to tie it up – threw his cape around his shoulders and marched ashore.

Brigitte was sitting on a swing with a guy, suddenly speechless, as Gunter Sachs emerged out of the water and the darkness.

He walked right up to them, said good evening, and sat down in between Brigitte and her date.

The other man soon got the message, excused himself and was never seen again.

'I think it's fair to claim that I romanced her,' Gunter says now.

That's an understatement.

One day in Nice, he went to the flower market and bought 100 dozen roses – he shrugs, 'You know, roses in Nice aren't very expensive. I hate to disappoint you, but they didn't cost too much. I can tell you the 10 carat diamond ring was more expensive' – then hired a helicopter, flew to her house, hovered above her head and dropped the roses all over La Madrague.

She spent the day picking them up, finding them everywhere, and later confessed that she fell in love with him, 'because it's not everyday a man drops a ton of roses into your backyard'.

True to character, his partiality towards helicopters continued. One day a year or so later, returning from a business trip, he chartered a helicopter from Nice Airport and, instead of landing at the pad in St Tropez, he directed the pilot to drop him off at La Madrague. The pilot tried to explain that there was no way he could land there. But Gunter already knew that. So with Brigitte in residence, the helicopter came in close – alarming her that tourists were invading – and, much to her utter amazement, he jumped out of it and into the sea, luggage and all.

A couple of nights after he waded ashore at her beach, he brought her back to La Capilla for a midnight supper. For light, he set up 200 candles along a wall overlooking the sea. At around

4 am, he and Brigitte were sitting on the terrace, bathed in candlelight, when he told her it was time to turn out the lights. She was just about to get up when he said, not that way. He handed her an air rifle and, for the next hour, they shot out the candles.

A few nights after that, he took her and a whole bunch of friends to a well-known Riviera restaurant just outside Monaco called 'Le Pirate'.

The owner, who dressed like a part-time gypsy, animated evenings by throwing plates into the huge open fire where the chef roasted food. He was famous for it. If he liked you, he'd also sometimes throw a chair or a table into the fire. If he really liked you, he'd let you throw a table or some chairs into the fire. That night, he was so thrilled to see Brigitte Bardot and Gunter Sachs in his place that he – with their help – threw the entire restaurant into the fire. Every table, every chair, everything!

A rough act to follow, Gunter, Brigitte and their friends decided to go from there to the casino at Monte Carlo.

'Normally', Gunter says, 'there are strictly adhered to dress codes at the casino. We were all barefoot, in jeans, with our hair soaked in champagne. But they knew me and when they saw it was Brigitte Bardot, the rules were bent.'

It might have been better for the casino if they hadn't made an exception.

Gunter, Brigitte and their friends came into the Salle Privée – the private rooms at the back of the casino – where everyone else was dressed in evening clothes. They sat down at a roulette table and Gunter covered the number 14. He played it every way he could – *en plein, à cheval, carré, douzaine, sixaine, transversale, manqué, pair,* and *couleur* – which all adds up to mean that he was also covering everything that surrounded his lucky number.

The wheel spun and, when it stopped, the little ball was sitting in the slot marked 14.

The people at the table shrieked and the croupier pushed some chips in front of Gunter and Brigitte.

Serge Marquand admits they were all a little drunk but even slightly tipsy Gunter knew what he was doing and saw right away that the croupier had made a mistake. Instead of putting 170,000 francs ($35,000) on the pile of chips, there was only 160,000 ($33,000). So Gunter said, stop, there's been a mistake. The croupier recounted, apologized and corrected the error.

A crowd began gathering around the table.

The croupier invited everyone to place their bets and Gunter again covered the number 14, every which way.

This time, number 12 hit. Gunter and Brigitte won again.

So the croupier counted the chips, pushed them towards Gunter and again, Gunter said, stop, there's been a mistake.

'This is the second time,' he reminded the croupier. 'Now, I know we all look a little drunk, like we've been having a good time, but don't take me for an idiot.'

The croupier apologized, 'I'm terribly sorry sir, it was my mistake.'

Gunter warned him, 'Please don't do it again.'

Once the croupier had put the correct amount of chips in front of them, he invited everyone to place their bets.

The crowd around the table was now several people thick.

For the third time, Gunter covered the number 14, every which way, and this time number 13 hit. The crowd roared.

The croupier pushed the correct amount of chips in front of Gunter and Brigitte and invited new bets

Gunter covered the table with chips in the usual manner and the wheel spun for the fourth time.

By now, absolutely everyone in the casino was standing around the table. There wasn't anyone at all playing at any of the other tables. Brigitte and Gunter had utterly stopped the place.

The croupier saw the little ball tumble into a slot on the wheel and announced, '*Quatorze*' – 14 – and the crowd went wild.

163

In the middle of absolute chaos, the croupier counted the chips and pushed a pile of them in front of Gunter and Brigitte.

And Gunter screamed, 'Stop!'

For the third time out of four, he was short again. This time, nearly 40,000 francs ($8,370) was missing.

Furious, Gunter demanded the director of the casino.

A dignified man in a dinner jacket showed up, pushed his way through the crowd and asked Gunter if there was something wrong.

Sachs roared, 'Is this a casino here or a grocery store.'

The director didn't seem to understand, so Gunter — whose French is perfect — told him in no uncertain terms just how angry he was.

The director tried to calm him down.

But Gunter wasn't going to let them off the hook. 'How come this man has been mistaken three times in four spins of the wheel? How come, every time the mistake has been in the casino's favour, never once in my favour?'

He had a mountain of chips in front of him — somewhere around 600,000–700,000 francs ($123,000–143,000) — and, in the midst of a barrage of the director's sincerest apologies, Gunter called for a basket.

Two croupiers soon made their way through the middle of the mob with a basket. Gunter swept all his chips onto it, and told the two men to take it to the cashier and deposit it in his account. Then he stood up and with Brigitte on his arm, they made their exit.

As they left, everyone in the casino applauded.

'It was an unbelievable spectacle,' Serge Marquand says. 'No one had ever seen anything like it. A bunch of beach bums without shoes, smelling of champagne – including Brigitte Bardot – march over to a roulette wheel, win 600,000 francs, give the croupier hell, give the director hell, shove the chips into a basket, and without even stopping at the cashier, no more than 23 minutes after we walk in, we're out of there.'

The following day, Gunter took the money he won, went to a jewellery store and spent it on a gift for Brigitte.

*   *   *

He called her Bardot or 'Mamou.' She called him 'Sachsi' or 'Planti' – a nickname she invented from the word *plantigrade*, which refers to the way certain animals walk with the entire sole of their feet, like bears.

At the end of those first few whirlwind weeks, he took her to Germany to see his home there, and put on the biggest fireworks display ever seen in Bavaria. Then he decided, 'Let's get married.'

'He romanced me like James Bond,' she says. 'I was seduced by the sort of madness Gunter put into seducing me.'

'I was in love with her,' he says. 'So I romanced her like a circus performer.'

Because they both agreed they couldn't possibly get married anywhere in Europe without turning the wedding into a media circus, Gunter suggested they make a fast run to Las Vegas, where he'd been told a couple could get married at any time of the day or night at very short notice.

Not having known each other a month yet, she granted that this was indeed short notice and said Las Vegas would be fine.

The problem was, they didn't know anybody in Las Vegas and neither of them wanted simply to show up and hope it would work. They agreed that they needed to plan the trip. She volunteered to phone Pierre Salinger. But Gunter had been friends with two of Jack Kennedy's sisters – Jean Smith and Pat Lawford – and through them he knew Teddy Kennedy. So he called Teddy, who said he would be happy to handle the suitable arrangements.

As his wedding present to Brigitte, Sachs had Cartier make three platinum bracelets of equal length so that she could wear them together. The first was encrusted with 50 bright red rubies. The second was encrusted with 44 brilliant white diamonds. The third was encrusted with seven bright blue sapphires. Together, they made up the tricolour of the French flag.

On Wednesday morning, 13 July 1966, with Brigitte and Gunter scheduled to leave in a couple of hours, Gunter drove from his flat at 32 Avenue Foch – where his neighbours were Prince Rainier and Princess Grace – to hers on the Avenue Paul Doumer to drop off something for her. To avoid drawing too much press attention, they were planning to drive in separate cars to Orly.

And avoiding the press was something they were intent on doing.

In fact, Gunter says, they were both very jumpy about getting found out and having their wedding turned into the usual three-ring circus.

After seeing her, he went downstairs and was just about to get into his car when he noticed a flyer for a magazine with her picture on it. She was standing next to a panther. He was staring at it when, suddenly, something nipped at his feet.

Not sure if it was the panther or the press, he jumped six feet into the air. 'It was only a little dog, but it was a pretty nervous morning.'

Five of them were booked on the flight to Los Angeles. Brigitte and Gunter had invited along Serge Marquand, Gérard LeClery and Brigitte's chum, photographer Philippe d'Exea. There were no reporters waiting for the party when they all met at Orly, but Air France had managed to screw up their reservations.

'We had first-class tickets from Orly to Los Angeles,' Gunter says, 'but when we checked in for the Air France flight' – they were using the names Mme Bordat and M. Scar – 'we were told that Air France had oversold first class and that we would have to fly tourist.'

A new experience for both of them. Gunter complained about it, to no avail. The only compensation the airline would make for their famous passengers was to give them the first rows in economy – 'You'll like it very much, sir, it's just behind first class, after all.'

Brigitte and Gunter had little choice but to accept.

So they got onto the Boeing 707 and sat in tourist class, and after a while their friends decided that seeing Brigitte and Gunter stuck in economy was so funny that Philippe d'Exea took pictures of them. When Brigitte and Gunter got back to Paris after their honeymoon, Gunter returned his first-class tickets and asked for a rebate. Air France refused, insisting that Brigitte Bardot and Gunter Sachs had surely not flown economy. Gunter produced all the necessary evidence but the airline wouldn't believe him. Ever conscious of good customer relations, they accused him of trying to rebate tickets he'd already used. It was nearly a year later that they finally returned his money, and then, only after he sent them Philippe d'Exea's pictures from the plane.

Adding insult to injury, someone at Air France had alerted the press that Brigitte and Gunter were on this flight. When they touched down in Los Angeles, photographers were waiting for them.

So were a pair of Leer jets that Teddy Kennedy had hired in Gunter's name, to fly them to Las Vegas.

They landed in Nevada 35 minutes later, met by a local lawyer friend of Kennedy's, Bill Coulthard. He took them to the Clark County Court House for the marriage licence and, from there, back to his house where Judge John Mowbray was waiting in his black robe to marry them.

The Coulthard living room was filled with flowers, a gift from Teddy Kennedy.

Brigitte and Gunter were still wearing what they wore on the flight from Paris. She was in a short, violet dress. He was in white slacks, with a dark blue blazer, white shoes but no socks. 'Naturally, I put on a tie for the wedding.'

The judge – a large, dark-haired man of 45 – asked who the witnesses were. No one in the wedding party spoke terrific English, so it took a few minutes to sort that one out. When the judge learned the witnesses would be Marquand and d'Exea, he showed them where he wanted them to stand. He put Coulthard and his wife next to LeClery, invited Brigitte and Gunter to stand in front of him, and started the ceremony.

Suddenly Gunter said, 'Please stop.'

Everyone glared at him.

'Please, would you wait another 20 minutes?'

The judge didn't know what this was all about. 'What for?'

'Please.' Gunter motioned to Brigitte to show her his watch. It was 11.40 pm.

She understood right away and together they urged the judge to wait a little while longer.

Mowbray didn't mind, so the eight of them stood around for the next 20 minutes.

It wasn't just that Gunter wanted to be married on the 14th because 14 is his lucky number. He says, 'It suddenly dawned on me that it would be very appropriate to marry the symbol of France on Bastille Day.'

Some eight minutes after midnight, when Mowbray pronounced them man and wife, Brigitte and Gunter kissed and then Brigitte asked the judge if she could kiss him. He said, 'Twice if you like,' and she did. Later the judge remarked, 'What a country this is. This afternoon I sentenced a murderer to death. Tonight I'm marrying Brigitte Bardot.'

Because it was so late and they were so tired – it was already morning Paris-time – as soon as the ceremony was over, Gunter asked the Coulthards if they had room to put them up. The lawyer and his wife were so thrilled at the thought of Brigitte Bardot spending her wedding night at their place, they immediately agreed and allowed Brigitte and Gunter to sleep in their bed.

The next morning, Mr and Mrs Gunter Sachs, together with Marquand, LeClery and d'Exea, got back into their Leer jets and flew to Los Angeles.

As Gunter explained to the press waiting at the airport for them, 'We decided to marry two weeks ago. We came here to make it fast and good. It is not possible to do it in Europe without all the photographers.'

168

Checking into the Beverly Hills Hotel, the newlyweds took up residence in Bungalow #1. For lunch that afternoon, Gunter had arranged a buffet on the lawn near the swimming pool. A number of people from the film business dropped by to wish them well, including James Mason and Danny Kaye.

Brigitte had briefly met Kaye in London – he'd been a guest on the set of *Babette s'en Va-t-en Guerre* – but Gunter didn't know him. Gunter was, however, impressed when someone told them that Kaye had a kitchen at home the same size as the one at the hotel, and that he was an excellent cook, specializing in Chinese food. So when Kaye invited Brigitte and Gunter and their friends for dinner that night, they happily accepted. Before long, Kaye was putting the story around that he'd personally flown them back from Las Vegas, thrown a wedding banquet for them because they were such old friends and, long before desert, had ushered them upstairs at his house to consummate their marriage.

News of Brigitte Bardot's wedding was a front-page story back in France, enough to put a dent in the coverage Charles de Gaulle got for his Bastille Day parade. And he was said to be furious.

To follow up, reporters in Paris now scoured the discos for her former boyfriends. Sacha Distel was quoted as having absolutely nothing to say. Bob Zagury replied, 'I was not aware that she was getting married.' Later, journalists would expand on his statement, claiming that he'd been waiting for her at La Madrague – he wasn't, he was in Paris – and quoting him as saying, 'I thought she'd gone shopping.' He never said it.

One paper in Rio de Janeiro reminded its readers that the marriage was the talk of Buzios. 'How', the newspaper asked, 'does M. Sachs' taste in beaches compare with M. Zagury?'

A newspaper in Bonn used the opportunity to make a political statement, as if their readers really cared. After pointing out how rich Sachs was, the daily *General Anzeiger* implied, 'Those years are now long behind us when French celebrities wanted nothing to do with us nasty Germans. The strength of our money has finally broken down those barriers.'

But some people were shocked. In an open letter to Brigitte, published in the weekly magazine *Vie Catholique Illustrée* (Catholic Life Illustrated), a French priest wrote, 'In eight minutes you got married again in Las Vegas. You no longer belong to M. Vadim, or to M. Charrier, or to M. Zagury, you belong to M. Sachs. If someone else comes on the scene tomorrow whom you do not know today, will you get married again? Will M. Sachs in turn use the words attributed to your last boyfriend, M. Zagury, when he heard about your recent marriage – that it is all a big joke?'

Objecting to a Bardot remark that her private life was her own business and that she didn't care if someone was offended by it, the priest said, 'No. Marriage is a public act.'

He explained that he wasn't attacking the concept of divorce, he was merely questioning Brigitte's views on marriage and the fact that she appeared to live with the philosophy that, once she'd had enough of one husband, she could discard the sanctity of marriage by moving on to the next one.

'That is not love,' he wrote. 'That is not proof of great maturity. But it is a way of living that is being shown to all who adopt the ideas of their idol.'

Bardot's response was typically acerbic. 'I suspect he preferred it when I had lovers.'

For three days, the phone in Bungalow #1 never stopped ringing.

Because Brigitte has always been one to answer her own phone, when an American journalist got through and she picked it up and he asked for her and she said, this is me, the man got angry. He couldn't believe that the biggest star in the world would answer her own phone. He snapped, 'I know you're her secretary and she tells you to say that, so stop fooling around and put her on the phone.'

Christian Barbier, a reporter for radio station Europe 1 in Paris didn't have that problem when he got through to her on the Friday night. Barbier reminded Brigitte she'd once said she would never marry again. Her answer, 'Only schmucks never change their mind.'

170

He asked, 'Who changed your mind?'

She answered, 'Gunter. I changed my mind because he exists. I didn't know he existed when I said I'd never marry again.'

Sachs then got on the line and explained that they didn't announce their wedding plans before leaving Europe because they wanted to get married for themselves, not for the press.

Nor was he being vague when anyone asked him where they were going on their honeymoon. Until that morning, he hadn't yet decided.

He now says, 'The thing was, we didn't want anyone to spoil our honeymoon. So we kept all our options open. I was thinking that our honeymoon should last three to four weeks and explained to Brigitte that I wouldn't tell her where we were going because it's more romantic that way.'

The truth is, he admits, he didn't have any idea where they were going until the Friday.

'I thought about the South Pacific, or Acapulco, or maybe just heading west and getting back to Paris after making our way around the world. But on Friday I decided it would be Tahiti, because I knew she'd like that. I bought us all tickets and on Saturday we left for Polynesia.'

Unfortunately, Tahiti did not prove to be quite as idyllic as he'd hoped.

By the time they got there, *Paris Match* was already waiting for them – although they did manage to stay a couple of steps ahead of the photographers for most of the time.

Also waiting for them was an invitation from a man who owned an atoll. But not just any atoll, this was the atoll that usually gets pictured in encyclopedias as an example of an atoll.

A photo and full explanation came with the invitation, and because neither Brigitte nor he had ever been to an atoll – and, certainly not an atoll perfect enough to be pictured in an encyclopedia – they accepted the invitation.

They were flown in a light plane from Papeete – having to fly was already one point against atolls on Brigitte's score card – and although they were well received by the atoll owner, within ten minutes she'd had enough.

'Too many mosquitoes.' She told Gunter that she hated the place and insisted he get her out of there.

Back at the beach where they were staying outside Papeete, things turned nasty when she stepped on some coral and cut her foot badly.

One of the few good things that happened to Brigitte in Tahiti, according to Serge Marquand, was that Gunter managed to keep the press at bay. 'We avoided most of the photographers during the honeymoon. In fact, while she was with Gunter she was more protected than ever before. They used to fly in private jets for no other reason than to avoid crowds. Brigitte was totally paranoid about crowds. So Gunter protected her. He always tried to find places where they could escape crowds and the paparazzi.'

Gunter's friend and lawyer, Peter Notz, arrived to spend a couple of days with them, and when he left so did they. From Tahiti, they flew to Mexico, to visit friends in Acapulco. And that might have been all right, except that Brigitte's foot wound opened again.

Throughout their honeymoon, Philippe d'Exea was their official photographer and both Brigitte and Gunter agreed that he could then sell the photos through his agency in Paris. D'Exea now claims that, several months later, Sachs rang him to ask for 50 per cent of the photo fees.

That's true.

But Philippe and Gunter disagree on the reason for it. D'Exea says it was for Sachs, which is difficult to believe because Sachs certainly didn't need the money. Sachs says it was for Serge Marquand, and Marquand supports this. They say that the deal with Philippe was contingent on Serge – as Philippe's assistant he had held the light screen and the extra cameras – getting half. But when the pictures were sold through Philippe's agency, there was a major misunderstanding because Philippe later claimed he was the photographer and that he was keeping the money.

Gunter and Serge have never spoken to Philippe since.

When the honeymoon party landed back in Paris, one of the first things the press noted was that Brigitte drove to her place in her car and he drove to his place his car. The rumour quickly spread that friends had already opened a betting line on how long the marriage would last.

D'Exea now insists, 'I knew the marriage was already finished.'

Again, Gunter's version is different. He says that, because they both had their cars at Orly, it was only normal that they would leave in separate cars. Furthermore, he maintains, the marriage was anything but over. 'During our marriage, while we were in Paris, she often spent the days at her own flat but almost always spent the night with me in mine.'

Years later she complained, 'I haven't even got a key to his house. It is a strange and unfamiliar place and it frightens me.'

The fact is, she didn't need a key. Gunter had staff in the apartment to open the door. But he does acknowledge that his taste was never hers. 'I had a library in the apartment, where the shelves were filled with leather-bound books. They weren't for reading, they were to create an effect, to look beautiful.'

That was precisely why she was uneasy there. Her bookshelves were then, and are now, not displays but the place where she puts books that she's actually read. 'His library is much more beautiful than mine, but you can't read any of the books.'

His apartment was also much more formal than hers, more sophisticated – decorator perfect, if you will – with the right furniture in the right setting.

'It simply wasn't her,' Sachs now concedes. 'What she said about the library, she's right. It wasn't her taste because there's nothing phony about her.'

They weren't back in Europe very long before the rumour spread that he'd only married her on a bet. The story that ran in the

173

papers — and Brigitte saw it — was that he'd wagered a lot of money with Serge Marquand that he could make her his wife.

But in those days Gunter had $100 million in his pocket and Serge Marquand probably didn't have 100 francs in his. 'So', Gunter asks candidly, 'how can you bet money with Serge Marquand? No. There was no bet. That was invented by the newspapers.'

Marquand also emphasizes there was no bet. 'Where the story came from is the fact that Gunter was determined to seduce her, to make her his girlfriend, and it wasn't evident that he could do it. She usually liked pretty young boys and he was already in his 30s. Making it even more difficult, she was with Bob Zagury at the time. So at first he looked at it as a challenge. But there wasn't a bet. No one ever put any money on the table. In his own head, he told himself he could do it and put all his energy, all his cunning, all his experience and a lot of money into the effort. The thing is, while he was doing it, he found himself in a trap of his own making. While he was wooing her, he fell in love with her. It all happened very quickly. And he was really very much in love with her.'

• * •

They were just settling into married life together, when she returned to work. Her new picture was called *A Coeur Joie* ('Two Weeks In September'). It was produced by Francis Cosne and, as silent partner, Bob Zagury. The studio work was done in Paris but there was location work in Scotland and London.

Arriving in London on Saturday 3 September, she was due to start filming in Scotland on the Monday. She was met by the press, who confronted her with the rumour that her three-month marriage was already on the rocks.

She snapped, 'I'm here to work so I'll only talk about my movie.'

174

But that wasn't what the reporters wanted to talk about. Since she was dressed in a mini-skirt, another reporter wanted to know if she still considered herself a sex symbol. Bardot answered sharply, 'A sex symbol is not myself.'

Her mood had quickly soured. She walked out of the press conference, and, together with Philippe d'Exea and her make-up lady, they drove 317 miles north to Carlisle in Cumbria. The production company had reserved a double room and two singles for them at the Crown and Mitre Hotel.

When they arrived – in a terrible rainstorm, just before midnight – Bardot found the lobby crammed with people. There were photographers waiting for her and guests from a local wedding reception. Flashbulbs went off. She turned on her heel, announced that she wasn't coming into the hotel with all those people there, got back into her car and drove away.

Half an hour later, the wedding party had broken up but the photographers were still hanging around. Pushing past them, she told the desk clerk that she and her friends were hungry. The assistant manager came over to explain that the kitchen was now closed, but he would personally prepare a chicken salad.

The three of them ate, but when they were finished Brigitte announced that the meal hadn't suited her. For that matter, neither did the hotel. She told the assistant manager that they wouldn't be staying there. The assistant manager tried to explain the trouble he'd gone to in preparing the chicken salad. 'I'm going,' she said flatly and asked for the back door to avoid the photographers.

The assistant manager, with typical British reserve, said, 'As you please,' and presented her with a bill for the rooms and the meal.

Bardot refused to pay for it. 'With all this publicity about my arrival, your hotel has got enough reward.'

The assistant manager explained that they didn't do business this way and insisted that the bill be paid. It was just over $35, which would probably represent ten times that today.

175

Clearly annoyed, she produced four £5 notes and stood there with her hand out while the assistant manager gave her the appropriate change.

Without saying another thing, she stormed out of the rear door, got into her car and drove the rest of the way to the Open Arms Hotel in Dirleton, East Lothian, where she'd been booked to stay during the filming. She arrived just before dawn and went straight to bed.

Whatever her feelings for the press, for her husband or for the film, everything was pushed aside on Monday morning when she started work. She was being paid to be Brigitte Bardot and she knew how to be that better than anyone else.

She knew her screen persona so well, she wouldn't even let somebody else's feet get in the way.

The shooting script of *A Coeur Joie* called for a close-up of Brigitte's feet as she runs along the beach. When the time came to shoot it, the director, Serge Bourguignon, decided there was no reason to bother Brigitte and instead used her stand-in.

But when Brigitte saw the rushes that afternoon, she was horrified. 'Those aren't my feet. Anybody can tell they're not my feet.' She insisted, 'You can't use it.'

The thing was, of course, like the rest of her, the Bardot feet were perfect and the stand-in's weren't. It didn't matter to her that nobody else could tell they weren't her feet because they were mostly in blur anyway. But she could tell. That's how precise she was in knowing who she was and what she projected onto the screen.

From Scotland, the crew moved south to London and her mood improved.

Staying at the Westbury, she noticed Philippe d'Exea going out one night on a date and, while he was gone, she emptied his room. She took every single piece of furniture and everything he owned out of there. If it wasn't nailed down or fixed to the wall, she removed it. When he came back late that night with his date, he found the room stripped bare – and Brigitte next door hysterical.

Sachs

(Turnabout was fair play a few years later when she cleared out her room. John Lennon had wanted to meet her, but stipulated that, before he'd come to see her, she'd have to take all the furniture out of her suite at the Mayfair. She complied, filling the empty living room with candles. It struck her as a little weird, but Lennon seemed to think it was all perfectly natural. It turns out that he always had a serious crush on her – there was a time in his life when he went out only with girls who looked like Brigitte Bardot – and had once hoped to make a film with her. The Beatles were interested in the idea and so was she. So Brigitte went to London to meet Richard Lester – he'd directed *Hard Day's Night* and *Help* – but nothing ever came of the project.)

Now on the set of *A Coeur Joie* she was equally playful, this time with a young actor named Mike Sarne.

Before coming to acting, he'd had a brief career as a pop singer. Easily handsome enough to catch Brigitte's eye, he claims they realized something was happening, went back to his place in West London, and stayed there together, holding up the film, for a couple of days. Once the film was over, she went back to Paris and that, he shrugs, was the end of that.

'She loves the *coup de foudre*,' Sarne says, 'that clash of bells and ringing of sirens when a certain man meets a certain woman. She was always looking for the bolt of electricity that brought life to Frankenstein.'

Although Gunter had gone to visit her in Scotland, he wasn't in London – he'd made the then cardinal mistake of leaving her alone – and she even told people on the set, 'I need to be taken care of and reassured all the time.'

The woman Mike Sarne says he was now reassuring struck him as someone who might have pretended to be a hippy, but in reality, never was. 'Deep down inside, she's a sensible, bourgeois, middle-class girl, very practical and with terrific common sense.

177

But she was never allowed to be herself. There's someone else inside the movie star.'

Central to her being, he feels, was the need to fall in love. 'That's what she did. She fell in love for two years or two weeks or two days. All of those affairs were about love, about falling in love, about hoping to stay in love. It was great if you happened to be the guy she fell in love with. At least for a time. Being with her meant your world had to revolve around hers. Brigitte was rich and famous and beautiful, but she only did whatever she wanted to. As long as everyone always understood that Bardot was an icon, she was terrific fun to be with, always in a terrific mood. Without that, she'd brood.'

It very rapidly became overbearing for Sarne because she seemed to encourage a kind of madness around her. 'There would always be dozens of people hanging around doing dozens of different things. And the phone was constantly ringing. It was a three-ring circus. It wasn't that she constantly sought attention. It was just something she expected. She never had to be demanding. No man could resist her. She expected that too. She knew how beautiful she was, even if she wouldn't admit it at times, because she was constantly being reminded of how beautiful she was. She was powerful and very passionate. And when you were with her, the real thing, you realized just how pale the imitations were.'

*   *   *

'When she wants to be, and she's in the mood, she can be so bright and wonderful.' Gunter is unequivocal. 'She also happens to be extremely intelligent. That's probably her least known asset. She expresses herself well and writes wonderful letters. She is also well known, among her friends, for correcting their spelling and their grammar. People never realize just how smart she is. Nor did people ever realize when she was in the movie business just how much she hated the movies.'

And when he says she hated it, that's exactly what he means.

178

'Each Monday the weekend take at the French cinemas would be announced in the newspaper. Like a bestseller list. And everyone in the business always checked the Monday listings to see how much money each picture was taking. Everyone, except Brigitte. She couldn't have cared less. I never once saw her open a newspaper to check the Monday listings. The film business simply did not interest her.'

Not even, he says, when it might have been good for her to pay a little attention to her career.

Producer Joseph Losey came to see Brigitte about a project one afternoon and Gunter received him. After sitting with Losey for a while, Gunter wondered where Brigitte was.

Excusing himself, he went inside and found her with Guapa, one of her dogs, who was apparently ill. Brigitte said she'd be right out. So Sachs and Losey chatted amiably for a while longer, until Gunter excused himself again to remind Brigitte that Losey was waiting. This time Brigitte said she had to take Guapa to the vet, leaving Gunter to explain to Losey that there would be a further delay.

Now Gunter promised Losey that Brigitte would be right back. After a total wait of three hours, Losey couldn't take any more of it and left.

Gunter shrugs, 'She has always had her own priorities. And animals have always come long before film producers.'

Nor did she seem overly eager to spend time with politicians. One day an invitation arrived for them to join French President and Madame de Gaulle for dinner at the Elysée Palace.

'He'd invited her four or five times and she'd never gone. When this invitation came, she was very proud of it, she'd never been to the Elysée, and put it on her dresser so that she could look at it. Of course, we accepted. Then, as we got closer to the date, she told me she didn't want to go. At the last moment I had to insist. She dressed in a trouser suit with a gold embroidered top that made it look like a uniform. It was the first time a woman ever came to

179

an evening at the Elysée in trousers. She looked like a soldier.'

Carrying on the theme of her outfit, instead of calling him Mr President, when Brigitte was presented to de Gaulle, she said, '*Bon soir, mon Général*'.

De Gaulle took one look at her and responded, 'That's the right thing to say.'

Gunter recalls that it turned out to be quite a funny evening. Once all the guests had arrived, the President walked around the room saying something to everyone. When he got to the sculptor César, he shook the little man's hand and proclaimed, 'I want to thank you for everything you've done for French medicine.'

When de Gaulle came up to Sachs — knowing that he was German — he said, 'We are very happy to see you here . . .'; there was a long pause before he added, '*vraiment.*' Truly.

Later, Gunter was speaking to the French cultural minister, André Malraux, about art, and in particular the work of a French still-life painter they both admired, Jean Fautrier. Malraux mentioned he had one in his office. Because Fautrier laid paint so thickly onto his canvasses — the pictures themselves are therefore very delicate — Malraux said he often went to work on a Monday morning and found little specks of paint on his desk.

Brigitte, who doesn't care much for modern art, turned to Malraux. 'That's very interesting. And if you put the little specks in a little box you can have a whole little box filled with culture.'

Chapter Nine

CALLING IT A DAY

Whether she was willing to admit it or not, her career was starting to wind down.

The reviews for *A Coeur Joie* were abysmal.

Her next film was with Louis Malle and Alain Delon, a short story as part of a trilogy of Edgar Allen Poe short stories, under the title *Histoires Extraordinaire* ('Tales of Mystery'). The other two were directed by Roger Vadim and Federico Fellini.

It didn't work.

Then came *Shalako* which put Brigitte Bardot on the same screen as Sean Connery. Years before, she'd been offered a role in a James Bond movie. She turned it down. When this project came along, she and Gunter went to meet Connery in Deauville. They got along and everyone hoped for the best.

It turned out to be a major mistake. 'If I had been offered better scripts throughout my career,' she explained, in an interview 10 years after the fact, 'maybe I would have made fewer mistakes in my career. But that's boring for me to talk about because everybody knows about them. For *Shalako*, I wanted to try my luck speaking English. So I tried. I tried. If nothing else, I learned English. It always comes in handy.

The great French actor Jean Gabin used to say that there are three elements that make up a great film: a great story, a great story and a great story.

Shalako more than proved his point.

The publicity ads read 'BB + 007 = TNT'. But the critics were merciless. One simply wrote, 'BB + 007 = 0'.

'I think I've been lucky,' she used to say, 'incredibly lucky. I turned down some fantastic projects and accepted others that were completely idiotic. I've often made mistakes, simply because I liked the person who brought me the project or I liked a certain subject. Happily, even after making some turkeys, I've always had the opportunity to catch up.'

Now her luck was running out.

In England, several critics had given her such a rough time for *A Coeur Joie* that, when they said she was even worse in *Shalako,* the French newspaper *L'Aurore* summarized, 'The British assassinated her.'

Brigitte, who never bothered with reviews in the early days and certainly cared even less about them now, responded, 'For a dead woman, I'm in not too bad a shape.'

In the summer of 1968 she made a film called *Les Femmes* ('The Women'). It was directed by Jean Aurel, the same man whom she'd had fired eight years before from *La Bride sur le Cou.* Also on that film was a young actor named Patrick Gilles. Before long, she'd move him into La Madrague.

It signalled the end of her days with Gunter Sachs. Although she says today she was devastated by her third failure at marriage, some people feel it was predictable. Among them, Roger Vadim. He recalls visiting her in Rome the year before, when she and Gunter had rented Gina Lollobrigida's house. He found her sitting in the living room, all by herself, crying.

He says she told him, 'I have a butler, three maids, four gardeners, a chauffeur, two duchesses, the ex-King of Greece or Spain, I don't re-member any more, the second-in-command of the Mafia in Nevada, friends like Serge Marquand, the Prince of Savoie, Paul Newman, Vis-conti, Ava Gardner and a husband who spoils me. And I'm bored. I'm bored like I've never been bored.'

Complaining to him that she couldn't stand being constantly

on the move, she told her Vava that with Gunter they were always travelling, and always going out at night. Worse still, she couldn't stand the fact that they were always surrounded by people. 'We are never alone.'

Later, she would complain about their honeymoon, 'I thought there would be just the two of us. Instead he took ten of his friends.'

Looking back, Gunter thinks it's fair to say that he showed her a different side of life. 'I'd like to think it was a life of class. That I took her away from her usual entourage.'

For a time, Brigitte did indeed adore Gunter's 'flying carpet ride'.

When he was dropping roses on La Madrague out of helicopters and serenading her the way he did, she kept saying, 'He loves me, he loves me.' But after two years she was telling people that Gunter was simply much too worried about the impression he makes. 'All Gunter ever wanted was to show me off to the Shah of Iran or important Swiss bankers.'

Today, he laughs when he hears that remark. 'Especially because I only met the Shah a couple of times and I think the second time was with her in St Moritz. When she was angry she could say anything and when she was happy she'd say the opposite. And as for Swiss bankers, you may not believe me, but I tell you, there are few things I like less than bankers and I've purposely never met a Swiss banker in my life.'

He confesses that Vadim had warned him that living with Brigitte was not easy. And he is quite frank in saying that his marriage to her was the most tempestuous three years of his life.

'It wasn't a simple matter being married to her. I couldn't tell ten minutes ahead what she was going to be like. Neither could she. Her moods change too quickly. She'd go from being wonderfully happy to being extremely annoyed in seconds. I began to feel she could have a nervous breakdown at any minute. By the end, I felt that the possibility of a nervous breakdown or even suicide was always hanging in the air. It's as if, from one minute to the next, her system collapses.'

He reiterates that he was very much in love with her and that life with her was very romantic at the beginning. 'The shadow hanging over our marriage, no matter what she may say or think, was her nervous system. Someone would invite us for dinner and she'd think it's great and then half an hour before she'd get afraid and wouldn't go. She'd want to go then she couldn't bring herself to go. She wasn't acting like a star. It was her nervous system getting the best of her. I never knew in which mood she would wake up. And that's very difficult to live with. When you go to sleep and both of you are happy and when you wake up and she's angry at you, it's very tough.'

In the end, the two of them simply decided enough is enough.

'As far as I'm concerned,' Brigitte moralized, 'to make marriage work, that is, to avoid the almost inevitable routine of marriage, two people must give themselves entirely to each other. But the way Gunter and I live does not correspond with this ideal. He lives on compromises and is incapable of giving up his past. He tries to take me into a social life that I detest and have always done my best to avoid. Our tastes are so different. He loves everything luxurious and loud and he loves photographers and publicity. When he gives me a present, it has to be a grandiose one, whereas I would prefer a key ring chosen with love.'

On 11 December 1968, just before leaving Paris for London to attend the opening of *Shalako*, Bardot announced, 'My marriage is over. I want a separate life and so does my husband. It's up to him to seek a divorce.'

He did. Their marriage was terminated on 7 October 1969 at the Albula District Court in Filisur, Grisons, Switzerland.

But it was not the last she would see of Gunter Sachs.

* * *

184

'There's no doubt that Gunter Sachs was attached to her and cared for her,' says Bob Zagury, the man who lost her to him. 'Even when the marriage proved much less successful than either of them thought it would, he still stuck around for several years.'

In a way, so did Zagury.

The television show he created with her put Brigitte on the small screen, singing and dancing her way into millions of French homes, with big screen charm. She was funny, she was happy, she was having fun.

One of the best musicians in Europe – Claude Bolling – was brought in to be her musical director.

She'd been singing all her life, Bolling says, but what she'd been doing was personality singing, not musical singing. And while that might have been fine for a bunch of friends sitting around a piano, he told her it wasn't fine for anyone standing in front of a big orchestra on a national television show. He convinced her she couldn't stand there and sing like a movie star. He forced her to sing like a singer.

'Claude pushed her,' explains Bolling's wife, Irène – the same woman who'd helped introduce Brigitte to Sacha Distel. 'It wasn't necessarily easy because Brigitte's hangers-on were too complimentary. They always told her everything was wonderful. She has a very strong tendency to beware of people who say they don't want anything from her, and she was never suspicious enough of her hangers-on. Claude told her if she wanted to be a singer, then she would have to work at singing.'

She worked at it, because she enjoyed it.

'As long as she was having fun', Irène Bolling continues, 'everything was fine. But that's always been the way with her. We used to play charades and cards with her. She liked to play cards and was fairly good at poker. Before she'd bet, she'd get up from the table and walk around looking at all the other players. She'd try to psych out everyone else. It's odd, because she can be so wonderful for a few days. In small doses. She can be great company. Then she goes off. She gets it into her head

185

that people are taking advantage of her or she gets bored, and simply goes away.'

Thanks to Claude Bolling, she worked with the best musicians, had the best arrangements and got help from the best song writers. Her New Year's Eve TV specials in the late 1960s were among the years' most watched programmes.

And for a time, Brigitte was a legitimate French pop-star.

'When I first met her,' reminisces French record magnate Eddie Barclay, 'it must have been at the end of the 1950s. She could play a bit of guitar because it's easy, although she didn't read music. There's no doubt that she never wanted to be a movie star. But she had fun singing and she had a unique voice, half little girl, half siren. She didn't sing a song as much as she talked a song. To be fair, hers isn't a great voice. But she had a terrific talent for putting a song across and she took her recording career seriously.'

She'd already recorded when he signed her for some songs.

'Normally,' he says, 'the technicians working in music studios have seen it all. They've met everybody. Those guys are always so blasé about everything. But the first time I got her into a recording studio, you should have seen how they carried on. I honestly didn't know they could get excited about anything. But when Bardot walked into the studio, they were like little kids. It was incredible, the effect she had on them. But she had that effect on everybody. You couldn't be in a room with her and not be affected by her.'

At one point Barclay suggested to her that the two of them should form a joint venture record label – he wanted to call it Barclay-Bardot, or B–B – and she was happy to discuss it with him. So they started going to lunch together, and then they started having dinner together, and there are some people who claim they also started having breakfast together. Barclay hints that they were lovers, but it wasn't so. They were certainly good friends and Barclay doesn't deny that he became so crazy about her he desperately wanted to marry her. However, Brigitte had no interest whatsoever in becoming one of the many Madame Barclays.

He's currently up to number eight.

The idea of the B-B record label did, however, amuse her. But it never went much beyond the amusement stage. He'd hoped she'd find recording artists she liked and could convince them to work for B-B, at which time he would arrange the sessions and distribution. But they never managed to get their act together and the label went largely unexploited. She was often travelling and didn't appear willing to do the work that maintaining a business like that required.

He describes her as 'instinctively intelligent. A superb animal who has managed to live instinctively. Her relationships were very well defined. Some people were only there for the night. Others were supposed to stay around forever.'

Like so many of her old pals, he hasn't seen her in years.

'That's the way she is these days. You phone and you're told Madame isn't in. So you call back and you're told Madame isn't in. And after 15 or 20 times of hearing Madame isn't in, you just stop calling. She's cut off all her old friends in a most brutal way. Slammed the door in their face. In the old days she loved to party. Today she doesn't know the word conviviality. She was always afraid that people would take advantage of her. That's a very real fear she's lived with. And she has been naive about a lot of things. But now she's on some sort of weird trip, retiring from everything. To protect herself, she's turned herself into a fortress. It terrifies her friends.'

On the Barclay label she had a huge hit with the song, '*Tu Veux? Ou Tu Veux Pas?*' ('Do You Want to or Not?') And these days, in record shops all over France, you can still buy CDs and videos of her musical specials and watch her vamp through all her hits, including 'Harley Davidson', 'Everybody Loves My Baby,' '*L'Appareil à Sous*', 'Comic Strip', the French version of 'You Are the Sunshine of My Life', accompanied by Sacha Distel, and the song she was supposed to have made famous, *'Je t'Aime, Moi Non Plus'*.

Perhaps the biggest disco hit of the late 1960s – in France it was 'the slow', and you didn't dance with just anyone when they put that song on – it was written for her by the peerless Serge Gainsbourg.

Of Russian extraction, born in 1928, his real name was Lucien Ginzburg and there's a fleeting glimpse of him in Brigitte's 1959 film *Voulez Vous Danser Avec Moi?* But his contribution to French society in the latter half of the 20th century far surpassed his meagre acting talents. Gainsbourg was one of France's greatest poet-songwriters.

Not terribly well known outside the French speaking world, he was a chain-smoking, unshaven, nervous drunk – a funny, almost pathetic-looking man, who took enormous pleasure in shocking people.

He owned a Rolls-Royce, but didn't have a driving licence and never took it out of his garage. Occasionally he'd remember it was there, sit in the front seat and smoke a cigarette, thinking how hilarious it was to use the car as an ashtray.

In public, no one ever knew what he was going to do or, even worse, what he was going to say. On a television programme one night, he unexpectedly took a 500 franc note out of his pocket and, to show his contempt for money, burned it. Another night, when asked to sing the Marseillaise, he did it in reggae. But none of that compares to the night he met Whitney Houston. After being introduced to her on a live television show, he turned to the host and told him how extremely beautiful she was, then turned to her and – in perfect English – announced, 'I want to fuck you.'

That was Gainsbourg.

His absolute genius shows in the beauty of his music, combined with his superb use of the French language – simple declarations of love and passion wrapped around intricate puns and double entendres – which earned him such a solid place in contemporary

French culture that, while he was still alive, his poetry was already being studied in schools alongside Baudelaire.

Brigitte recorded his song 'Bubble Gum' in 1960 and had a hit with his 'Bonnie and Clyde' in 1967. When she then asked him to write a love song for her – 'The most beautiful love song you can think of' – his answer was *'Je t'Aime, Moi Non Plus'*.

Loosely translated to mean, 'I love you, me neither', it was four minutes and 20 seconds of very slow, very grinding music with non-stop, very heavy groaning. They recorded it one midnight, in January 1968, with only a small crew in the studio.

Word leaked to the press that Bardot and Gainsbourg might have recorded their own love-making, which pleased neither Brigitte nor Serge. They hadn't. Yet she sounded so wanton in an overtly sexual way that some people at the record company –which had been planning to bring it out later that sum-mer – felt they should put a warning on the sleeve, 'Not to be sold to minors'.

When Gunter Sachs heard the song, he couldn't believe she would ever allow such a thing to be released. It was so explicit, Gunter recalls today, 'Serge Marquand *and* I were shocked, which means something!'

Brigitte told Gainsbourg about Gunter's reaction, and Gainsbourg locked the master tape in a safe, announcing that the song would stay there forever.

Not long afterwards, when Gainsbourg and the British actress Jane Birkin became one of France's great modern love stories, he re-recorded the song with her. That was the version that raised the temperature in discos around the world.

Still, he had second thoughts about it, believing that he had perhaps hurt Brigitte by doing that. But then, when he told Jane for whom he'd written it, he hurt her too.

Gainsbourg once said to Birkin, 'With the muzzle I've got, imagine it, I've jumped all the most beautiful girls in France.'

Among his conquests, she reveals, was Brigitte.

'They had a little fling in the '60s. It was nothing that lasted very long, but when it was over Serge was hurt. He liked her. He told me that Brigitte was always so easily shocked and that amused him. He also used to say, she is very straight. Contrary to what many people think, he used to tell me, there's nothing perverted about her.'

They shared, she says, a great affection.

'Years later, when Serge was dying, Brigitte rang him one day, out of the blue. They talked on the phone. And for the last few months of his life they called each other and just talked. They didn't see each other, even though, at times, they were only a few blocks away in Paris. But they talked and that meant a lot to Serge. He was alone and very lonely and just by talking to him on the phone, I think he rediscovered a genuine friendship.'

*   *   *

It took three years to make her last six films.

'The day I can no longer be Bardot on screen,' she had been telling people for several years, 'I'll pack my bags and go away and be forgotten.'

Her interest in the movie business had long since ebbed. She was weary of constantly having to defend herself – from the press, from her fans, from people she'd never met.

As she once divulged, 'People often see in me something I'm not. For example, they see things in my films that never happened. I'm criticized for having a bad influence on youth. "Bardot is amoral." And, "Bardot is immoral. She has no principles." But people say that not only about my films, but also about the way I choose to live. Yet I believe I have certainly been more honest and frank than most people. I could have lived my life the way other people wanted me to. But I think we should live the way we want to and not worry about living the way we're told to. I'm living my life. That's all.'

That's all she ever wanted to do, she maintained. But the movie business kept getting in the way.

190

'The cinema is an absurd world. I decided to live my life as I am, not as anyone else wanted me to be. When I'm working, that's fine. But when I stop and think about all of that, I am horrified by the extraordinary image that has been created around me. I am neither superficial, nor an ingrate. I know very well what's going on. I want to keep my balance and not let my life become twisted. It's not easy. Because the life of Brigitte Bardot, movie star, and the life of Brigitte Bardot, a Parisian like millions of others, is incompatible.'

In *L'Ours et la Poupée* ('The Bear and the Doll') she worked with her young lover Patrick Gilles, and a chap named Xavier Gelin – the same Xavier Gelin, now all grown up, Vadim had been babysitting for the day he found her photo on the cover of *Elle* magazine.

Next came *Les Novices* ('The Novices'), which decidedly stretched the imagination, as nuns in bikinis require a hefty suspension of belief.

Then, in *Boulevard du Rhum*, ('Rum Boulevard') she worked with the man who replaced Jean Gabin as France's leading male star, Lino Ventura.

Lino didn't know her when they both signed for the picture, but he thought he knew about her reputation for involving her co-stars in press speculation and he wasn't having any of that.

The absolute antithesis of the movie star, Ventura was proud of the fact that, when he left the studio, the star on his dressingroom door stayed there. He never brought it home with him. His friends were not show business people, they were the same friends he'd had 20 and 30 years before, at the time when Gabin discovered him.

Boulevard du Rhum was his film – Brigitte's character was not the lead – and he set down a rule. There would be no photographers hanging around to take pictures on or off the set. And, except for stills from the film, there would be no photographs of him with Bardot.

He would come onto the set each day, do his bit and then leave. He never socialized with anybody and kept a very cool, and very noticeable, distance from her. At least, that's the impression he wanted to give. It turns out that, in the evening, he'd go to where she was staying with Olga Horstig-Primuz, and the three of them, away from the glare of the press, would sit around playing cards.

Lino was an actor with the tough exterior of a Bogart and a marshmallow centre – a kind, loving, warm and deeply caring man. It was, then, typical of him that he would, in small ways, become a bit protective of her. At a press conference, when reporters started asking Brigitte about her private life, Lino put on his tough guy expression and told them, 'Messieurs, I am not here to discuss the private life of Madame Bardot.' He stood up, glanced at her – a signal that all she had to do now was follow him – and walked out.

Unfortunately for her, she hadn't picked up on the signal. The result was that she wound up sitting right where she was, alone, facing more questions about her private life.

Her next film was *Les Petroleuses* ('The Legend of Frenchy King'), co-starring Claudia Cardinale, a picture that was actually worse than *Les Novices*.

And Brigitte knew it too.

There was no escaping that fact. It was reflected in her paycheques. From the big money she'd earned in the mid-1960s, her fees had dropped to around 800,000 francs ($145,800) per film.

In the days when her salary was the highest of any movie star in France, she was honest enough to tell interviewers, 'First, I am a woman, and only second an actress. I am not like some actresses who only come alive when they are in front of the movie camera. I live when I am not filming. I am a better actress if the director takes hold of me and is masterful. I like that. Some people think you have to be old and ugly before they will say you are good. I prefer to be beautiful and not so good.'

Now, faced with a string of failures, she was equally frank. 'I never had acting in my blood. I'd say to myself, "In two months, we start. In one month. In one week." Then, I'd get spots. So we'd have to wait a while and I'd say to myself, "I've gained that much time!" During each film I was frantic. And yet I have done more than 40. One would have thought I was a beginner who had never set foot on a set. I think it's shyness that makes me like that. I don't know how to apply myself, to prepare my parts. It comes by itself or it doesn't come at all. I'm not a real actress, I think, or a good audience either. Not at least for the movies.'

It was clearly time to go.

She looked to the one man who might help her make her exit a memorable one. For the last time in her film career, she turned to Roger Vadim.

His idea in *Don Juan* was to get her out of the BB character and into a fairly difficult theme. Unlike *And God Created Woman*, where she was the woman-child, he wanted her to play a woman who was really man, to go to the outer limit of women in society. When he conceived the project, he saw it as a serious film with a serious point to make. When he first explained it to her, he stressed how serious it was, even if there were tender and funny parts. He then asked her if she wanted to play the part and she said she did. But when she saw the script she told Vadim she was afraid of certain scenes and asked him to rewrite them. Playing a woman who was really a man was a far cry from playing Brigitte Bardot.

He agreed to change a few things for her. 'But when it came to her character, she went right back to making herself up like Brigitte Bardot. The result was a baroque film with a few interesting moments. But it wasn't the film I wanted to do. Brigitte wasn't able or wasn't willing to cross over from being Brigitte Bardot on screen to being an actress on screen. She couldn't get away from being herself. It was probably her last chance to keep making movies because she'd grown too old to continue playing Brigitte Bardot. But she understood that, too. That's why she stopped making movies.'

One of her co-stars was Jane Birkin.

'Brigitte is an innocent who plays the little girl. "Bri Bri is thirsty." "Bri Bri is hungry." "Bri Bri needs love." There were times

193

when she'd come onto the set with puffy eyes and I could tell she'd been up all night crying. She was so vulnerable. So distressed. And yet at the same time she has always been dangerously beautiful.'

The script called for the two women to do a nude scene. And the first thing Birkin did when they got into bed together was cover her own feet. Brigitte wanted to know why.

Jane told her, 'Because my feet are so ugly.'

Brigitte said, 'Not to worry,' and placed her own feet in such a way that they looked like they belonged to Jane.

'I lay there next to her and looked at every inch of her and couldn't find a single fault. Then, to make me feel good, she told me, "Your nose is prettier than mine." It isn't. But it was sweet of her to say so.'

While technicians moved around them, setting up the scene, Brigitte asked Jane, 'What shall we do now?'

Birkin looked at her. 'What do you mean?'

Brigitte decided, 'Let's sing.'

'Good idea,' Birkin said.

Bardot suggested, 'How about, "My Bonnie Lies Over the Ocean"?'

Jane said, 'Great,' and they started singing that.

They hadn't got far before they realized they'd forgotten the words, so now Brigitte proposed, 'How about that song we both know.' And together they went into *'Je t'Aime, Moi Non Plus'*.

＊　　＊　　＊

By early 1973, Bardot retirement rumours were again circulating through the French press, and were now accorded the same space that might be given a government about to fall. They promised that, this time, Brigitte's decision was final.

In an interview with *L'Express* on 19 February, she let fly with both barrels. 'I detest humanity. I'm allergic to it. I see no one. I don't go out. I have created my own universe that is as I want it

194

to be, which is that of my childhood. I find my balance in nature, in company with animals.'

Even the normally staid *Le Monde* agreed that the time had come. Reviewing *Don Juan*, they wrote, 'What Vadim doesn't see is what Vadim refuses to see. Myths don't have the right to get old.'

She'd long since realized herself that the cinema couldn't bring her anything else, nor could she bring anything else to the cinema. Like a couple who've separated, she and the movie business had nothing left to say to each other. It was time to go their separate ways.

She'd convinced herself, 'It's not because we've had a few glorious moments that we have to hang on to that for the rest of our lives.'

Originally, she'd planned to retire to a farm at the age of 40. She'd intended to live there as a total recluse. In her mind, she was willing to accept that, in the beginning, people would say, there's BB the actress. Her hope was that, after a while, they would simply change that to, there's Brigitte the lady from the farm.

By spring, the papers were guaranteeing, 'She will step down from her pedestal as the world's leading film sex symbol.' Others quoted her as saying, 'Those wrinkles scare me. I'll quit soon.'

The fires were fanned during a TV interview in which she admitted, 'I've noticed signs of ageing in the last two years and even feel a little frightened when a new wrinkle appears.'

However, she assured her audience, 'There is no need to panic. What's more beautiful than an old lady with white hair, grown wise with age and able to tell lovely stories about her past?' She claimed she would rather see a woman accept advancing age gracefully, than turn into one of those 'grannies dressed up to look young'.

This from a woman who was just 39 and whose figure was the same as it had been since she was 16.

Promising she would not resort to face-lifting – 'It's against nature' – she confessed it was becoming a chore to look beautiful from early morning to late at night. 'It's terrifying.'

And anyway, she felt, 20 years of movie-making were enough. 'After 40 comes 50 and then 60. I don't want to be haunted and made unhappy at 50 by the thought that less work is coming my way. I shall retire because, if I do not abandon films, they may abandon me.'

Screenwriter and director Nina Companeez had approached Brigitte to take a role in the awkwardly named, *L'Histoire Très Bonne et Très Joyeuse de Colinot Trousse-Chemise* ('The Edifying and Joyous Story of Colinot, the Skirt Puller'). Companeez had already worked with Brigitte, having scripted *L'Ours et la Poupée*. Sensitive to the fact that this was a woman director – which was still a novel idea in France – Brigitte agreed, but only on condition that she would not have to be on the set for more than ten days. So Bardot's final appearance on film turned out to be in a supporting role.

'In those days', Companeez observes, 'she surrounded herself with some pretty awful people. They were always hanging on. Especially boyfriends. She always needed a guy. She always needed to be in love. I guess she needed them to be there because she hated acting. It was painful for her. It wasn't something she enjoyed. She did it seriously, she took her work seriously, but she didn't like it and didn't enjoy it. She never much liked rehearsing. But she has a good memory, so she always knew her lines. The trick with her was to get it on the first few takes because that's when she was at her most spontaneous. After that, she started to get bored.'

Companeez notes that, unlike so many other actresses, Brigitte never played the star, that she wasn't in the least capricious.

'She never needed to mark her territory. She was never out to impress anyone with who she was. She took directions very easily. The only time she was at all demanding on the set was when she got depressed, usually because some man had left her or was about to leave her, and then she'd start to cry, so we'd have to re-do her make-up. Any problems on the set could always be traced back to some man.'

Much like Marilyn Monroe, she goes on, Brigitte was also

criticized for bad acting. 'I don't think she was a bad actress. I think she was just too irresistible and too dangerous. So people had to find something bad to say about her. It was a natural reaction because they were afraid of her. Actually, she was one of those rare actresses who liked other actresses. She never felt threatened by them and oddly, found everyone else more beautiful than her.'

However, she wasn't quite as relaxed with everyone.

'Film-making was not only painful for Brigitte, some things about it frightened her. Some directors scared her. For instance, I know that she was afraid of Truffaut. She was also afraid of the unknown. Spending two or three months making a film somewhere with people she didn't know scared her. I can tell you that she also happens to be very prudish. She was shocked by the sexual revolution on film. She is also extremely sentimental. Her attitude towards nudity and men was seen by the world, at the time, as very sensational. But when she was nude, it was completely natural. She was never provocative. She was like an animal. She wasn't being an exhibitionist. It just seemed right for her to be like that.'

One of the assistants on the film had invited his ageing mother onto the set. She was a little old lady and, Companeez says, no one knew what to do with her because everybody was so busy. Immediately, Bardot took charge. She'd never met the old lady before, but never left her side. Whenever she wasn't working, she was with this old lady.

'That is very typical of Brigitte,' Companeez notes. 'She has an enormous heart. I don't think there's any doubt that she's had a difficult life and people who live difficult lives often come out of it badly. She didn't raise her child because she didn't feel capable of raising a child at that point. She was unbalanced and living in a unreal world. Her life has always been a very complicated trip. But she hasn't completely burned out and been ravaged by it. She's come out of it slightly better than most. She quit because she'd reached a point where she was miserable. She wanted to be left alone but no one would leave her alone. That may be why, today, she wants nothing to do with her past. She hated all of that. I don't think she has many good memories. I wouldn't say that her life was *Sunset Boulevard*. Not as much as it was *The Misanthrope*.'

During her last ten days of filming, Brigitte told Gilbert Picard, a reporter from the Yves Mourousi radio show on France Inter, 'Finishing this film is a way to leave gracefully.'

Companeez also knew this would be her last film. 'There was no doubt about it. She came onto the set one morning in her costume and said to me in an exasperated way, "I just can't do this any more."'

Still, a few French papers were dubious. They reprinted her previous promises to quit. At the same time, some foreign papers took the position that it was just as well she was retiring because she was getting too old to play sexy roles. In Britain, for example, the *Daily Mirror* published a fairly unflattering photo of her – 'The New Look Bardot' – with the headline, 'The Sex Kitten Retired – Defiantly, BB Shows Us Her Wrinkles'.

When her announcement was formally made, on 7 June 1973, it was reported as if the inevitable had finally come to pass.

'Oh yes, I'm going to quit,' Brigitte confirmed. 'There's no reason to make such a thing about it. The world isn't going to stop turning.' She said that, after appearing in something like 48 films in 21 years, that was enough. 'I can't keep working at a profession that doesn't do anything for me.'

Getting off a merry-go-round, she said, was never easy. 'But I've had enough. I've never cared about the success or failure of my films. I've always been more concerned with happiness. That's what I've always run after.'

Money would not be a problem, she explained. She'd earned plenty, and put some aside. She hinted that if one day she had serious financial difficulties, well, then, she might be back. 'But right now, you know what I want to do? Nothing!'

Having left the door slightly ajar, some people were entirely convinced that, within a year or two, she'd return, looking for the right project.

But two people who knew her very well were persuaded beyond any doubt that this time she meant it.

The first was Vadim.

The second was Mama Olga.

Vadim says that it was during the filming of *Don Juan* that she ultimately made up her mind. She confided in him that she wanted to stop and that she was going to stop.

'No one believed her,' Vadim adds, 'except me. I knew she'd quit and knew she was right to quit. It would have been a tragedy if she'd kept on going. This way people remember her as Brigitte Bardot, they remember her at her best. And even if she made a lot of films that were absolutely awful, totally stupid – and unfortunately she made most of those really stupid ones towards the end of her career – there still weren't enough to erase the best work she did. So she remains Brigitte Bardot and will always be Brigitte Bardot. I don't think she's ever regretted her decision or missed making movies for even a minute.'

Olga Horstig-Primuz realized it too. 'I knew her well enough to be certain that she was quitting. Her decisions are final. She never changes her mind. Scripts continued to pour in for the next several years. And I dutifully forwarded all of them to her. But she never read another one.'

For BB, the movie actress, it was over.

But Brigitte Bardot, the woman, was determined to have a second chance.

Life Two

BORN AGAIN

———

'You have to understand that I have been born again, that everything before my work with animals has nothing to do with me. The woman who made those movies, that's not me. She's someone else. I have nothing to do with her or with that entire period of her life. My life today is only about animals. Nothing that came before is me.'

Brigitte Bardot, 1994

Chapter Ten

THE MADNESS CONTINUES

It is impossible to say what might have happened had any one of Vadim's pals been home that day in 1949, before he finally got around to ringing Brigitte.

Or what might have happened to their lives if she'd been out when he dialled her number.

Or what might have happened if, when he called, her mother had refused to let him drop by, which she surely would have done had she answered the phone.

In parallel universes, the way they write about such things in science fiction, there is an infinity of probabilities and all of them exist. In this universe, on that particular day, he put his last token in the phone and found her. In another universe, he never met her.

Roger Vadim acknowledges that he has occasionally considered the question, in that other universe, did Brigitte Bardot become Brigitte Bardot?

'My answer is, I don't think so. At least I'm 98 per cent certain that, if Brigitte and I had never met, she would never have become such a phenomenon. She might have had a career as a dancer. She had a real talent for dance and might have been a big name in that world. Perhaps she might have met someone eventually who proposed that she make a film. But the way in which she became a star, that all happened very fast and you have to remember that, when I looked at her, I didn't see an actress, I saw Brigitte Bardot.'

When it comes to movie stars, personality and stardom are often equated. But, he alleges, wrongly so. There are some people who have the most incredible personality and who are also incredibly beautiful and as soon as you put them on the screen, it doesn't work. In fact, with many great stars, when you meet them in person, it's hard to understand what it is that makes them a star.

A case in point, in the very early 1960s, Vadim was staying in one of the bungalows at the Beverly Hills Hotel and had asked for his breakfast. When it didn't arrive after waiting for what seemed to be a very long time, he dialled room service again to ask where it was. They said they'd just sent it, that it was on its way. So he went to the door and spotted a young woman walking across the lawn with a tray. Assuming it was for him, he took it from her and said thank you. But instead of leaving, she stood there staring at him. He said, again, thank you. She said, but this is mine. He didn't understand. She explained, I'm staying at the bungalow next door, I went to get my breakfast and this is mine. He apologized and handed it back to her, stared at her for a moment and only then realized it was Marilyn Monroe.

'Whatever it is that makes someone a movie star,' he speculates, 'it isn't necessarily an explosive, amazing quality that you can see in life. Marilyn, the woman, needed three hours to disguise herself, to become Marilyn, the movie star. Once she was made up and in character, it all seemed perfect. But she was completely fabricated. I'd met her before, in New York. I was coming downstairs in an elevator and found myself next to this creature out of my dreams. But that day she was made up, with her hair done, wearing one of those dresses that showed off her figure. She was disguised as Marilyn Monroe, the movie star. The morning in Beverly Hills, she was just herself.'

With Brigitte, whether she was made up or not, dressed or not, with her hair done or not, at any hour of the day or night, it didn't matter, she was still, always, Brigitte Bardot.

'There is no difference between Brigitte Bardot the person and Brigitte Bardot the movie star, they are immediately one and the same. And that sets her apart. Of course, that alone isn't enough to become a movie star, and certainly not enough to become the kind of international phenomenon that she became. Frankly, I don't know what makes someone a movie star. Except that there are certain people who have something special and are able to transmit that onto a screen. When I first saw her and realized she was so unique, such a remarkable human being, I wasn't thinking of her as a movie star, I was thinking of her as a person. What struck me immediately when I then saw her on the screen was that what she transmitted was 100 per cent of herself.'

And in being herself, he says, she was a paradox.

'She wasn't afraid of anything. At the same time, she was afraid of everything. There was never a fraction of a second when she thought to herself, I must conform to a certain image that society has of beauty or I must conform to a certain standard that society sets for the way a young woman should behave. She had her own ideas and her own view of life and it was all incredibly natural. I don't have any idea where God found the mould to make her or how he got her onto this earth, but after he made her he broke the mould, that's for certain, because there isn't anyone else in the universe like her.'

Some people believe that, by the time she'd retired from the movies, fame had already stolen her life.

'The thing about Brigitte', Vadim underlines, 'is that she never wanted to be a celebrity. She couldn't have cared less. She always found it a pain. All she ever really wanted was to be with her friends, to live her way and to be left alone. So when the moment arrived and she was faced with all the inconveniences of being a star, she didn't enjoy any of the pleasures of being famous. This woman became a movie star without being an actress, without enjoying movie making. She used to say to me, like the time when I wanted a little electronic chess board, if you do the scene in one shot, I'll buy it for you. She didn't find anything in her career that recompensed her for the inconvenience of it.'

She resented having to live under the enormous pressures that came with her enormous fame and one day simply stopped being a movie actress.

But, no matter how much she wanted to, she couldn't simply stop being Brigitte Bardot.

At the very beginning of her career, when she first got involved with the cinema, she said that she wanted to make movies because that was an easy way of earning enough money to buy a farm where she could then live surrounded by animals.

It very quickly became too late.

French fashion designer Louis Feraud first met Brigitte at the Cannes Film Festival in 1953. He had not yet become prominent in *haute couture* but she liked what he did so he began dressing her, both privately and for the screen. Thanks in large part to her, he burst onto the fashion scene with a dress that had little pastel *vichy* checks – *vichy* is French for gingham – with guipure lace.

It wasn't until her marriage with Jacques Charrier that the Bardot-Feraud style really made its mark. For the summer season, 1958, Feraud – with his then partner Jacques Esterel – was showing a line of gingham that Brigitte loved so much she had Feraud make one up for her wedding.

'Immediately,' Feraud says, 'the Bardot effect in particular, and French fashion in general, exploded throughout the entire world. That's thanks to Brigitte Bardot. She was the reigning symbol of womanhood in the 1950s.'

Shops in Paris now reported that they couldn't keep their shelves stocked with gingham. The rage spread from France, through Europe and into North America. From high fashion houses to High Street bargain basements, everything was gingham. First it was pink and white, then blue and white, then yellow and white – gingham was everywhere. There were gingham skirts, dresses, slacks, shorts, bathing suits, waistcoats, underwear.

One store owner on London's Oxford Street reported that 20 young girls a day were walking into his place, looking very English, and all of them were buying gingham dresses so that they could walk out looking like Brigitte Bardot.

Nor was gingham a one-summer fad. It went on for nearly five years, and still keeps coming back. But then, for more than 20 years, it wasn't only Brigitte's fondness for gingham that caught on, it was just about everything she wore.

After putting a steel helmet on her head in *Babette Goes to War*, a Parisian milliner began making helmets out of felt. They sold out immediately. Astoundingly, her 'Babette' phase was still noticeable in 1993, when the parachuting outfit she wore was put in France's new fashion museum. Minister for Culture Jack Lang described it 'as important for our cultural history as a 17th-century French painting'.

Then there was the hippy-chic rage. She picked up some of those clothes from a designer working in St Tropez named Jean Bouquin, who in the mid-1960s was considered pretty far out when he created styles mirroring San Francisco's Haight-Ashbury crowd. Once Brigitte started wearing his clothes, the mode took off.

Unlike other shops that shut down in the heat of the summer between 1 and 5 pm – when everyone is at the beach and St Tropez looks like a ghost town – Bouquin stayed open. That's one of the things she liked about his place. It meant, at least in theory, she could sneak into town, do her shopping and get away before the crowds returned.

Except most of the time it didn't work like that.

Simone Bouquin, who ran the boutique with her husband, recalls one afternoon in the middle of the summer of 1964 – she swears that there wasn't a soul on the streets – when Brigitte drove up in her Citroën 2CV and parked in front of the boutique. She was barefoot, as usual, and had a male friend in tow, as usual. Ten minutes later, there were two dozen people standing outside – as usual – fighting to get a glimpse of her through the front window.

With so many people trying to wear what she wore, it's hardly surprising that, when Bouquin dressed her in shorts for an evening, with a long sleeveless velvet coat, every young girl in France was suddenly going out for the evening in shorts with a long sleeveless velvet coat.

In fact, for some young girls, coming to St Tropez early in the season to check out the boutiques – to see what the Brigitte Bardot look would be for the summer – was like a religious pilgrimage. They wore their hair like her, tried to walk like her and tried to speak like her. They also tried to pout like her – that craze came to be known as *'La moue à la Brigitte'* – holding in their cheeks, pushing out their lips and staying like that for hours so that no one could possibly miss the point.

Gunter Sachs was so amused by the rage that he opened a boutique with a line of clothes called Mic Mac. He sold t-shirts – boldly inscribed Mic Mac St Tropez – for 100 francs ($18) at a time when you could buy the same t-shirt, still boldly inscribed St Tropez but minus the Mic Mac, at every overpriced souvenir stand along the port for 40 francs ($7.20).

Then there was a boutique she liked called 'Vachon'. She dressed 'Vachon' – which was a faded blue cotton look – so everybody dressed 'Vachon'.

She finally got the message and jumped onto her own bandwagon with a collection of clothes, under the label 'La Madrague'.

Aiming essentially at 'women like myself, who feel good about themselves and know their femininity', Bardot simply commercialized the various styles she had always worn for herself.

It was all part of the craze that came to be known as *'Bardolatrie'*.

Supposedly, the word means, 'The love of Bardot'. At least the French used it to mean that and it easily slipped into English. Except it probably ought to be 'Bardotolatrie' – which is, admittedly, pretty clumsy as far as words go – because when you translate the French word directly into English, at least according to the *Oxford English Dictionary*, it means 'a love of the bard' – as in Shakespeare.

Brigitte has always found the whole idea pretty silly. Every time someone mentioned it to her, she would give them her stock response. 'When I was making movies, they never stopped criticizing my style of comedy, my style of hair-do, how I dressed, how I lived. Now that I've stopped for good, they make such a big thing of it. You might say that it's laughable, no?'

But then, in those days, when it came to clothes she could never win. 'If I go out in a simple dress or in jeans, I hear people growl, with all the money she makes you'd think she could dress decently. Then, if I make an effort, if I put on my prettiest dress, my best coat and my diamond ring, the same people say I'm playing the movie star.'

Still, the concept behind *Bardolatrie* was not lost on the masses.

It might have taken a remarkably long time before Brigitte Bardot finally made it into wax at Madame Tussauds, but that's not because they hadn't 'Bardolotried' sooner. Although wax sculptors moulded her face at the end of the 1950s, they had problems getting her body right. In the past, female bodies on display were always suitably well covered, so it never much mattered. The Queen in a bikini would have been unthinkable. So too Bardot in ermine robes. Being a family-minded establishment, they settled on a mini-skirt, which they acquired from a Paris fashion house. But the expanse of thigh and uncovered shoulders worried the Tussaud management. 'We have never been able to make a convincing woman's body before and we felt that we could not show Miss Bardot without getting the body right.' So it wasn't until 1967 that she was elevated to waxdom.

They weren't quite so slow about *Bardolatrie* in the rest of the world. By the late 1950s, even the famous Barbie Doll had long blonde tresses and figure that matched hers and sported gingham clothes.

Some people were shrewd enough to pick up on the craze and business boomed in the States, where there were all sorts of 'BB' products – from leotards, sunglasses and make-up to everything imaginable in gingham. There was also a line of lingerie, featuring 'the Bardot bra' – the mind does boggle – which was made by a company called Lovable Brassieres. Honestly! And just so that none of the department store buyers would miss the point, when the company put on fashion shows they hired blonde Bardot look-alike chorus girls from the Copacabana as models.

Even just being Brigitte's chum was sometimes enough.

Jean Bouquin had flown from Nice to Spain to bring her some clothes while she was filming there. With his long hair, hippy costume and flowing scarf, he attracted quite a bit of attention at Madrid Airport – especially when he stepped up to the immigration desk and couldn't find his passport.

The Spanish authorities insisted that, without a passport, he couldn't get into the country. To avoid being sent back to France, he tried explaining that his visit to Madrid was very important, that he was meeting his friend Brigitte Bardot.

They didn't know what he was talking about.

'Brigitte Bardot,' he kept saying, 'Brigitte Bardot. I'm bringing these clothes to her.'

Still no reaction.

He happened to be carrying a poster with her photo on it, so he unrolled it and held it up for them to see. 'Brigitte Bardot.' He told them, '*Mon amie. Mia amiga.*' My friend.

'Ah,' the Spanish border guards suddenly understood. 'Brigitte Bardot.' They kept saying, '*Si, si, si.*'

With nothing more than her picture, he was allowed into the country.

*　　*　　*

One of France's best television journalists, Christian Brincourt – who has known her for more than 30 years – saw her power defined in several other ways.

A first-class reporter and seasoned war correspondent, he

realised the extent of her fame when during one of his tours in Vietnam, American medics at Da Nang brought in the body of a young soldier who'd just been killed and when they emptied his pockets they found two photos – one of his mother and one of Brigitte Bardot.

'Brinc' and 'Bri' – as they called each other – had never been lovers, which was clearly one of the reasons they maintained such a long friendship. They'd nursed each other through various marriages and had been there for each other through difficult times. And the soft-spoken, bearded Brincourt has seen her in all her moods.

'When she gets angry, she gets furiously angry, crazy angry, and doesn't care who's on the other end. She isn't at all shy. She speaks her mind. She's been taken advantage of so much in her life that she's had to learn how to defend herself. And she isn't afraid of anyone. She'll stand up to anyone who tries to get in her way. Yet she's also a very fragile woman and breaks down in tears like a teenage girl, when love goes sour.'

He also knows, better than most people, just how painful fame has always been for Bardot.

'She hates the myth and hates the legend that surrounds her. She doesn't want to hear about that. She doesn't understand it and never did. She doesn't want to know that she's a legend. She realizes that she influenced a generation of young people. She accepts that. But the rest, the legend thing, she doesn't want to know and definitely doesn't care.'

Although there have been rare exceptions.

In 1965, after three tours reporting from Vietnam, radio station RTL sent Brincourt to the wilds of northwestern Canada to retrace Jack London's footsteps. While there, Brincourt heard about a French monk, Father Robert Lemeur, who'd spent the past 20 years tending to a small community of Eskimos in the extremely remote village of Tuktoyaktuk. Formerly called Fort Braban and now known simply as Tuk, this is Canada's most northern inhabited settlement, sitting on the edge of the Beaufort Sea.

Some 450 people lived in darkness half the year and daylight the other half, permanently surrounded by ice. North of here there is nothing – and no one – but the top of the world.

It was a one-missionary village.

And Brincourt was the first Frenchman Father Lemeur had seen since leaving his native Brittany two decades before.

A quiet, gentle man with heavy eyebrows and opal blue eyes, Lemeur lived a spartan life, even by local standards. Fascinated by his genuine humility, his deep and his special life in one of the world's least habitable outposts, Brincourt decided to forgo, at least for a while, his Jack London story and put together a major piece on this unique man. Returning some weeks later to Paris, over dinner one night with friends – including Brigitte Bardot – he told them the story of Robert Lemeur, and Brigitte was very moved by it. Christmas was just around the corner, so she wrapped a package that she asked Brincourt to send to the priest. Inside were some French delicacies, including three bottles of vintage Bordeaux, plus a photograph of herself – chastely dressed, of course – dedicated to 'my unknown friend'.

A few years later, Brincourt returned to the Arctic. Father Lemeur told him that the name Brigitte Bardot meant something to him and, on thinking about it, he recalled seeing a photo of her cut out of *Life* magazine, nailed to the wall of an old trapper's hut.

Brincourt's next task was to arrange a visit for Lemeur and two Eskimo children to France. On that trip, he took the three to meet Brigitte. Lemeur was struck by her simplicity and gentle kindness. He also recognized how spiritual she really was. Several months after Lemeur returned to the Arctic, she received a message from the missionary in the form of a tape recording where he spoke to her of his own loneliness, and compared it to hers. He explained how they shared this solitude, him in the middle of nowhere, her in the middle of enormous fame. His message, so down to earth and so very perceptive, brought her to tears.

A few years after that, Lemeur conceded to Brincourt that he'd come up with a rather whimsical – and successful – way of bringing more Eskimos to his Sunday mass.

'That photo of Brigitte Bardot,' he said, 'I've hung it on the door of the church.'

*　　*　　*

When she turned 30, she shrugged off advancing age in a birthday interview with radio station Europe 1.

'I wonder why everyone makes such a song and dance about it. Certainly it is a milestone. But I do not feel the change. I would be sad if I remained the way I was ten years ago. But make no mistake, although I have calmed down, it does not mean I have become a stick in the mud. I am now sensitive to a lot of things I've never felt before. My feelings can be touched by injustice, poverty, sickness, treason and suffering.'

On her 35th birthday, she told an interviewer, 'In general, when I leave a man it's because the rules of mutual honesty have not been observed. On top of that, I get jealous. Sick with jealousy. If there was a medicine I could take against being sick with jealousy, I'd swallow a very large dose. I have hurt a lot of people around me with that stupid fault.'

Now, at 40, to much of the public, her life was still a stage on which she played out her non-stop party girl existence. As the Bardot myth fed on itself, they continued to feel perfectly entitled to take their places in the audience.

For many people, she would continue to symbolize all that was right about freedom and liberty. For others, she would forever symbolize all that was wrong with it. She could be seductive, but she could also terrify. She was a forerunner of the Women's Movement without ever knowing it, without ever trying to be, without ever understanding the consequences of vanguarding an attack on the established world order.

Some women hated her because she was an object of scandal and a symbol of sexual liberty. Many men looked at her as an

erotic fixation. Here was a woman who would have affairs with
anyone she wanted. She would leave one man for another. She
had a child, was frank enough to say she wasn't capable of raising
him and allowed the boy's father to do that. These were all things
a man could get away with. But in the 1950s and the 1960s and
now into the 1970s, a woman couldn't.

Yet she did.

She lived her life the way a man does. What's more, she
was arrogant and she mocked opinion. She infuriated people by
flaunting her independence, by not giving a damn about what
anyone thought. She provoked, which excited some people,
drawing them towards her. And she threatened, which had the
same effect.

In several ways, she was what Marilyn Monroe was never
permitted to be. Everything she said was quoted. Everything
she wore became fashion. Every man she went out with became
interesting. Everywhere she went became a media event. No one
seemed to care that she never wanted any of it. That she never
liked being seen the way the world saw her. That she never pursued
it. That she hated the way her life became torturous.

'They tell me that I'm as popular as Rudolph Valentino,'
she once remarked, thoroughly unamused by the thought. 'But
Valentino is dead and I want to live.'

For her 40th birthday, there was a terrific party in her honor
at Club 55, along Pampelonne Beach. All of her friends showed
up, and music was provided by a group then called *Chico et Los
Gitanos* – Chico and the Gypsies – who later became the Gypsy
Kings. Brigitte adored the group and loved to sing and dance with
them. In fact, for a time, she hung out with them as a fully fledged
honorary Gypsy.

She'd been having dinner in a restaurant with friends when
she first heard them. It was her kind of music, so she got up
to dance – she did a flamenco – and she sang with them too.
When the night was over, Chico told her if she ever wanted
to work with the group again, she'd be welcome. Thinking

he was joking, she told him to call anytime they needed a singer-dancer.

And he did.

He rang her one day to say that the group was supposed to play at a wedding. He offered, if you really want to have some fun, come along. So she put on her finest gypsy frock, made herself up to look like a member of the group, and worked the wedding with them.

Not surprisingly, people came up to Chico during the course of the evening and mentioned to him how his singer-dancer looked a little something like Brigitte Bardot. But, as legend now has it, no one actually recognized her.

There was a time when she used to criticize anyone over 40 as being 'ready for chrysanthemums'. Now here she was, bringing in her 40th with great spirit.

It was, in many eyes, a milestone worth noting. *Playboy* ran a special, featuring a nude study by her then 30-year-old live-in lover, photographer Laurent Vergas, which in its own right heralded the beginning of the 'older woman' vogue that swept men's magazines in the mid-1970s. The magazine quoted her as saying, 'No man can have any security in loving me. The problem is to hold onto me and that is difficult.'

One of the wire services heralded the event as Brigitte's arrival into adulthood. 'When I was 20 I liked men who gadded about, who danced, who owned nice cars, who told stupid jokes. Today I demand something deeper from a man. Why, if I had kept the same man for 10 years I would have died of boredom.'

While a French paper came up with a quote that showed even more awareness of a new age. 'I am a woman who has undoubtedly made a success of her career, but not of her private life. The myth of Bardot is finished. But Brigitte is me. Perhaps in five years I'll finally be able to live like everyone else. I'm waiting for that moment. I'll no longer be a beautiful object, but a human being.'

A year later, for her 41st birthday, she reserved the Palmiers

215

restaurant, just down the beach from Club 55, and put together another big party.

'Bardot, at 41,' a newspaper observed, 'still manages to conjure up in the public's mind the image of the liberated, free-loving teenager who pioneered a whole new lifestyle for her generation. No actress has inspired more unmistakable imitation. Not only other actresses, but young girls all over the world copied her blonde, seaweed hairstyle, her minimal make-up, her preference for simple, clinging clothes (gingham dresses, jeans and sweaters that were more like a second skin), her daring – in the 1950s – belief that a woman should be allowed to take her pleasures and her lovers as brazenly as a man.'

But the day before, she cancelled the party.

A few weeks later, there was another incident when she took one too many sleeping pills.

So much had changed between those two birthdays.

She'd quit being BB the movie star. Yet the madness continued. It was like trying to break a habit, only to discover the monkey was still clinging to her back.

There were still people banging on her front gates, writing her hate mail and following her through the streets. There were still people sneaking onto her property, installing themselves on her beach and sitting in boats off-shore taking long-lensed photos.

The popular press was relentless, with a mountain of fodder – although none of it was supplied by her on purpose – as she waltzed her way through a string of younger men, almost as if recapturing her own youth was the reason for the binge.

'When a man attracts her, Bardot goes straight to him.' French author Marguerite Duras wrote, 'Nothing stops her. It does not matter if he is in a café, at home or staying with friends. She goes off with him, on the spot, without a glance at the man she is leaving.'

Interestingly enough, Jacques Charrier claims she was never one to play the *femme fatale*. 'When she was with a man, he was the only person that mattered. But when it was over, she could turn it off completely. When it was over, everything ended and she'd move on to the next one without ever looking back or giving the last one a second thought.'

Vadim wholeheartedly agrees. 'When she left one lover for another, nothing remotely hypocritical stopped her. She had a gift for infidelity, that's true. And she always suffered if she had an affair with more than one man at a time. Passion was a drug to her. And, as with any drug, she would be enslaved by it all her life. Yet, when she told a boy she loved him, she was entirely sincere. Except of course, she was equally capable of forgetting him the next day.'

In the old days, the press measured out her life by her films. Now they were measuring out her life by the men she was with.

Christopher Wedow was a handsome, 6 foot 2 inch guy from London who'd met Mijanou and her husband Patrick in Paris in 1968 and through them had been introduced to Brigitte. But it wasn't until he bumped into her again, this time at a dinner party in St Tropez late that summer that sparks flew. He was her type of guy. She was 34. He was 22.

Without any hesitation, she brought him home and he stayed with her for three weeks – he recalls, 'It was like being in a dream' – and when the summer was over, he left.

When the papers got word of it, they turned it into something much more than a summer romance. Describing him as a timid boy from Wandsworth who didn't chase girls, they interviewed his mother, extracting from her the quote, 'I think at the moment they are friends.' Then they decided they could do better and the story got out that Mrs Wedow had been so worried about her little boy in the clutches of Brigitte Bardot that she phoned La Madrague and told Brigitte, 'Send my little boy home.'

It didn't happen. But that's a perfect example of the sort of thing that did get printed, then reprinted and reprinted yet again, a good example of how, the more you keep repeating fiction, the more it becomes believable.

Then there was Patrick Gilles, a 21-year-old political science

217

student who showed up in a couple of her films. And then there was Christian Kalt, a 30-year-old bartender and former ski instructor whom Brigitte spotted one night in 1972.

She was in Meribel with Philippe Letellier and his wife, and Jicky and Anne Dussart, and the whole group of them went over to Jacqueline Veyssiere's restaurant in Courchevel, which is where Kalt was working. She noticed him behind the bar, found him cute, asked Jacqueline who he was and said she wanted to meet him. Jacqueline agreed that he was cute but reminded Brigitte that he was working. So Brigitte said, figure something out and I'll come back tomorrow night. Jacqueline again protested, but he's working. It was down to Philippe and Jicky to come up with a solution. The next night, Philippe and Jicky ran the bar while Christian Kalt dined with Brigitte. That relationship lasted several years.

Of course, every new love affair hit the headlines. Colour photos on a cover guaranteed increased sales for the weekly magazines. And every new man in her life – especially this string of younger guys – was rumoured 'by inside sources' to be the next Monsieur Bardot.

There was so much publicity surrounding her younger lovers that Olga Horstig-Primuz once asked her about them, hinting that some of them were, at best, rather dubious. Brigitte told her candidly, 'I have always adored beautiful young men. Just because I grow older, my taste doesn't change. So if I can still have them, why not?'

Talking one afternoon on the beach with André Pousse, Brigitte told him about a married woman she knew who was having an affair, and how the woman's husband not only accepted it but used to invite his wife's lover to come along on holiday with them.

'It's beyond me,' she said. 'I just can't understand how some women can manage to have two men in their life at the same time when I can't seem to deal with even one at a time.'

'It's no wonder,' Pousse replied. 'How can you expect to keep a man when every time you take him to bed there are 14 dogs in bed with you.'

Pousse, who saw her often during those years, believes that she was routinely deceived in love. 'Not with one man, but with the whole group of them. Part of the problem has to be, when you're a star the magnitude of Bardot, you have to keep asking yourself, are the men here with me for me or are they here because I am who I am?'

In many cases, the answer was obvious.

Ten years later she would ask herself whether men ever truly held an important place in her life. By that time, she was finally learning to live on her own. She hadn't yet managed it, but she was certain that leaning on a man was no good. 'A man is not a white stick.'

She was even willing to admit that some of her affairs might well have been mistakes. 'I went to bed with people I shouldn't have. It just happened.'

Those were the days when she was convinced she would never get married again. She used to say she didn't see the point in it, that three was enough and anyway, it was always such a fuss to get divorced. The problem was that she wanted to get married every time she fell in love. 'If I'd followed my own advice, I would have got married ten times.'

Now a lady of leisure, she could take the time to fall in love. But whatever she might have been looking for, she seemingly wasn't able to find it. At least, not with this crowd of younger men.

*   *   *

She is, by nature extremely, *'fleur bleue'*. It means romantic, of the hot blushes, no appetite sort, the way a schoolgirl falls in love for the very first time.

'The thing about her that has always been especially touching', Christine Gouze-Renal points out, 'is how every time she fell in love, she thought it was for life. But you have to understand that

219

she's not a realist. That she's never truly lived in the real world. Maybe now she does. But she didn't in those days. Most of her friends have always felt terribly sorry for her, because they've known how lonely she is. They also know that, in many ways, she's created this loneliness herself. She has never learned how to keep a lover, a friend, a servant or a husband.'

In moments of extreme loneliness, she's cried to Gouze-Renal, 'There is no shoulder for my head, no hand for my hand. I'm all alone.'

Gouze-Renal tried to be there for Brigitte when she needed a friend. But that hasn't always been easy. 'My friendship with her comes from a young friendship. We were young together. And I owe her so much. She was there when I started and when she became a star she stuck with me. But I was always careful never to become part of Brigitte's court, part of her entourage. When she's not in the middle of some dramatic affair of the heart, she's amusing, she's funny, she's great company. However, and I say this affectionately, in a lot of ways, she's a lunatic. She is eternally infantile. Frankly, I don't think she's ever really known love. Vadim will always be special in her life. She can't forget that he was the one who taught her about life. But the others? I wonder.'

She says you have to be a very strong personality to resist Brigitte. To stand up to her. Otherwise she'll hurt you. 'She doesn't realize she's doing it. But that doesn't make it any less painful for the people she hurts. The way to avoid it is not to be at her mercy. The reason she surrounds herself with animals these days is because they are at her mercy. The few friends she has left aren't subject to her extreme mood swings. The only way to stay friends with her is to avoid her when she's in one of those bad moods. Her friends know she'll come out of it and, when she does, she's wonderful and irresistible.'

Mike Sarne saw her up close and, even if it was for only a few days, there was no mistaking what he saw.

'Her femininity is so powerful that when she walks into a room, suddenly, every colour in the room is different. Her presence is remarkable, absolutely extraordinary. There's more of her face than you expect, more hair, more body, and everything about it is perfect. There's nothing minor about her.'

Her thing, he says, was falling in love, and doing that in a very straight way. 'She didn't have that democratic, orgiastic California lifestyle. She didn't easily separate sex from love. Many people, Vadim for instance, can use sex like a disposable commodity. That's not what Brigitte was all about. She lived for love, and in many cases that's meant hopeless love. It's that weakness in this strong, male character of hers that makes her such a terrifying woman. Terrifyingly argumentative. Terrifyingly beautiful. Terrifyingly sexy. Terrifyingly famous.'

Oddly, he thinks, women have always understood Bardot better than men ever could. 'They never felt threatened by her. She was so far out in space compared with the rest of the human race. They couldn't compete on any plane, so they didn't even try. Instead they dressed like her and wore their hair like her and tried to walk like her and tried to pout like her and tried to be as free with love as they thought she was.'

Her great dilemma was that she easily upstaged men. He says it was unintentional but it was also unavoidable.

'When she falls in love with someone she takes over that man's life. It's very hard for her to compromise. It's got to be her way. It's also the only way she knows. And no matter how secure she tries to make a man feel, and she does try, there is a male ego somewhere that keeps whispering, I'm not in control.'

Now, in those first couple of years after she retired from films, Brigitte Bardot was discovering that growing up is tough. No one was there to help her get through the stage from girl to woman. One day she was just older. In a way, she'd been tricked into the dream and had made the mistake of buying it herself.

It didn't matter that she was going through a whole string of younger men. Her promiscuity has always been France's honour.

221

The French would want the world to believe that only they truly understand love.

It's rather that she was so badly served by so many men.

They wanted to own a Stradivarius and it never mattered to them that they were incapable of playing any music on it.

Chapter Eleven

SAVING THE SEALS

Gérard Montel, the fellow known around St Tropez as *le perruqier* – the wig maker – rang Brigitte one day to tell her, '*Le Shah est mort.*' The Shah is dead.

But she thought he said, '*Le chat est mort*' – the cat is dead – and was desperate to know, 'Which one?'

Gerard wondered, 'Which one what?'

She repeated, 'The cat is dead. Tell me, quickly, which cat?'

'No,' he explained, '*Le Shah d'Iran est mort.*' The Shah of Iran is dead.

'Oh,' she said, 'What a relief.'

.   .   .

As early as 1962, Bardot had publicly protested against the treat-ment of animals in slaughterhouses, the first celebrity in France to take such a stand. She'd pressured the French government to proscribe the more antiquated killing methods then in use and, after a lengthy campaign, saw an act passed that obliged slaughterhouses to use the faster, less painful electric-shock pistols. That legislation came to be known as 'the BB Law'.

Over the years, she'd also crusaded for more compassionate treatment of animals in zoos. Her efforts resulted in the permanent closure of four French zoos where animals had been held under appalling conditions; the temporary closure of nine more, to allow for badly needed improvements; plus 18 official warnings and fines at zoo parks where conditions had been decidedly less than ideal.

She'd launched a crusade against the fur trade and had made public the plight of animals injured by hunters. On several occasions she'd personally paid for animals to be nursed back to health after hunters had seriously wounded them, then sadistically left them to suffer an agonizing death.

So, by the time she quit making movies, she'd made a lot of serious enemies.

High on the list of people who believed they had a grudge against her were hunters and butchers, especially butchers specializing in horse meat. They've insulted her, threatened her, terrorized her and even killed some of her own animals. They hate her for the troubles she's caused them and, in the case of horse meat butchers, the damage she's personally done to their business with her campaigns. Even in their calmer moments they spit when you mention her name, insisting that she is the original misanthrope – someone who hates mankind.

The venom that spews forth from hunters and butchers – but in particular horse meat butchers – is a sure sign that, even if she hasn't won all of her battles, at least the other side knows they've been in a fight.

In retirement, she now spoke out more often, and even more vehemently, against animal abuse. In return, her critics began referring to her as an ageing actress with nothing else to do. But she was about to prove them wrong. She was on the verge of a truly outstanding success – although it began with a series of frustrating and decidedly embarrassing false starts.

When her two-year affair with Laurent Vergas ended, she took up with a muscular, blond French-born sculptor of Czech parentage, eight years her junior, named Miroslav Brozek. They met while she was skiing at Meribel.

Saving the Seals

She called him Mirko for short, and, after living with him for a few months, she began telling people, 'I'm mad about him. He's a solid man. With him I feel protected. I feel secure. I can count on him.'

Asked about her plans for the future, all she'd say was, 'I'm just an old-fashioned girl. It's better to think things out very carefully before you marry. After three failures, I should know.' Before long, however, the press was predicting that Mirko would become husband number four.

It wasn't to be, but it was during her years with Mirko that she took up the cause of the baby seals.

When she first heard about the culls in eastern Canada and learned how tens of thousands of seals were murdered each spring on the ice flows – the Eskimos traditionally clubbed the seals to death so as not to ruin their fur – she was so utterly disgusted that she told everyone she met about it.

Not surprisingly, that was the main topic of conversation, one night in early March 1976, at a dinner party with a group of friends, including Christian Brincourt and Philippe Letellier.

Brigitte told them about the seal cull, getting more and more agitated, soon growing angry enough to warn her friends that it wasn't going to happen this year because she was personally going to Canada to try to stop it.

Letellier, who was now working as editor-in-chief of *Parents* magazine – a stable-mate of *Paris Match* – said the story interested him, and that he would cover it for the entire *Paris Match* group. 'If you go, I want to come along.'

Brincourt, by now a senior journalist with the television station TF1, immediately said he'd sign on too. 'I'll bring a camera crew and we'll film the whole thing.'

So a hasty plan was put together to get Bardot and her friends from Paris to Newfoundland. Letellier and Brincourt both had to clear it with their offices and Brincourt then had to arrange for a camera man, a sound man and a lighting man. Together with Brigitte and Mirko, they also had to buy special protective clothing. But once that was set, the trip was on.

The best way to get there, they discovered, was to fly from Paris to London and change at Heathrow for an Air Canada flight to Newfoundland. Bardot was, as usual, apprehensive about flying, but the group agreed to meet at ten Sunday morning, 28 March, at Charles de Gaulle Airport for their 11 o'clock flight to London.

By 10.15, Brigitte and Mirko still weren't there.

By 10.30, Letellier and Brincourt were trying to convince Air France to hold the flight.

Just as the ground staff informed Letellier and Brincourt they absolutely couldn't wait any longer and would have to close the gate, Brigitte rushed in, wearing a long cape, with Mirko hurrying after her.

It was obvious that she and Mirko had been fighting.

And the first thing she said was, 'I'm not going.'

It took several minutes before Letellier and Brincourt could calm her down – and all the time the Air France people pressed them, are you going or not and if you are going, would you please board the plane – and then several more minutes of assuring her that everything was going to be all right before she would get on the plane.

Once they took off for London, she seemed to settle down.

Brigitte sat next to Mirko, holding his hand, with Philippe and Christian just behind them. And for the entire 35 minutes it took to get to London, she kept turning around to say, not to worry, we'll get there.

Both of her friends knew that she was afraid of flying and that she was especially apprehensive about the long journey to Canada. They also knew she'd been run-down for several weeks and was not feeling well. But now she seemed all right and Philippe thought to himself, we're on our way.

Her mood quickly changed in London.

They had to switch terminals for Air Canada and were on their way when a photographer working for the *Daily Mail* caught up with her. He'd been tipped off that she was there. He started taking pictures and that sent her into a rage.

She began screaming at him, threw her cape around herself, tried to get away and dived into the nearest ladies' room. When she finally came out she announced that she was too ill to continue and wanted to return to Paris immediately. Letellier and Brincourt got her into Air Canada's private lounge and the airport doctor was summoned.

With Brigitte lying on a couch, the doctor took her pulse and examined her as best he could. After speaking with her for a few minutes, satisfying himself that this was nothing serious, he assured her she could continue her journey. But she kept saying no, she wasn't going and told Philippe and Christian that she wanted a flight back to Paris.

They tried to reason with her but she was resolute.

Outside in the hallways, the *Daily Mail* photographer was soon joined by the small team of photographers and journalists who regularly cover the airport, and they demanded to be told what was wrong. Mirko was dispatched to deal with them, explaining that she was ill, that she had a fever and that she was returning home to see her doctor.

In the meantime, Letellier stayed with Brigitte while Christian went to book some seats to Paris. Unfortunately, everything going that way was full. At least there was nothing until much later Sunday evening. That would mean sitting around Heathrow for the rest of the day. He explained that to Brigitte, hoping she'd change her mind. But now she said, either get me on a plane to Paris, or charter a flight to Paris, or, if need be, take me to the boat train for Paris, because I'm going home now!

It took a lot of doing – and a considerable amount of name dropping – but Letellier and Brincourt eventually managed to secure two seats to Paris on a flight leaving early in the afternoon. That's when Mirko pulled the two men aside. Sensing a chance to make a few headlines for himself, he suggested they send Brigitte home alone, and continue the trip themselves, filming him with the baby seals instead.

As that wasn't quite what *Paris Match* or TF1 had in mind, they said, thanks anyway. And only a few hours after the whole group arrived in London, Brigitte and Mirko were on their way back to France. In the meantime, Letellier, Brincourt and the three man camera crew were stuck in London.

The following day Brigitte issued a statement explaining that the very thought of the seal slaughter had upset her so much she hadn't been able to continue.

Nine days later, on 6 April, she showed up at an organized protest in front of the Norwegian Embassy and found herself in the middle of a crowd of 5,000 people. When reporters finally got close enough to speak to her, she publicly damned the Norwegians for also killing seals, said she fully intended to carry on her fight against culls no matter where they took place and, through the press, asked for a meeting with Canada's prime minister, Pierre Elliot Trudeau.

Even though she'd not got anywhere near Newfoundland, her media prowess had greatly increased the public's awareness of this annual bloodbath.

The public's response – overwhelmingly supporting her efforts – encouraged her.

In an ominous way, it was as if she'd uncorked a bottle and the Genie who'd popped out was not merely ugly, he'd come to haunt her. Her morning mail – which now jumped from the usual 200-400 letters a day to sometimes as many as 1,000 – brought case after case of animal mistreatment to her attention.

Experience told her she'd taken on more than she could handle all by herself. Facing well-organized opposition on almost every front – the world's fur trade, for example, was a powerful political lobby – she realised she needed the weight of an organization behind her. So she decided to form the Brigitte Bardot Foundation.

She used the access her name gave her to petition support

from two internationally known conservationists: marine explorer Jacques Cousteau and Arctic explorer Paul-Emile Victor. Both agreed to lend their name to her effort and to take up positions on her board of directors. Victor also offered the administrative services of Philippe Cottereau, who was then secretary-general of the Paul-Emile Victor Group for the Defence of Man and His Environment.

The mission of her foundation, she announced, was to declare war on the horrors that are daily inflicted on animals throughout the world, to use the full weight of the resources she could muster to defend their rights and interests and to protect endangered species. Each year, she said, there would be one major endeavour. She would do battle against the sea cull, the fur trade, hunters, zoos, the use of animals in medical experiments, the use of animal products in the cosmetics industry, and the cause of abandoned animals.

Asked if she was putting cruelty to animals before cruelty to humans – a facile and therefore frequent criticism – her answer was characteristically to the point. 'It's an easy step from cruelty to animals to cruelty to humans. War is born out of hunting. Blood calls for blood. You've got to seek out the roots of the evil. I have always profoundly respected animals who, for me, have never been objects. What I really want to be is a catalyst who leads a great movement of public opinion, because without public opinion, I can't do anything.'

Within days, letters of support together with small contributions came in from France, Belgium, Switzerland, Canada and the United States.

Working with Cottereau, the Foundation's budget was set at $2.6 million for the first year. Bardot committed herself to giving 30 per cent of her earnings to the cause and was looking for the rest to come from the public. What she hadn't counted on was that the public might be more interested in her than in her work, and that running a foundation meant running a business, not simply a vehicle for her undeniably sincere ambitions.

A champagne reception at the fashionable Pré Catelan restaurant in Paris in June had to be abandoned when huge crowds of fans showed up, reminiscent of the mob scene madness that marked the height of her movie career. Bardot had intended to say that the planet was in a state of war and that, unless there was action by its habitants, irreversible damage to the survival of the species would surely occur. But she never got the chance. Mayhem took over, the police had to be called and, for her own protection, they whisked her out of the restaurant. Philippe Cottereau was left to deal with the remaining crowd. He didn't bother making any sort of statement because, in the end, the reporters and the photographers were off chasing her.

Three months later, the Brigitte Bardot Foundation was dissolved.

Thoroughly discouraged, her explanation was that the problems the Foundation was being asked to solve were too complex, and too costly, for such a small group. She said that there were simply too many obstacles and, while she'd been greatly moved by the abundant generosity of people who'd answered her cry for help, the Foundation's overheads far outweighed the money available for good causes. She said she now found it more honest and more efficient to continue all by herself, using her own funds.

'I'd hoped it could have been a collective effort of good intentions aimed at a single goal. But the volume of mail we received, and the scope of the problems posed, necessitated a management and administrative structure which couldn't be handled by volunteers and I didn't want the donations we received to go to bureaucrats.'

Over the course of the next several months it came out that the Foundation's demise was based on more serious problems than just funding. She'd not been getting along with her partners – namely Victor and Cottereau – had grown suspicious of them and had questioned their bookkeeping. It all came to a head when she'd discovered that salaries, rent, office supplies and postage accounted for more than twice the Foundation's income.

Incensed at this use – or, as she saw it, misuse – of funds, she lashed out, 'I would have done more good had I bought 25,000 cans of dog food and distributed them to strays.'

An insulted Cottereau fought back, accusing Bardot of being little more than a dilettante. 'She is just a wealthy lady who prefers to play cards with her friends at her villa in St Tropez rather than do something to help animals.'

According to him, CBS television in the States had been willing to donate two million francs ($466,200) to the Foundation if Bardot would appear in a documentary they were taping at a wildlife park in the States. When he approached her with their offer, she refused, on the grounds that she didn't like flying.

He was willing to admit, 'She certainly loves animals,' but was fast to add, 'the only trouble is that she is not prepared to lift a finger personally to help them.'

By January 1977, with acrimony spewing forth from both sides, Bardot filed suit against Victor and Cottereau. She was looking to recoup 72,000 francs ($16,875). Included in that was rent paid to the Victor Environment Group, which she claimed should have been waived, Cottereau's salary, which she claimed he wasn't entitled to, and the cost of 20 animal sculptures that Cottereau had purchased without her approval, first to decorate the reception at the Pré Catelan, then to resell at a profit for the benefit of the Foundation. Symbolically added on to the total was one franc damages for what the two had done to the image of the Brigitte Bardot Foundation.

Cottereau responded that his salary was the same as it had been when he worked for Victor, that the Foundation didn't pay rent – but was obliged to pay, and had agreed to pay, monthly charges – and that every time he tried to get Bardot to verify the

Foundation's expenses she refused to discuss it. He said at one point he even flew down to St Tropez to confront her with the accounts so that she could see where the money was going, but in a fit of temper she grabbed the accounts and threw them on the floor.

Victor now filed a counter-suit for slander, saying that she had brought serious harm to the cause of animal protection. What's more, he noted, instead of working for animal's rights, she spent too much time getting a suntan in St Tropez.

Bardot retorted that she did love animals, had been prepared to sacrifice a part of her life for them – which was the reason she started the Foundation in the first place – but vehemently objected to seeing the Foundation's funds being spent on bureaucrats. Anyway, she said, she'd seen Victor's suntan, recently acquired in Tahiti, which was 'several shades darker than mine'.

Her lawyer, Gilles Dreyfus, stepped into the fray and issued a statement. 'Mademoiselle Bardot fulfilled her obligations, but she obviously could not be expected to spend 24 hours a day working for the Foundation. That is not her job. As a beautiful woman, she is not prepared to enter the Holy Order of Animals.'

Animal rights activist and French television producer Allain Bougrain-Dubourg had become friendly with Bardot at that time. He would eventually become her lover and lived with her for many years. Together they would produce television shows about animals and do a three-hour TV series on her life.

He recalls the anguish she went through over the demise of that first Foundation. 'She was terribly depressed about it. But Brigitte wasn't mature enough at the time. Neither were the people she asked to take charge of the Foundation. The administration was clumsy. She was too naive about how it should run. She wanted to see every penny go to the benefit of animals. She couldn't understand, for instance, that there were administrative costs.'

Nor did she have enough experience with animal rights work. 'She didn't have the depth of knowledge that she now has. She shut the first Foundation because she felt like a prisoner inside an administrative structure. Today she understands that these things must be run like a business. Today she understands that administration is part of it. Today she also has a deep working knowledge of the issues and is able to deal with complicated problems. Paperwork bores her to tears and she hates reading dossiers, but she can handle them, and does. She has genuine expertise. However, that's all these years later. The first Brigitte Bardot Foundation just happened too soon.'

*　　*　　*

On Tuesday 15 March 1977, the day the seal cull began off St Anthony in northeast Newfoundland, Brigitte Bardot petitioned the Queen of England, in her role as Canadian sovereign, to stop the massacre. She knew that there was nothing the Queen could do, but Bardot wanted to play every public relations card she could find.

The following day, with scores of anti-hunt protesters already gathered in St Anthony, she set out for Newfoundland in a chartered jet, with Mirko, Swiss environmentalist Franz Weber, and photographers from the Sygma Photo Agency. They were along because she'd convinced Sygma to pay for the trip.

Warning that, 'at the present rate of killings, the last of the seals will be finished by 1985', she intended to put the Canadian government on notice. 'The whole world has risen up against the baby seal hunt and Canada runs the risk of diplomatic conflicts if the situation doesn't change.'

She promised that she would go to the ends of the earth to stop such savagery and asked, again, to meet Trudeau.

The Prime Minister's office, understanding that they ignored Brigitte Bardot at their own peril – no one had to remind them that, if it came down to which of them could get more international press attention, Bardot or Trudeau, it would be no contest — suggested that if she wanted to meet him 'the correct procedure would be for her to phone his office or send a letter'.

In the meantime, protesters, including Greenpeace and the International Fund for Animal Welfare, reported that, in just the first day of the cull, hunters had slaughtered 11,930 seals.

The police had their hands full with the protesters, and violence broke out on the third day of the hunt. The last thing the government now needed was Brigitte Bardot. So on Friday 18 March, when her jet landed at Blanc Sablon on the Quebec-Labrador border, they were ready for her.

First, they impounded her plane, claiming that the pilot had landed in Newfoundland on his way to Blanc Sablon but had not cleared Customs there as he was legally obliged to do.

Next, a Royal Canadian Mounted Police official demanded that the pilot produce papers certifying his current flying status. In other words, he wanted to see a valid commercial pilot's licence. He also insisted on seeing a valid flight plan with pre-clearance by Canada's aviation authorities granted them landing rights.

Finally, an airport official slapped the air crew with a bill for several hundred dollars in landing fees.

A detestable attempt by the Trudeau government to keep her at bay, the ploy half-worked. Bardot missed her helicopter flight to the cull.

However, she instantly raised the stakes by allowing her temper to show. And here the government plot backfired. What would have been a photo-feature — and might not have attracted very much attention — swiftly turned into a news story which attracted a lot of attention. It was no longer just Brigitte and the seals, it was Bardot versus Canada.

With her air crew trying to satisfy the idiots who were using officialdom to keep her grounded, Brigitte chose to wait them out in rented accommodation. She moved into the only house in the village with a bed.

By this time, the baby seal death toll had reached 50,000.

Just when it seemed that she might win – that, in fact, all the necessary paperwork was in order – the weather closed in on her. For the next three days she sat by helplessly, stuck in a snowstorm.

She used the time to make the hunters a deal. If they would give up the killings, she would help them set up a synthetic fur industry in the area, creating employment for them. Additionally, she would allow them to use her name, free of charge, to commercialize the business.

Her offer was mocked by the hunters, who berated her for using their livelihood as a personal publicity stunt.

She lashed back at them, 'I hate publicity. I can't understand how they can say such things.' But to no avail.

As soon as the weather cleared, she piled into a helicopter for the 90 mile trip. But, again, luck was against her. They flew straight into a snowstorm and with visibility way below the legal minimum – while being tossed around in high winds – the pilot was forced to turn back.

Bardot returned to Blanc Sablon distraught and in tears.

'The ice was red with blood. I saw it from the plane, streaked with red for miles and miles and strewn with tiny carcasses. They kill them with iron hooks, little two-week-old seals, defenceless little balls of fur and life and love. They skin them on the spot and you can see their little hearts still beating in the bloody mass that remains.'

Although she never got to the cull – never got to throw herself in between a seal and a hunter the way other protesters did – she did manage a photo session with some baby seals. She lay down on the ice with them, face to face, producing a picture that would come to symbolize the world's revulsion at the cull.

The response from the Trudeau government and the Eskimo hunters was to remind the world that here was an old actress who might just be looking to make a come-back.

Two days later she was back in Paris with a warning for the Canadians. 'I don't care what people say about me. I'll do it again next year.' In all, some 170,000 baby seals had been savagely clubbed to death.

She refused to give in and spoke about the seal cull whenever and wherever she could. She kept the public's awareness high. She petitioned her own government and refused to allow the Trudeau administration off the hook. At the end of the year, she wrote again to the Canadian prime minister to tell him, yet again, of the savagery that he seemed all too willing to endorse.

In January 1978, she brought her battle into the Council of Europe and went to Strasbourg to argue in favour of a motion proposing a two-year ban on the hunting of Greenland seals — which through Denmark came under Common Market jurisdiction — and a quota limiting the killings in future years.

Danish and Norwegian parliamentarians first defended their positions by criticizing Bardot for showing up so informally dressed. She wore a sweater, a skirt and boots instead of, one presumes, something more akin to some obscure Scandinavian tradition of attending parliamentary sessions in an evening gown, tiara and high heels.

Next, they criticized her for turning the session into a circus with the crowds she attracted. Unfortunately, hardly anyone bothered to remind the Scandinavian delegates that, until she showed up, they functioned in near-total but richly warranted obscurity.

At a press conference, Bardot heralded the proposed legislation as a step forward but insisted the fight had to go on.

One journalist, about as aware of the world as the Scandinavian parliamentarians, asked if it was true that her campaign was nothing more than a publicity stunt for her come-back in the movies.

When she refused to dignify the question with a response, other journalists noted, 'She refused to answer the question.'

No sooner was the press conference over then Canada's Vice-Consul in Strasbourg handed her a message from Pierre Elliot Trudeau.

Responding to her letter of the previous month, Trudeau made lame excuses for something that many people now consider to be inexcusable. He wanted her to understand, 'Seals are killed in a quicker and more humane manner than are most domestic animals in civilized countries.'

As if that made sense, Trudeau went on, 'We impose a certain method of killing to avoid needless cruelty. The clubbing on the ice flows and the use of the felling axe in the slaughterhouses are not tender gestures, but what counts is that they make the animal unconscious.'

It was a pathetic attempt to justify the unjustifiable by an otherwise intelligent man.

Today, the fact that seal fur is outlawed in many nations across the world, including the European Union, is almost entirely down Brigitte Bardot.

*   *   *

Four months after she returned from Newfoundland, Christian Brincourt received a message from a French fishing boat off the Canadian coast that they'd heard about Brigitte Bardot's campaign, had just found a seal pup on an ice cap, and wanted to bring him back as a gift for her.

When Brincourt phoned Brigitte to tell her the story, she answered, right away, 'Yes, yes, I want my baby seal.' So Brincourt made suitable arrangements with the boat captain.

A few weeks later, the fishermen slipped into the port of Fécamp, in Normandy, just up the coast from Le Havre. The quayside was filled with anxious wives and children who hadn't seen their sailing men for nearly five months. But just as the crew was about to dock – to everyone's astonishment – Brigitte Bardot arrived.

To the great chagrin of the waiting wives, the fishermen turned their attention to her.

It took some time before everyone finally settled down. Once the wives had reclaimed their men, the crew presented Brigitte with the baby seal, which she promptly named Chou-Chou. Overjoyed, she put him in a crate she'd specially prepared for the journey and drove him home to Bazoches.

He lived for a time there in her swimming pool, eating nothing but round fish – a dietary quirk that Bardot discovered only after a rather frustrating few days of trial and error.

But by then the seal didn't seem well, so she summoned a vet and a couple of seal experts, who decided to give him some shots. Afraid they would do more harm than good, she refused to allow that.

After three months, she was willing to admit that the seal needed more suitable accommodation, so she gave in to her emotions and offered him as a gift to Marineland in Antibes.

And over the next few years, every so often, Brigitte Bardot could be seen at Marineland, standing at the side of the pool, screaming 'Chou-Chou'.

However, the night she brought him home from Fécamp, Letellier and Brincourt were having dinner when Philippe wondered how Brigitte and Chou-Chou were getting on, so he phoned her to ask.

She told him, 'He's warming up under the radiator.'

Letellier wondered, 'What are you going to do with him?'

'Not to worry,' Bardot answered with typical élan, 'I'll make a man of him.'

Chapter Twelve

THE BATTLE OF ST TROPEZ

There is the St Tropez to live in from September to May. And there is the St Tropez to suffer in from June to August.

Off-season, there are fewer than 5,000 people, who quietly go about their lives – a morning coffee at a café, a late afternoon *pastis* on the Place des Lices.

In season, everything changes.

The invasion force is more than 100,000 strong. They come in buses and campers and in Mercedes too, forcing the natives into retreat. They line up their big boats along the *quai*, fill the red canvas chairs at Le Senequier, fill the blue canvas chairs at Le Gorille, and fight for the few foreign newspapers that arrive at the cramped newsstand at the port that is otherwise stocked with picture postcards of young women on the beach, topless, or in string bathing suits, or even without any bathing suits at all, and with the words 'Greetings from St Trop' in bold colourful letters across the top.

Store fronts closed most of the year, many of them once stables at the bottom of a small house, open their doors to hawk swim masks and swim fins and t-shirts in six languages that say, 'My parents went to St Trop and all I got was a lousy t-shirt'.

They sell Piz Buin suntan oil and Fuji disposable cameras and Seattle Mariner baseball caps. They sell inflatable buoys in the shape of fish to go around a child's waist, bathing suits decorated like the Union Jack, with *espadrilles* – canvas beach shoes – to match.

In season, breakfast at the five-star Hotel Byblos – one cup of coffee with two croissants – costs $20. Out of season the place is closed.

There are pizzerias and clothing stores where the owners need to make their year's living in under five months, and *patisseries* which sell baguettes to the natives and *pan bagnat* sandwiches to the tourists.

At any *tabac*, you can buy multi-coloured phone cards, which you need to make a call from the public booths at the end of the quay or next to the little parking lot in front of the police station, bearing appropriate advice from France Telecom – 'Say Yes to Condoms'.

When the day-trippers arrive in their air-conditioned buses with hostess service and two toilets on board – Germans and Finns and Brits and Japanese and Guatemalans and Americans and, these days, Eastern Europeans too – they swarm through the town, buying whatever they see, then flock to the beach for the day, where they walk around dressed, cameras hanging off their necks, looking for people who are not dressed.

Tour boats leave from the port every hour and La Madrague is still the grand finale.

Police officers patrol the streets – 'No parking', they bark in French, Italian, German and English – while tourists line up in front of banks and the *bureaux de change* to exchange their travellers' cheques for French francs so that they can pay for a badly boiled hot dog at a back-street *épicerie*, or buy a watercolour from any one of the 25 sidewalk artists who live for a year on what they flog here each summer.

At night, the restaurants spill their tables onto the street, as tourists walk by, staring at their *prix fixe* menus – in six languages – wondering how much 120 francs is, and asking harried waiters, is service included? And, does that include wine? And, is the *tarte Tropezienne* really good?

Guitar-strumming musicians come into the restaurants – they make the rounds, moving from one to another, all night long – and play a few songs before passing the hat. They're followed by a young woman selling roses. And the artists come here too, bringing their watercolours to the tourists in case there are any who might have missed them at the port.

Later, when the discos open, with their throbbing music and $30 drinks, the men are, *de rigeur*, in tight white trousers and open-necked black silk shirts and white shoes with no socks. And the women are, *de rigeur*, in tight white trousers and open-necked red silk shirts and high-heeled white shoes, or no shoes at all.

The men say they are actors, in between films, or stunt men – that's better because who would recognize a stunt man – or just rich enough to hang out on a boat. The women say they are actresses, in between films, or models off the Paris catwalks. It doesn't matter what anyone says, because these places are not made for talking.

The music pulsates non-stop until morning, when the cafés start to fill up again and the day's bus loads begin to arrive. It goes on like that all summer.

Brigitte makes it a point to leave before it starts, some time in early June, and often doesn't come back until late October, long after it's ended.

Although that doesn't necessarily stop the reporters who, like the tourists, also show up, faithfully, every year.

In the days when she was working, if they had nothing to write about they invented foolishness. They rationalized the exercise by claiming that they were helping her career and that it didn't matter what they wrote, as long as they spelled her name correctly. They took it as their mission to sustain the myth.

But she never saw it that way. As far as she was concerned, she never felt she owed them anything. If the press promoted her career, it wasn't because they were being philanthropic.

Now that she's not working, they continue to invent foolishness.

One newspaper continues to dredge up the old chestnut that she owns a chain of snackbars and laundromats. She doesn't. But the tax man keeps seeing that story and he keeps dropping by every few years to look for his share of her profits.

Another paper recently sent its reporters to sift through whatever rubbish they could find outside La Madrague. It never dawned on them that this might not be her garbage. After all, she has a caretaker living on the property. Nor, presumably, does it matter much that for decades she has been a near-vegetarian and only very rarely eats meat. After sorting through someone's rubbish, their conclusion was that Brigitte Bardot lives almost entirely on canned meatballs.

Still, there have been some rare moments when she's found herself in St Tropez being treated like an ordinary human being.

One night, when she was with Bob Zagury, the two of them were walking along the port a few hours before dawn. No one was around. So they stopped at the quay where the fishing boats were tied up, and sat there talking.

After a time, two, young, local policemen came up to them. They both saluted. And one of them politely asked, '*Papiers, s'il vous plait.*' Your papers please.

Brigitte was stunned. 'My papers?' She couldn't believe it. These were not gendarmes, who might not have been raised in the area and who – as implausible as it sounds – might not have recognized her. Nor were these officers from the Police Nationale, perhaps sent down from Paris to help keep the peace during the summer. No, these were two kids on St Tropez's municipal police force.

She stared at them for the longest time, then said, 'But surely you know who I am.'

Sheepishly one of them responded, 'Yes, Madame, we do. But we have to ask because we've got orders to search for a blonde.'

* * *

As legend has it, Tropez was a Christian centurian beheaded by Nero. His body was put into a little boat, along with his head, one rooster and one dog. The boat was then shoved out to sea. Nero's guys reckoned that, when the dog and the rooster got hungry, they'd eat poor Tropez. But, miracle of miracles, when the little boat finally washed ashore, the body was still intact.

So the spot where the boat was found was named after the uneaten, headless, Christian centurian.

An independent republic from the 15th to the 17th centuries – some locals say that buried deep in the civic subconscious is a nostalgia for lost autonomy – St Tropez was, until the last century, an out of the way port, largely inaccessible except by sea, that lived off a small but thriving commercial maritime industry. It wasn't really until the painter Paul Signac arrived in 1892 that St Tropez became known in the rest of France.

Singularly impressed by the sunlight he found there – he later described the village as 'the eighth wonder of the world' – he convinced other artists, like Henri Matisse, Kees van Dongen and Pierre Bonnard, to visit and inadvertently changed the place forever. St Tropez soon became the home of the school of art known as 'pointillism' – a precursor to the French Impressionist movement.

Writers followed painters. Guy De Maupassant worked here and so did Colette, who arrived in 1934 to write *L'Eté 34* – although she quit the following year because she found it already too crowded, too *à la mode*.

The Parisian theatrical crowd followed the writers. And the cinema world came too.

Then, so did the Germans.

Hitler's army occupied much of southeastern France, and stayed in the area until the night of 14–15 August 1944, when 15 American soldiers – the first wave of the Allied landings – parachuted in. The Yanks were targeting the stretch of beach from Ste Maxime to St Raphael but were blown off course. So the invasion of the French Mediterranean coast actually began in St Tropez, by mistake.

In the late 1940s and early 1950s 'Le Tout St Germain des Prés' – everybody who was anybody in Left Bank Parisian circles – came to St Tropez in search of quiet amusement. By that time tourism was already an important element of local life.

Thanks to *And God Created Woman* the place took on mythical status. There are still people who, when you speak about Vadim, can tell you how he used to park a metallic grey California Ferrrari inside Le Gorille, with its nose up to the bar.

Being part of the legend pleases him. 'Either you're a real snob or you're not a snob at all. You have to go all the way.'

He did. But then, those were intoxicating days. It was a time, he says, when a person with no money could live like a millionaire and a millionaire could live like a bohemian.

As a family, the Bardots had spent time in St Tropez long before she made that film there. Brigitte visited for the first time in 1948, with Pilou, Toty and Mijanou. They returned in 1951 when the Bardots rented a small house. Shortly thereafter, Pilou bought his first villa there, La Miséricorde. In 1964, after he retired, Pilou and Toty bought a new place, in a small wood in the middle of the cape, called La Pierre Plantée.

By the time Brigitte owned La Madrague, St Tropez was very much in fashion. What she did – unintentionally – was to banalize it. If bus tours arrived bringing hordes of people, it wasn't because they cared about the sunlight or quiet amusement, it was because they wanted to get a glimpse of her.

The names St Tropez and Brigitte Bardot became inextricably linked and, almost immediately, the word nudity was thrown in for good measure. St Tropez became one of the most famous villages on earth because it was where she lived and she was one of the most famous people on earth.

Before she moved to St Tropez, the beaches were nearly empty.

The Madrague wall (Popper)

The provincial life at home (Popper)

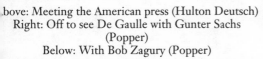

Above: Meeting the American press (Hulton Deutsch)
Right: Off to see De Gaulle with Gunter Sachs
(Popper)
Below: With Bob Zagury (Popper)

Saving the seals (Sygma)

A woman and her animals (Popper)

A retired 40 year old (Hulton Deutsch)

As Marianne (Associated Press)

Below: Going to court with Allain
Bougrain-Dubourg (1) and Gilles
Dreyfus (r) (Popper)

Above: With pal
Jo de Salerne

The principal players today:
Above left: Roger Vadim
(photo Dominique Nabokov)
Above right: Jacques Charrier
Left: Mijanou
Right: Nicolas Charrier
Below: Gunter Sachs
(private photos)

At home with Bernard D'Ormale (Michel Luccioni, Angeli)

(photo Michel Luccioni; Angeli)

People took off their clothes to worship the sun and swim in the sea and no one much cared. When Bardot took off her clothes, a lot of people cared and now the beaches changed too. She accidentally incited a new wave of nudism – exciting a generation of people who wanted to see and wanted to be seen – where sun worship was replaced with voyeurism and exhibitionism.

*   *   *

It was never difficult to find her house.

Even if some locals tried to do their best – when asked by tourists, 'Where's Brigitte's place?' they'd point in the wrong direction – it was usually only a matter of time before the tourists got there anyway.

Within five years of buying La Madrague – five years of being constantly under siege – she was starting to wonder if there was any way she could protect herself, if there was any way she could ever be safe.

One afternoon in August 1962, she was sitting on the terrace at La Madrague quietly having lunch with Eddie Barclay when, suddenly, a man walked out of the water and started coming towards her.

'Would you please be kind enough to leave,' she called out. 'This is my home. Would you please leave me alone.'

But he didn't stop. He stepped up to the terrace and, without saying a word, raised his hand, as if to slap her. Barclay jumped up to grab the man, who swiftly turned, fled back into the water and swam away.

'Every day it's the same thing,' she told Barclay. 'I'm never left alone here.'

Later she would start asking friends, 'Why is it that the first reflex of so many people when they see me is to be aggressive?'

Protecting herself has been made all the more difficult – owing to the way the house is exposed to the sea – because there's a law in France, dating from 1681, which says the first four metres (about

14 feet) of land from the shore line belongs to all the people. In other words, in France, there is no such thing as a private beach. Anyone can use any beach, as long as they stay within those first four metres.

Technically, anyone who wanted to picnic in front of her house could not be arrested for trespassing. They might have met with the disapproval of her dogs, and they would certainly have met with the fury of Madame herself, but the police would have been otherwise helpless.

So she got it into her head that if she built a high wall, going from the side of her house five or six metres (17–20 feet) into the sea, at least it would keep people from walking along the beach and onto her property. She applied for a building permit. But because her wall might restrict the right of access to a beach – and therefore be against the law – building permission was not automatically granted.

On the one hand, she had to admit that, of course it restricted right of access to the beach. That's why she wanted to build it. On the other, she knew, anyone determined enough to come onto her property would only have to walk into the water and around the wall. If they allowed her to build it, from now on, trespassing tourists and photographers would just have to get their feet wet.

The debate, whether or not to permit her to build the wall, went on for months. She finally got a ruling in her favour in 1963. But she was granted only 'temporary' permission.

Not waiting for anyone to question what that meant, she built the wall and convinced herself that she was safer with it than without it.

Almost as soon as it was built, objections were raised. Letters came into the town hall at St Tropez from other wealthy local residents who wanted a wall on the beach in front of their houses. She argued this wasn't about trying to create a deluxe beach for herself, this was about her personal security. But, her neighbours grumbled, if she could have a private beach, then they could have a private beach too.

The question of the legality of her wall slowly made its way through the bureaucracy that is French government. Meanwhile, the tourist invasion continued.

By the time she married Gunter Sachs, she was just about ready to call it quits. The harder she'd tried to pull away from the limelight, the brighter those lights became. Unlike Garbo, who managed to find some anonymity, Brigitte had totally failed and the result of that failure was that armies of people continued to arrive every summer, looking for her.

'My life in St Tropez is intolerable,' she complained. 'I can't stay any longer.'

Now a second solution presented itself. She might sell La Madrague and move someplace new with him. Gunter suggested Deauville.

The Normandy weather wasn't quite as good as what she'd grown used to in the Midi, but Deauville had its charm and it was evident that she could be much better protected there. Gunter bought an acre on which he planned to build and she put La Madrague on the market. Her asking price was 2.5 million francs ($450,000).

Needless to say, the people of Deauville were thrilled. They knew that she would bring tourism to the town and that she was good for business. The Mayor promised that the lot next to theirs – which was still undeveloped – would not be sold to autograph hunters. And the director of the casino was so pleased that he waived the dress code for Monsieur and Madame Sachs, just in case they wanted to come to gamble while she was wearing slacks.

One French journalist was so amused by the idea of her selling La Madrague for 2.5 million francs that he rang round some likely buyers to see what they thought of the price. Among the people he called was Jacques Charrier.

His response, 'You've got a nerve to ask me that question!'

The only thing that stopped her from selling La Madrague was that there were no takers. By the time her marriage with Sachs was over, she was just as glad still to have it. A few years later, Gianni

Agnelli, the chairman of Fiat, offered to buy it at her price, and she came close to selling it. In the end, she rationalized that maybe the way to avoid being molested on her own beach was to build a swimming pool. So she told Agnelli no and installed a pool.

During those years when she lived with Mirko, he was there to protect her.

One afternoon, a guy arrived in a row boat just off the shore in front of La Madrague. There was a tarpaulin covering it. And under the tarpaulin he had a camera. The fellow stayed there all afternoon, trying to photograph Bardot when she stepped out of the house, much to the annoyance of Bardot and everyone else.

Eventually, Mirko lost his temper.

He climbed onto a raft and paddled out, going around the side to sneak up on the guy in the boat. Once he was there, he reached inside and grabbed all the man's film.

Brigitte was delighted.

Except that the man then called the police and, when they showed up, they gave Brigitte and Mirko a hard time for stealing the film.

Mirko fared almost as badly the day the maid started shrieking that someone had stolen her purse with all her money in it. She said that her entire week's savings were gone.

Brigitte couldn't understand it because there didn't seem to be anyone around. The only people on the property were her and Mirko. At least that's what she thought.

The maid told her she'd noticed a young blond guy wearing shorts. So Brigitte called Mirko and he came running – a young blond guy wearing shorts.

She knew he hadn't taken the maid's money and couldn't understand how the maid might have mistaken him for the thief, when she spotted someone on the roof of La Petite Madrague – a young blond guy wearing shorts.

She phoned the police, begging them to come quickly because the man was escaping. They asked her what he looked like and she described him. While she was on the phone, Mirko climbed up onto the roof and caught the thief. He brought him down and tied him up with a rope. But when they searched the guy's pockets, the maid's wallet wasn't there.

So Mirko climbed back onto the roof to see if it was up there somewhere.

That's when the police arrived to arrest the young blond guy wearing shorts who was hiding on the roof.

No, Mirko cried, I'm not the one you want.

Sure, the police responded, that's what they all say.

It took Brigitte, who was, at this point, hysterical with laughter, to explain that, odd as it may sound, she had two young blond guys wearing shorts and that the one on the ground was the one they needed to arrest.

*   *   *

The wall came back to haunt her.

Various municipal officials in St Tropez, departmental officials in the Var and government officials in Paris kept trying to decide if it was legal. While they debated the point, copycat walls went up all over St Tropez.

Leopold, the King of Belgium, felt entitled to a wall for security reasons. As did orchestra leader Herbert von Karajan. As did the von Opel family next door to Brigitte.

She managed to hold off any official decision until 1981, when François Mitterand was elected. The matter went as high as his socialist/communist coalition cabinet, and they encouraged the Minister of the Seas, M. Louis le Pensec, to enforce the law.

He dictated, there would be no special privilege extended to those people who usually enjoy special privilege. To show that he meant business, the following summer he personally bulldozed a wall. Except that the wall he bulldozed belonged to Mme Lucette Thomazo, a particularly well-known personality in the French

Communist Party – she'd been on the board of the communist newspaper *L'Humanité* – which brought serious objections to his ardour from within the cabinet.

So much for people of special privilege.

Brigitte, who by now regularly took refuge every summer at Bazoches, let it be known that, if M. le Pensec bulldozed her wall, she'd move to Mexico. He responded by withdrawing her temporary permission to maintain the wall and issuing an order that it had to be at least partially destroyed by midnight, 31 December 1982.

She appealed and only an eleventh hour reprieve saved it. Rather than create an awkward confrontation, the Mitterand government put the affair on the back burner, where it was intended to stay.

Fearing that another government could always try again, and exasperated by the ever-present tourists and paparazzi, she bought a tract of land on the other side of the cape, and began construction there of a small ranch. If all else failed, she decided, she'd have somewhere to run and hide.

What she hadn't counted on was that, while the wall would remain, it was St Tropez that would go.

•   •   •

Each year, with the beginning of good weather, she rounds up all her dogs, drives with them from St Tropez to Toulon and flies privately to Le Bourget, outside Paris.

In the autumn, she heads south the same way.

It costs her a fortune to charter planes, but she refuses to allow her animals to be shoved in boxes and stored in the hold of a commercial flight.

Since starting her annual migration in the 1980s, each year she's found her summer season at Bazoches stretching longer – her exit from St Tropez being made hastier.

In 1986, with tourists and photographers as obsessed with her as ever, she announced, 'I'm sick and tired of being Mickey Mouse in this Disneyland. I'm leaving.'

She went off in a huff for her longest absence to date. But eventually she returned, and when she did, so did the tourists and the photographers.

Three years later, she couldn't stand it any more. The straw that broke the camel's back was her run-in with Mayor Alain Spada.

A slim, dark-haired man then in his mid-40s – a military engineer by trade – he was a local boy who'd raised his family in the town and deeply cared about St Tropez. They'd known each other for years. He'd been the mayor for one term at the beginning of the 1980s, had lost the town hall to a cardiologist named Jean-Michel Couve, and in 1989 had reclaimed it from Couve.

Thinking that the beaches had become too crowded – and much too commercialized – one of Spada's first projects was to convert a small, little-used stretch along the water into a family beach. He wasn't going to allow any private facilities – no cabanas, no sun-loungers, no bars, no restaurants – because there were already more than enough beaches where people could find those things. He wanted this beach to be a quiet spot, the sort of beach St Tropez used to have, the kind of beach he remembered from his youth.

But that was the beach where Brigitte walked her dogs.

A sign went up saying *Interdit aux Chiens* – no dogs allowed.

When a couple of gendarmes spotted her there one day with her dogs, they tried to give her a verbal warning. She told them off in such a way that they beat a hasty retreat.

In normal circumstances, she wouldn't have given the incident a second thought. But now she was more and more troubled by what she saw as 'the dreadful decadence that has come to symbolize St Tropez'.

In her mind, St Tropez was supposed to be about charm and elegance. She was against the organized nudity that seemed almost contagious along the beaches, and was offended by the

251

crass behaviour of the tourists who piled into town. 'They have no shame.'

She also resented the sign that forbade dogs on that beach, and took it down.

Spada ordered another one to be put up.

That one came down too.

She told him, 'You can keep putting up all the boards you want to every day and I'll keep taking them down every night. If you're looking for your signs, you can always come and get them back at my house. But each time you put one up, I'll take it down.'

Before he realized what was happening, the world's press descended on St Tropez to watch her lock horns with the mayor.

In an open letter to Spada, she exploded with a diatribe of accusations. 'Shamelessness, exhibitionism, vice, money, homosexuality have all become sad symbols of the degradation of the village for which you are responsible.'

Brigitte noted that each year, when summer arrived, she was forced to flee from tourists who were, for the most part, low class, dirty and rude. Furthermore, she took it as a personal insult to her campaign to defend animals when her own town outlawed dogs on the beach.

'Human turds, condoms, and all kinds of rubbish are polluting the bay and the beaches. Human filth is spreading like a black tide.'

Feeling like a stranger in her own home, she said she didn't want to live in St Tropez any more. She announced that she was giving up, 'leaving everything to the invaders', and going away.

Spada was stupefied. 'She's very capricious, everyone knows that. But she couldn't understand, she didn't want to understand, that this was a public beach and not her private domain. People don't want dog crap on their beaches. I put a stop to it and she took it as a personal affront.'

She retorted, 'The town is overrun by hoodlums, drug addicts, crooks of all kinds and garbage. It's Miami. The little, gleaming port of the 1960s, when there were pretty girls, models, cover girls, is gone. Today French fries and sausages are king.'

At first, he ignored her verbal assaults. 'I tried to let it roll off my back. I told myself, she's just tired and irritable. I decided she didn't see the whole picture. But then she began attacking the town, life here, the people here, and I couldn't sit by any longer. I knew her well enough to know that I had to put a stop to it before she caused some real damage.'

She was older, more reclusive, angrier – some people thought, less rational – and clearly determined to have her way. There's no denying that she has always treated St Tropez as her mini-fiefdom. But, for her, this wasn't her second home – as it was for so many other people – it was her life.

In Brigitte's opinion, 'The village was never protected from anarchistic urbanization, any more than it was from frantic industrialization. No one in St Tropez ever tried to put on the brakes, or control what was going on. That explains the anarchic construction, the invasion of the crazies, who turned these sublime beaches into tourists' bordellos.'

St Tropez hadn't improved with the years, and no longer corresponded to the life she wanted to lead. She wanted a place where she could live in peace with her animals, without local policemen giving her tickets when she walked her dogs on the beach.

'As if a dog is dirty or more dangerous than empty syringes lying there on the sand.' She said she would always have the old St Tropez in her memories, and that's where St Tropez would have to stay. She said she was not coming back.

Requests for interviews poured into the town hall from all over the world. This was not only a story widely covered by the French and Italian media, it seemed to fascinate newspapers, radio and television stations as far afield as the BBC in London, the CBC in Montreal, ABC News in New York, plus wire services in Japan and daily newspapers in Australia and New Zealand.

And the mayor's desk was inundated with mail.

Someone from southwest France wrote, 'She has contributed to the enrichment of your town, and this is how you thank her?'

Another, this one from the Var region, noted, 'Shame on you, Mr Mayor, for creating such misery for our dear Brigitte Bardot.'

A woman from Nice wanted Spada to know, 'We were alone on the beach and by about noon I'd just finished making a *salade Niçoise*, when suddenly, some 30 metres from us, the star herself appeared, with a boyfriend, three dogs and a donkey. All of that menagerie walking freely. One of the dogs came racing towards us and splashed sand into our salad.'

While a grandmother from Lyons had her say, too. 'When Madame Bardot criticizes exhibitionism and immorality, I think she has a short memory.'

Someone else sent Spada some nude photos of Brigitte published in *France Dimanche*, suggesting, 'When one has been an international star of that type, we are astonished by her disgust. She shouldn't talk about imprudence.'

A woman from Brest felt, 'Brigitte's success in favour of animals has gone to her head.'

But a woman from Paris didn't agree. 'Madame Brigitte Bardot is always a celebrity in our eyes no matter how she behaves. If she leaves, there will be a certain emptiness in St Tropez.'

A local woman concluded, 'In effect, everyone who created something in St Tropez, who opened up business in St Tropez, who earned a lot of money in St Tropez, who has a good job in St Tropez, who exists in St Tropez should never forget that it is thanks to Brigitte Bardot. St Tropez exists because of her.'

And a man from Perpignan concurred. 'You and your citizens owe a lot to Madame Bardot. She represents a feminine myth to our generation, as striking as Marilyn Monroe for the previous generation. She has brought prominence to your village, to France, to French culture throughout the world and to the courageous campaign that she leads for animals.'

•　　•　　•

In June 1992, they had another run in.

Spada had initiated a plan to modernize the village sewer system. In order to complete the job, some minor work needed to be carried out on the road that leads up to La Madrague. The council's engineers were obliged to block it off. The entire task – crewed by a few guys with shovels and one small trench digger – was set to take two days. But Brigitte wouldn't have it.

She protested to Spada, 'I am violently opposed to being a prisoner of your fantasies for 48 hours. It is a blow to my liberty. I have the right of passage, to do my shopping, to walk my dogs, to receive my friends. I have the right to come and go as I please, I pay my local taxes and I don't intend to be subjected to forced confinement just because the mayor has decided that.'

Adding that the work endangered the lives of some 60 cats who lived in and around her property, and who would now be prevented from being taken to their veterinarian, she ordered her attorney to go to court to get the work stopped. It took three days before she could get her case heard, and in that time the work was finished. Naturally, the judge ruled against her.

In this case she proved to be a good loser and sent the mayor a bouquet of flowers.

•　　•　　•

The Place des Lices is covered with plane trees, and old men playing *boules*.

Lices apparently means joust and it's said that in the Middle Ages, when St Tropez was just an isolated fishing village, this was the piece of land where the jousts were held. It's a pleasant enough story, and possibly even true. Although it's difficult to imagine fishermen jousting.

On Saturday mornings, *le marché* takes over.

From just before dawn until early afternoon, the Place des Lices is filled with covered stands – with white and red and blue striped canopies – where people sell fruit and vegetables, t-shirts, spices, children's underwear, sausages, cheese and fresh pasta.

And open stands, with souvenirs and imitation provençal pottery, new paintings, old wooden tools, second-hand record albums, movie posters and a few pieces of antique French silver.

In the market in St Tropez on Saturday morning you can buy 30 sorts of olives out of large earthenware pots and 50 sorts of *saucisse* that have been tossed into wooden baskets. As far as the eye can see there are oranges and cheese and piles of fresh tomatoes and small white jute sacks filled with herbs and spices and nearby someone is selling soap, handmade in Provence, that smells of camomile and linden. There are stalls covered in fresh fish. And someone sells fresh mint. And someone else sells sweets, with miles of old-fashioned licorice laces curled up in the centre of his stand.

Not far away there's an old man making music on an accordion and children queuing for the merry-go-round.

Brigitte comes into the market late in the morning, buys her cheese, her fruit, her vegetables and her bread, stopping only at the stalls of the traders she knows. She rarely if ever makes eye contact with the regulars – who know enough to avoid her – and never when the tourists are here.

Her temper is famous, both for its ferocity and for the way it is apparently set on a hair trigger.

One morning, a couple of years ago, a pair of tourists spotted her, walked up and without saying anything, took a picture. It's a scene that has been played literally thousands of times throughout her life. But when it happens here she flies off the handle. She cursed the tourists for taking her picture without her permission and slapped the person holding the camera.

Yet once, it was very different for her.

It was back in the days when she could take her time, when people didn't look at her like one of the objects on one of the stalls — didn't stare at her as if she was a Cavallon melon or the best *fougasse*, which is provençal olive bread — when she could smell the fruit or taste an olive or just stroll barefoot through the Place des Lices.

'The minute she became a star,' Alain Spada says, 'people took an interest in her life. When she slipped from stardom into becoming an international social phenomenon, any last chance she might have had to lead a normal life was gone.'

Her chum Jo de Salerne concedes, 'It's sad.' Because for him and the other locals, *le marché* is not only about cheese and fruit, vegetables and bread, it's also about saying hello and gossiping and being a part of village life.

In season, he does a local radio programme live from the market. But it is out of season, when the tourists are gone, when the natives have taken back their town, that there is time to fill your senses here.

You taste it and smell it and see it best walking through the market with him.

He shakes hands with old men. He tips his latest prize baseball cap at old ladies walking past. He explains with his rolling provençal accent why these olives are better than those olives. He convinces the lady behind one counter to let you taste her *paté* — the best *paté*, he assures you, because she makes it herself. He hands you a *piment* and promises it is the best *piment* you have ever tasted.

It's when you hang out with the locals at the Saturday morning *marché*, and sit with them afterwards at the Café des Arts, taking a *pastis* before lunch, and someone puts a fresh fennel on the table and someone else slices some fresh tomatoes and suddenly some raw artichokes appear there too – that's when you understand what *le marché* means.

And that's when you suddenly realize that this simple pleasure has been taken away from her.

'She comes here but she never stays very long,' de Salerne explains.

He says, 'She can't. She can't stop being Brigitte Bardot.'

He says, 'You understand, she can't just turn off her celebrity status. She'd like to. But it isn't possible.'

And, with the winter sun pouring that special light through the plane trees, he quietly adds, 'Maybe it never was.'

Chapter Thirteen

LITIGIOUS LADY

B rigitte Bardot is extraordinarily litigious.
For close on 40 years, she has actively used her lawyers and the courts to bludgeon people whom she deems to have displeased her. Not surprisingly, living by such a sword, she has also spent a great deal of time and money defending herself from being sued.

Her cantankerous passion for jurisprudence hasn't been replaced with the grace of age. If you listen to some of the nastier rumours about her, there are those people who insist that Bardot supplements her income with whatever she can win in court. It happens not to be true. But some people nevertheless believe that money is the most logical explanation for so much time spent seeking justice. Others say it is just her way of reminding the world, I am still here.

Her father's successful use of attorneys to protect her virtue in 1952 when she made *Manina Sans Voile* obviously left its mark.

A few years later, when she felt that a Parisian magazine had misquoted her and not satisfactorily represented her views, she flexed her own legal muscles and asked her lawyers to obtain an order removing the magazine from the newsstands. But she was new at this and up against adversaries who'd been in the ring before. The magazine successfully defended the case, replying that

Bardot had authorized, in writing, publication of several articles about her.

Father and daughter joined forces in December 1958 to stop the Comédie Caumartin – a Parisian repertoire theatre company – from calling their latest revue, '*Ça va Bardot*'. By this time she'd become the country's number one box office star and hung her case on the flagrant exploitation of her name. The producers agreed to change the title to '*Ta Bouche, Bébé*' – literally, 'Your Mouth, BB' – but she refused to back down and even threatened to send bailiffs into the theatre to stop the performance. She should have quit while she was ahead because when the judgment came down it said that the producers weren't being harmful.

That led the *Paris Journal* to observe, 'Today she is such a prisoner of her own stardom that she trembles with fear over everything that might be written about her. A mere hint, even of a friendly pen, and BB already hears loud echoes reverberating off the walls of the Grand Canyon.'

She sued a German film distributor in 1960 for using photos of her to publicize a movie because she hadn't authorized those photos to be used. And when, during the World's Fair in Brussels that year, a wall of her photographs appeared in one of the pavilions to symbolize 'the evil spirit of the flesh', Brigitte's parents were so horrified that her father beat her to the punch and sued to get the photos taken down.

It was around the same time that she was sued by a French record company for breach of contract. A year or so before, she'd agreed to record a series of fairytales. But she never managed to find the time to show up at the studio. Eventually the company's patience ran out and they sued her for 10,000 francs ($2,080). The judge agreed that she was in breach and awarded damages.

In turn, she sued another French record company for using her picture on an album sleeve without her permission, when neither the songs nor the recording artist had anything to do with her.

That same spring, she went to war against Perrier. The French bottled water company had recently purchased a source in the

Alps that happened to be called Charrier. Because bottled water is good for infants, they launched a massive advertising campaign with the photo of a 15-month-old boy holding a bottle of mineral water and the three-word slogan, '*Bébé aime Charrier*' – Baby loves Charrier.

Bardot saw red and told her lawyers, 'Phonetically, Bébé is me, no matter how it's written. Charrier is Jacques. And by consequence, they're speaking about us.'

There was no doubt, her lawyers explained, that Bébé – or BB, whichever way it was spelled – had become the international trade mark of their client and that no one could mistake the intended pun. But they weren't sure she had a case.

A friend, businessman Jean-Claude Simon, argued with her that she'd lose. He suggested she forget paying lawyers and turn the matter into something profitable. He approached the Vittel water company and they agreed to pay her a small fortune if she'd allow them to put up huge posters throughout the country showing a photo of her with their water and the captain, 'Yes, but Bardot Drinks Vittel.'

No, Brigitte said, she was going to sue Perrier, and she did.

Perrier's lawyers maintained that, by including the photo of the baby, they were making it very clear what they were talking about. Anyway, they pointed out, no one said 'BB loves Charrier'. The campaign read, 'Baby loves Charrier', which was not the same thing. Furthermore, as the spring had been in operation since 1930, 'Babies loved Charrier since before Mme Bardot was even born'.

The judge agreed with Perrier.

She decided her name was being misused again in November 1963 when the singer Guy Beart came out with a record called 'Bobbob BB'. As she was living with Bob Zagury at the time, it struck her that Beart had overstepped the bounds. In fact, he'd gone so far as to mention a few more of her chums in the song – Roger (Vadim), Jean-Louis (Trintignant), Sacha (Distel), Jacques

(Charrier) and Sami (Frey) – along with commentary about her affairs with them.

Adding insult to injury, Beart's record had been published by her pal, Eddie Barclay. But even their close friendship wasn't enough to stop her from taking out an injunction against him. Joined in the action by Roger Vadim, the court ruled that Bardot's affairs were not the stuff of pop music and ordered the discs recalled.

The same day that she beat Beart and Barclay, she was the defendant in a case brought by a would-be screenwriter who sent a story to her. It's a very typical situation and most people in the arts have gone through it at one time or another. I sent you my idea, you used it, where is it, pay me! So most people in the arts – especially those who have been this route – know that they can never read anything that comes in over the transom. Scenarios, scripts, songs, manuscripts, whatever arrives in the mail unsolicited, is usually returned immediately. This particular guy didn't go so far as to say that she'd stolen his idea, he was merely incensed that she never returned his screenplay and wanted 200,000 francs ($40,700) compensation. Her case hung on the fact that she neither asked to see the script nor received it, and therefore had no obligation to him. For the second time that day, the courts came down on her side.

In 1965, she challenged seven newspapers for publishing photos of her that had been taken without her permission. The pictures were all shot through telephoto lenses while she was on private property, either at La Madrague or at Bazoches. 'I hate photos taken without my knowledge. I cannot tolerate telephoto lenses.'

The press retorted, 'Brigitte Bardot, probably the most photographed female in the world, is getting shy.'

Her answer to them is one she's often repeated. She likens herself to the Indians of the Amazon who hate having anyone photograph them because they believe that it robs them of a part of their soul. 'Some will say this is naive or primitive. Well, then,

262

I must be naive and primitive, since, for me, each photograph carries with it a portion of myself.'

The courts agreed with her, and awarded one franc in symbolic damages. She announced, 'I'm delighted,' while newspapermen in Paris avowed, 'She's just committed professional suicide.'

She had another double-date with justice in 1966.

In the morning session, her lawyer tried to evict a young man who was living in a studio apartment Bardot owned on the Rue Compagne-Premiere. He'd been there for 14 months, without paying any rent, and now she wanted him out. But he was refusing to leave. The courts invited him to find other accommodation.

In the afternoon session, she sued a cosmetics company for using a photo of her and Jeanne Moreau from the film *Viva Maria* to sell lipstick. The company in question had issued two shades of the product, one called Brigitte, the other called Jeanne. Their argument was that they'd run the campaign only after having secured proper permission from the film's producers. But Bardot's lawyer arrived in court with a copy of her contract for that film, which specifically carried a clause forbidding any such thing.

Anyway, she'd beaten everyone to the punch by registering the name Brigitte Bardot as a legal trademark on 17 January 1959. It protected her against any unauthorized use of her name, including any and all exploitation for 'perfumes, cosmetics, suntan lotions, soap, creams, toothpaste, rouge, make-up, beauty products and dolls.'

*   *   *

In 1981, Brigitte Bardot celebrated her 47th birthday by getting herself sued for slander.

There was a rumour running through St Tropez that a local florist – 70-year-old Mme Odette Giraud – had beaten her cat to death with a stick. When Bardot heard it, on 28 September 1981, she went to Mme Giraud's shop and demanded to know if it was true.

The florist told her, 'It's none of your business.'

Brigitte insisted it was her business and let fly with her wrath. 'You savagely killed your cat. You're a slut and a criminal.'

As Mme Giraud had not been the one to kill the cat, she took Bardot to court. It turns out to have been Mme Giraud's son who killed it because, he claimed, it had gone crazy. In fact, he believed he was doing the cat a favour by putting it out of its misery. That he'd crushed it with his feet, then tossed the cat's dead body into the rubbish bin didn't help win much sympathy for the Girauds.

The case was heard 17 months later, on 14 January 1983, in Draguignon, which is the county seat for the Var *departement*. While Mme Giraud did not bother coming to court, Brigitte was there.

She arrived in a white Range Rover, to be greeted by 50 photographers who pushed and shoved their way towards her to get a better shot. Accompanied by two lawyers, Bardot forced her way through the crowd.

Inside, the pandemonium continued.

As she took her place in the dock, wearing leather boots, tan velour jeans and an Indian knitted waistcoat, photographers yelled, 'BB, look here,' and 'Brigitte, this way,' and 'BB, how about a little smile.'

And all the time fans crammed into the courtroom, yelling, 'Brigitte, we're with you,' and 'Good for you, Brigitte.'

'Look this way.' Flashbulbs went off.

'Bravo Brigitte,' screamed a little old lady who queued most of the night to get a front row seat.

'Smile, BB, come on.' More flashbulbs.

Bardot turned her back to them, faced the wall and defiantly refused to play their game.

The judges took their place and the presiding magistrate screamed at the photographers to stop. 'Enough. No more pictures. Enough.'

'Come on BB.' They didn't stop. 'Brigitte, just one more.'

'Enough.' The judge continued banging his gavel. 'If you don't stop, I'll throw you all out of here.'

After a few minutes, the photographers stopped taking pictures.

But they refused to budge from the back of the room, where they continued to jostle for a better position.

Eventually there was enough quiet for the presiding magistrate to ask Bardot how she wanted to plead.

Jumping to her feet, she launched into a brief but angry monologue. 'I stand by what I said. I try to protect animals. I am fighting against the stupidity and cruelty of humans. I don't regret anything I've said. If people continue to act this way I will continue to speak up. You don't kill animals for any reason under those conditions. That cat, if it was mad, could have been put down correctly.'

The judge was clearly not immune to the power of her presence. 'So when you heard about this, you simply exploded.'

Bardot nodded.

'Everyone knows that this animal was cruelly killed,' the judge said, 'We understand your anger, Mme Bardot.'

Mme Giraud's lawyer jumped up. 'You don't regret anything?'

'Of course not,' Bardot snapped. 'If Mme Giraud had killed a child, no one would have reproached me for anything.'

The crowd in the courtroom applauded.

'Animals can't speak up for themselves,' she tried to say over the commotion. 'So I speak for them . . .'

The crowd applauded again.

Mme Giraud's lawyer argued that the death of the cat was not what this was all about. It was, instead, about Mme Bardot's quick tongue and misinformation. It was, instead, about the dignified reputation of a local businesswoman, which had been irreparably tarnished. 'To attack my client in such an unjustified manner is a repulsive blot on the reputation of Mme Bardot, which is also part of the reputation of France.'

It was only by chance, Mme Giraud's lawyer pointed out, that, in the face of such false accusations, his client had not taken her own life. 'Then there would have been a cadaver and Mme Bardot would have been responsible.'

On behalf of his client, he was asking the court for only 8,000 francs ($2,160) in actual damages, enough to pay her expenses. And, as a show of good faith, his client would settle for one franc, as a symbolic payment, to repair the moral harm Mme Bardot had done.

In response, Bardot's lawyers argued that what had taken place, the savage killing of a defenceless animal, was unconscionable. And that in reacting to such a heinous episode, Mme Bardot had in fact used the correct word – *salope*. Translated in English as 'slut', her lawyers then produced a dictionary definition of *salope*: 'A woman who has shown contempt for morals or generally accepted behaviour.' In this regard, the attorney claimed, Mme Bardot had not in the least defamed Mme Giraud. In fact, she had chosen her word with great accuracy.

The public, crammed into the courtroom, loved it. This was the best show in town.

And the press loved it too.

They wrote about how Brigitte had triumphed, even though the judge elected to delay a verdict in the case for 15 days. They wrote about how she couldn't lose. 'Such passion in defence of animals merits everything except a guilty verdict. Who could doubt for a moment the outcome of this case?' They wrote about how this wasn't just anybody in the dock, this was 'our last idol', and 'she's untouchable'.

It came as no surprise to anyone when, two weeks later, the decision went in Bardot's favour.

She was back on the offensive a month later when the satirical magazine *Hara-Kiri* published a photo-montage in February 1983 depicting a nude Bardot with a decrepit, cellulite-plagued body. She hit them for 50,000 francs ($8,000). The judge noted that she'd been a symbol of beauty all her life and felt that this photo-montage—which pretended to represent her but in reality did not – was malicious. He said, that because it might lead someone to believe she'd lost her finesse and grace, it was, therefore, dishonest.

For her 50th birthday, the Spanish magazine *Interview* published a feature with the cover line, 'Bardot Nude at the Seaside'.

Photos on half a dozen pages, in full colour, showed a less than flattering image of her, taken with a telephoto lens that could have been up to one-third of a mile away. Bardot, who was by now using the same lawyer Jacques Charrier had engaged to defend him in their divorce suit 20 years before – Gilles Dreyfus – went after the magazine, demanding 200,000 francs ($22,300) in damages.

Unflattering photos – long-lensed or not – constantly draw her indignation.

In September 1986, the editors of the magazine *Courier du Coeur* ran a photo-montage that they called 'The Incredible, Mysterious Photos'. It might well have been entitled, 'Whose Boobs Are These?'

They published half a dozen photos of a nude woman – careful to leave off her head – then wondered if their readers could identify her. Giving a hint or two, they suggested that the hips and thighs and chest on view might belong to Catherine Deneuve, Jeanne Moreau or Claudia Cardinale. But then again, they might not.

Bardot claimed the photos were of her, taken 30 years before, and that publication of them constituted an invasion of her privacy today. She ordered her faithful Dreyfus to sue for 500,000 francs ($55,750).

She attacked a British men's magazine for publishing a full-frontal nude photo of her without her permission, even though she'd posed for it and even though they'd bought it legitimately through a French picture agency.

She went after *Hara-Kiri* again when they published a photo of her that had been faked to show her with only one tooth. The headline read, '20 Years Ago I Had All My Teeth.'

That was more than enough to send in Dreyfus.

'For the entire world,' he said, 'Brigitte Bardot is a symbol

267

of beauty. This photo mutilated her, giving the impression of an old and ugly woman. The photo was retouched without her permission, and attacks her right to her own image.'

The magazine responded, 'We know BB has good teeth. She simply can't stand being 45 years old.' The courts ruled the photo did tarnish Bardot's image and awarded her nearly 25,000 francs ($6,210).

When another French magazine used a retouched photo of her as an old woman to advertise a miracle cure for wrinkles, she dispatched Dreyfus into battle and this time he came home with 45,000 francs ($11,180).

Any magazine or newspaper that uses telephoto-lensed photos of her, anywhere in the world, risks her outrage. Almost automatically, when she finds out about it, they receive a letter from her lawyers. And many of them have subsequently found themselves in court. For instance, in 1992, when the French magazine *Voici* published seven photos taken with long lenses while she was having lunch on a boat with her husband and some friends, including politician Jean-Marie Le Pen, Dreyfus swung into action, not only against *Voici*, but against two foreign publications – one Spanish, one Italian – for invasion of privacy. This time the bill for the offending photos came in at 250,000 francs ($62,100).

*   *   *

Not surprisingly, she has lost a few along the way.

Brigitte was found guilty in June 1989 of defamation for a remark she'd made the previous December on a television programme where she'd accused the staff of an animal refuge of mistreating their charges. She was fined 10,001 francs ($1,800). A week later, she was found guilty of defamation again, this time for having accused a noted medical researcher of being a torturer. She'd made public the fact that he cut the vocal chords of dogs used for experiments to keep them from barking. He sued Bardot and two magazines that published the word 'torturer' – and he was, bizarrely, awarded 4,000 francs ($720).

But, on the whole, her batting average is pretty high.

When a French eyeglass manufacturer produced, without her permission, a series of photos that were distributed to opticians, showing Bardot wearing glasses, she pursued them.

When a German furniture manufacturer produced a range of chairs with backs that resembled her lips, she slapped a $45,000 suit on them.

When a newspaper suggested that she'd stopped work in the middle of one of her films because she found three wrinkles on her face and immediately had her face lifted, she sued for 25,000 francs ($4,200).

She sued the revue *Minute* for 80,000 francs ($13,500) when they published articles suggesting that she was personally profiting from her campaign to save baby seals.

And she sued French journals *VSD*, *Jours de France*, *Ici Paris*, *France Dimanche* and *L'Union de Reims* when they published articles alluding to a suicide attempt that she claimed never happened.

Gilles Dreyfus, who has, to date, purportedly acted for Brigitte no fewer than 150 times over the past 15 years or so, even won a suit in January 1987 against a French author who'd labelled her 'a myth'. Bardot apparently objected to the word and won 60,000 francs ($8,250). It was odd because Brigitte had appeared happy with the generally benign tone of the book and, anyway, calling her a myth was hardly an original thought.

*   *   *

On two occasions, she has – rather uncharacteristically – allowed her emotions to involve her immediate family.

In the early 1970s, when she purchased a new apartment on the Boulevard Lannes, on the edge of the Bois de Boulogne, she decided to sell a two-bedroom flat that she'd owned for some time on the Rue Clement, in the 6th arrondissement, next to the St Germain des Prés market. The problem was that Mijanou was living there at the time with her husband Patrick Bauchau and their eight-year-old daughter, Camille.

To facilitate the sale, Brigitte proposed that the Bauchaus should move from the Rue Clement to her old flat on the Avenue Paul Doumer. She said that her sister's family was welcome to live there under the same conditions as in their current flat — that is, without paying rent — and could stay as long as they pleased. But Mijanou balked at the idea, claiming that Brigitte had given her the apartment ten years before as a wedding present. What's more, she'd grown very attached to the livelier 6th arrondissement, wasn't in the least interested in moving to the 16th arrondissement, and had plans to open a small shop nearby. It got a bit out of hand and, in a pique, Brigitte called in her lawyers. The case was referred to a judicial referee who, instead of making a decision, proclaimed a three-week cooling-off period. That gave the sisters enough time to sort out the problem among themselves and the Bauchaus did eventually move.

The second case surrounded the death of her mother, at the American Hospital in Neuilly-sur-Seine on Tuesday 1 August 1978. Toty was 66.

She'd been admitted to the hospital three days before — Saturday 29 July — and was operated on for an intestinal tumour on Monday afternoon. Brigitte had come to see Toty, who was still in intensive care, on Tuesday evening. Sometime around 7.20–7.30, her mother started complaining of chest pains. Brigitte later claimed her mother told her, 'I am going to die.'

In a panic, Brigitte tried to get help. But she couldn't find a doctor or an on-duty resident. The only person to come to her mother's aid was a nurse, who did nothing more than administer an electrocardiogram. According to Bardot, the nurse explained that a specialist would be coming on duty at 8 that evening.

Now Bardot's mother began asking for her own heart specialist.

At about 7.55, the surgeon who'd originally operated on Toty arrived. Bardot tried to make him understand that her mother's condition was worsening. The surgeon phoned Toty's doctor and asked him to come and see his patient, saying that she was apparently suffering from an irregular heartbeat.

That doctor later explained that he didn't sense any urgency in the surgeon's request.

Anne-Marie Mucel Bardot passed away a few minutes later.

On 16 December Bardot – still reeling with anger about her mother's death – sent a registered letter to the hospital's administrators, complaining that her mother hadn't been properly cared for and demanding an explanation. She said that when she had arrived at the hospital, it seemed deserted.

The administrators were forced to consider Bardot's comments because it is an offence under French law to fail to help someone in danger. But she would have had better luck arguing with a brick wall.

They claimed that a resident physician was on duty.

She argued, nobody could find him and that he wasn't there when her mother needed him.

They refuted her insinuation that they'd been at all negligent in their treatment of her mother and tried to write off the incident with the conclusion that Bardot had been under great strain because of her mother's death. They even went so far as to acknowledge, it is perfectly understandable.

That was not the answer she wanted to hear.

'When you lose your mother,' she said at the time, 'that's when you become an adult. When she's around, there's always an umbrella over your head to protect you, there are always a pair of arms you can snuggle into without offering an explanation. Even if at times she was judgemental, she was my mother. Now she's

271

gone. It's insupportable, unjust and yet the only great certainty in life is death.'

Furious with the hospital's attitude, she filed a suit, in the city of Nanterre, against an unnamed person for having failed to render proper assistance to a person in danger.

'The doctors did not do everything within their power to save her,' Bardot claimed, in explaining the action.

The hospital contested the action.

She never got much satisfaction out of it, but at least she had a chance to vent some of her anger and to make a few people around the hospital sit up and take notice.

* * *

Friends, ex-lovers, former employees and used car dealers are not immune either.

In 1960 she sued Alain Carré when he announced that he was publishing his memoirs after four years in her service. He'd taken the precaution of giving her a copy of his manuscript, asking for corrections and her comments. Her answer, four months later, was to send him packing in search of an attorney.

Oddly, Carre's ten-article series was a fairly tender portrait of his employer. However, she claimed it contained both untruths and unkind statements. He retorted that three months prior to Bardot's complaint, both she and her husband Jacques Charrier had expressed their satisfaction with the manuscript. Bardot cried foul and demanded that the manuscript be seized. The case was heard in July, in Paris. The judge ruled that the law did not permit him to seize a manuscript which had not yet been published. In essence, the courts cleared the way for publication.

After Carré, who'd been paid 1,000 francs ($204) a month by Bardot, was allegedly paid ten times that per instalment, another Bardot employee – a butler named Guido Albert – also decided to take up journalism. He wrote an article, which

272

Bardot was also unable to stop, about wild sexual abandon at La Madrague.

Trying to put a halt to such things, some former employees now say they were asked to sign a contract of silence, much like that demanded of everyone in the employ of the Queen of England. The French press had always suspected as much and once spitefully wondered how long it would take Bardot to ask her future lovers to agree to the same conditions.

A few years later, one of her maids decided what she'd seen and heard was far too interesting to keep to herself and so she sold her story to the tabloids. By the time it reached publication, it had been thoroughly embellished, padded out with great chunks of purely salacious fiction, because the market dictated that the dirtier it was, the more the tabloids would pay for it.

In 1985, she sued Sacha Distel after he wrote a kiss and tell autobiography. Distel claimed she often walked around in a sulk, was frequently bad tempered and was tight with her money. Besides insisting that there was never any food in her refrigerator, he said she frequently embarrassed him by stroking and kissing him in public and that, in the end, she was unfaithful to him. He said that when he came to see her one day, he found her getting dressed, with a man hiding in her bathroom. Furious, he broke a glass door and stormed out of her flat. He said that she then sent him a bill for the door. Bardot, who was 'shocked, hurt and disappointed' by a man she'd once loved, went after him for 150,000 francs ($36,270).

Five years later she went after Eddie Barclay, for the second time. He was in the midst of producing a video cassette about St Tropez and was putting clips of her in it.

She announced, 'I will not permit anyone to use my personality, my name, my voice or my image without my permission. I have not yet fallen into the public domain. I am opposed to all this abuse and will continue to oppose it.'

What particularly annoyed her was that Barclay – 'who wrongly pretends to be my friend!' – never even bothered to phone her to ask her permission to use the footage of her.

Barclay confides, 'Dreyfus gets her 10,000 francs or 20,000 francs or 50,000 francs whenever she finds something in the papers about her that she doesn't like. There are people who believe she lives on that.'

She fought fashion designer Paco Rabanne in 1968 after posing for a photo spread in Vogue wearing a brown metallic Rabanne dress. Once the shoot was finished, she took the dress home. Rabanne asked her please to return it as he'd already sold it to someone else. When it became obvious that she intended to keep it, Rabanne sent her a bill for 2,400 francs ($500) plus 15 per cent value added tax.

'I am not making any presents of my work to Madame Bardot,' he declared. 'I know of her reputation. I know that she never pays the people who supply her with things. But with me it's not the same thing.'

Believing that she had made a present of her work – and without being so rude as to cast aspersions on his reputation – Bardot simply sent Rabanne a bill for her modelling fees – 2,400 francs plus 15 per cent value added tax.

These days Rabanne seems too embarrassed to discuss it. The best his spokesman could come up with was, 'It's polemic'.

A few months later she took on the might of Mssrs Rolls and Royce.

In 1965, she'd bought a second-hand Rolls – the same 1958 model that the Queen of England was riding in at the time – for 35,000 francs ($7,115). Four years later the heater packed up so she took it to the Rolls concessionaires in Paris and asked them to repair it.

They not only fixed her heater, they billed her for 121 hours of labour, which included extensive body work, and the total came up 11,000 francs ($2,315). When Brigitte refused to pay it, the garage refused to return the car to her.

She complained directly to Rolls-Royce in London. The French concessionaires then sued her for one franc damages, saying that going over their heads was prejudicial to them. Carrying the matter into the realm of utter silliness, their lawyers even claimed, 'Madame Bardot shows herself to be very thrifty. But if she is no longer rolling in money, she should not be rolling along in a Rolls.'

Bardot's attorney retorted, 'Rolls-Royce wants to be the height of fashion of the automobile business but they comport themselves like common off-the-peg traders.'

Eventually she got rid of her Rolls, using the excuse that it was 'a bloke's car'.

In the middle of all this, she also sued her Vava.

In 1986, a full decade after publishing his first autobiography, *Memoirs of the Devil*, Roger Vadim decided to tell the story of his life with three of the most beautiful women in the world, and wrote *Bardot, Deneuve, Fonda*. He'd sent a copy of the manuscript to Jane Fonda, who took a typically American attitude and shrugged it all off, but Catherine Deneuve and Brigitte Bardot were hardly so nonchalant.

In unison, both summoned Dreyfus.

'It's very strange,' notes Vadim. 'Brigitte doesn't stop suing people. She sues everyone. She wasn't like this when I was with her.'

He sometimes wonders if it's Gilles Dreyfus who points out the opportunities to her. Dreyfus also represented Deneuve, and Vadim can just imagine how he might have told Brigitte that Catherine was suing and how Brigitte might have figured that sounded like a good idea, so she joined in.

When the judgment was handed down, he says, although he had to pay them each 30,000 francs ($3,350), he wasn't required to make any changes. 'Not so much as a comma.'

He sees Dreyfus as an intelligent man who would easily recognize an occasion to sue for his clients. And because whatever he wins for them is tax free, it is understandable that his clients would be more than happy to take their chances.

Vadim has also heard the rumour that Brigitte lives off those lawsuits, but is fast to discount it. 'No, I don't think there's any truth in that. I don't think Brigitte is very rich, she doesn't have a great fortune, but then she isn't poor either. She certainly doesn't need to work, the proof being that she doesn't work. And even if she's earned a million francs (£100,000) over the past ten years, it's not much when you compare it with what she used to earn. So no, I don't think she's gone into the lawsuit business to earn a living. Although, it's true what Brigitte has always said, there's no such thing as a small profit.'

*   *   *

Her most bizarre legal battle – at least, to date – has got to be the one over a donkey's testicles.

Jean Pierre Manivet is a tall, white-haired man with a thin white moustache. A retired Lyonnais industrialist, now in his early 70s, Manivet never met Brigitte Bardot. But as her neighbour in St Tropez – he has a house on the slope that leads down to La Garrigue – he'd occasionally seen her swimming at the beach. There had also been times in the past when he found a stray cat or dog and took it to the front gate of La Garrigue to return it to her gardener.

In April 1989, he bought a donkey named Charly from an antique dealer in town for 4,000 francs ($650). His intention was to keep the animal over the summer when he was in St Tropez, but to leave Charly with the antique dealer over the winter. Manivet had agreed to pay for Charly's food, while the antique dealer agreed to look after Charly for free, in exchange for servicing her female donkey. But that would require Charly to be capable of such things.

One afternoon, the following month, Manivet happened to spot Brigitte's friend Mylene de Muylder walking some of Bardot's dogs along the street past his house. As he was planning to go away for a few days, the thought dawned on him that he might be able to leave Charly with Bardot. So he politely asked Mylene if Mme Bardot would look after Charly. Mylene explained, that because Brigitte had so many animals at La Garrigue, she wasn't normally open to the idea of taking in any new ones. However, she promised to ask.

A day or so later, Mylene returned to tell Manivet's gardener that Brigitte would do it.

Normally, Manivet says, he would have taken Charly to a small corral at the other end of the beach and left him there. 'But this was also the chance to meet my famous neighbour.'

So a few days before he departed for Lyons, Manivet asked his gardener, Gilbert, to go to La Garrigue to tell Mme Bardot that he'd bring the donkey by. He rang the bell at the gate but no one answered. So Gilbert located a friend of Bardot's in the village who promised to get in touch with her. Manivet claims that friend rang Gilbert the same evening to say, everything is all right but Brigitte wants to know if the donkey is 'complete'. In other words, Manivet explains, 'She wanted to know if Charly had already been castrated.'

This part of the story has always been denied by Brigitte.

Manivet and Gilbert left Charly at La Garrigue with Bardot's caretaker, on Sunday 21 May.

'I went on my trip thinking I'd done the right thing,' Manivet says. 'After all, who better than her to look after an animal? I even sent her a little note to say thanks and signed it Charly.'

A fortnight later, Gilbert phoned Manivet in Lyons to say that he'd bumped into Brigitte's gardener who told him, 'She's castrated Monsieur Manivet's donkey.'

According to Manivet, her gardener told Gilbert that he'd personally tried to intervene to stop Bardot from taking such a drastic step, but that Brigitte didn't want to know. He said that she claimed she was within her rights to do whatever she wanted to on her property.

But this does not correspond with Bardot's version of events.

Where the stories meet is that Charly turned out to be a less than suitable house guest. As soon as he moved in, to Brigitte's horror, Charly began making passes at her 32-year-old mare, Duchesse, whom she'd saved from the slaughterhouse. Greedy sod that he was, Charly also made passes at her donkey, Mimosa, who happened to be in heat.

Convinced that much animal suffering is in part due to animal overpopulation, she is a strong advocate of sterilization for pets, so she rang her vet on Thursday 25 May.

Dr Jacques Aubertin, who is based in nearby Ste Maxime, arrived at La Garrigue a few hours later and supposedly warned her that, if Charly got Duchesse pregnant, the old mare would die. As she was unable to keep the animals separated and equally unable to reach Charly's owner, she insists she had no other choice but to have Charly neutered.

Manivet finds it an odd claim to make. 'Have you ever seen a donkey chase an old mare when there's a young female donkey in heat nearby? And how could a veterinarian say that Charly posed a mortal danger to Duchesse when he must have known that a mare over the age of 30 hasn't been fertile for many years. Anyway, if Charly was too active, and I can't deny that Charly would naturally run after Mimosa, the worst thing that could have happened was that Charly would have got her pregnant and, when you love animals, there's nothing more adorable than a baby donkey. I would have thought she'd have been thrilled.'

When Manivet phoned Aubertin to ask on what grounds he'd taken the action, feeling that any responsible vet should have asked questions – 'At least he might have wondered whether or not the donkey belonged to his client' – Aubertin told him he didn't want to discuss 'this masquerade'.

Later Aubertin would claim that it wasn't his business to ask whether or not she owned the donkey. And these days he sees off enquiries with the rather astonishing excuse, 'I have to respect the medical secrecy of my client.'

Accepting the mystifying possibility that medical secrecy could exist when your client is a donkey, Aubertin refuses to say why, for instance, he didn't give Charly a shot to calm him down, or at least recommend that Charly simply be separated from Duchesse and Mimosa.

Anyway, the moment Manivet heard the news, he returned to St Tropez and went to La Garrigue to reclaim the unquestionably 'incomplete' Charly. But when he got there he was informed that Madame Bardot was not in residence, that she wouldn't be back until late September and that, unfortunately, she'd left instructions not to release the donkey to anyone without her permission.

When Manivet enquired on what grounds she was holding his donkey, her gardener said it was because she wanted to be sure that Monsieur Manivet treated his animals well.

Already miffed that poor Charly's bray was now a few octaves higher and that no one had ever bothered apologizing to him for what had happened, he was utterly speechless that she would now try to keep him from taking his own animal home. He demanded an apology. When none was forthcoming, he rang his attorney, had a bailiff fetch Charly, then filed a suit against Bardot.

As there is no distinction in French law between an animal and any other sort of property, the basis of his claim was that he'd asked her to take care of an object that belonged to him and, after agreeing to do that, she had not returned it to him intact. He sought 4,500 francs ($730) in material damages for the castration and 10,000 francs ($1,620) in moral damages.

The case was heard in St Tropez on 23 October 1989.

Manivet's lawyer agreed that Charly had been randy – the French term is '*chaud lapin*' or hot rabbit – but that he'd been forced to pay a cruel price for his passion. 'This affair amounts, after all, to the theft of family jewels in a village where we no longer count such things.'

Unable to attend, Brigitte wrote a letter to the judge, on Bardot Foundation stationery and in her own hand, dated 16 October. She apologized that she could not attend the hearing because she had to be in Paris to prepare a television show on animal rights. Then she explained how shocked she was when Manivet had asked to take back Charly.

'Like all the animals that are brought to me, I thought this little being' – referring to a donkey who weighs 250 kilos – 'was mine. I never saw or heard of M. Manivet, or his caretaker, and no one ever approached me to look after the animal. My good faith is evident. I *never* look after animals for other people because I become attached to them.'

She said that she castrated Charly – whom she'd renamed Perichole – only after he became aggressive with Mimosa and Duchesse. 'I am sorry that this affair has turned into something ridiculous, sorry not to be able to see Perichole again and sorry that French justice is mixed up in all of this.'

When the ruling came down, it was an unambiguous home-town decision. The local judge decided there was no evidence to prove Manivet had made it known to her that he was Charly's owner, that she had believed she was the owner and, in so believing, she was entitled to act as she did. Therefore, Manivet had no claim. What's more, the judge felt, Manivet had caused moral harm to Bardot's reputation as an animal rights activist and fined him 20,000 francs ($3,440).

Manivet was stupefied. 'He fined me! He felt that my action put into question Madame Bardot's personal reputation and her good work as an animal rights activist. It's the world turned upside down.'

So Manivet appealed.

On 1 October 1992, the case was heard in the Court of Appeal in Aix-en-Provence. They overturned Manivet's fine. But they did not overturn the original judgment. This court agreed that there was no proof Madame Bardot knew Charly was not a stray and actually belonged to Monsieur Manivet. Apparently, in French law, an object of less than 5,000 francs ($860) in value, left in someone's care, is deposited at the owner's risk, unless he has first secured a receipt for the object. No receipt, and the absence of any witnesses to testify to the contrary, meant the lower court was correct in ruling that Manivet had no case.

Shaking his head in total disbelief, Manivet wants to know, 'How could I have gone to her and said, you've been kind enough to keep my donkey for the next two or three weeks, now would you mind giving me a receipt?'

Mail flooded in to everyone involved with the case. One postcard arrived at the town hall in St Tropez with the message, 'Brigitte prevents me from making "cric-crac" – she made me "cric and crac".'

Another, bearing the photo of a donkey, read, 'Here we're not in pieces. Life is beautiful. Not like Charly in St Tropez.'

A third said, simply, 'Poor Charlot, now Charlette.'

During the appeal hearing, the judge made reference to the mythical character of the donkey. Which is how Manivet now thinks of this case.

'It was all about the meeting of two unequal myths. All about the mythical quality of the donkey versus the mythical quality of Madame Bardot. Frankly, if I had to choose whether to spend eternity in heaven with Charly or with Brigitte Bardot, I wouldn't hesitate to pick the donkey.'

Chapter Fourteen

SECRET LADY

Friends arrived at La Madrague for dinner one evening, with dinner. They'd brought 10 absolutely beautiful Mediterranean *langoustes* – spiny lobsters.

Of course, the lobsters were all still very much alive.

The moment Brigitte saw that, she yelped, castigated her friends for being so cruel to animals, grabbed the lobsters, ran to the beach and threw them all back into the sea.

*　　*　　*

When Brigitte and Jacques Charrier divorced in 1962, custody of two-year-old Nicholas went to his father. The next time the boy and his mother spent any real time together was when he was seven. During those five years, when Nicholas asked about his real mother he was told that she was very busy with her films and that she was travelling.

Eventually Charrier remarried. He and his wife raised Bardot's only child alongside theirs, in the countryside, not far from Bazoches.

'Babies change women,' Jacques Charrier says. 'There's something about having a baby that brings out all sorts of natural instincts in them. But having a baby didn't change Brigitte. It's incredible. There were a few moments when she was maternal, but it didn't last very long.'

Vadim first met Nicolas when he was only a few days old.

'It's never been a secret that Brigitte doesn't like children and somehow coming to grips with the fact that she now had one was not easy for her. I went to see her right after the baby was born. She was leaning over Nicolas's crib, wearing a big hat. The baby was screaming. I suppose he was afraid of the hat. But she kept saying to me, he won't stop crying because he hates me.'

There was always, it seems, a great deal of misunderstanding when it came to this mother–son relationship.

When the boy was just 12, he went to St Tropez to see her – in those days he idolized her – but because all sorts of friends were staying at La Madrague, there wasn't room for him. So Jacques Charrier made arrangements for him to stay with Vadim and his wife, Catherine Schnell.

The next morning, when a chauffeur came to pick up Nicolas, the boy was all excited. His mother gave him a guitar lesson and they went out on a boat for a while. Then she explained to him that she would have loved it if he could have stayed for dinner but it was impossible because a whole bunch of her friends were coming.

He was back at Vadim's house by six, in tears.

In 1983, Brigitte tried to explain why she didn't raise Nicolas. 'I wasn't able to take care of myself, so how could I raise a baby? I did not feel capable. I needed a mother, not a child. I needed a shoulder to lean on, roots. I could not be those roots on my own because I'd been uprooted, unbalanced, lost in a crazy, mad world. I could not cling on to a little child who'd just been born. What would I have shown that child? The life of a mad woman, the life I'd led, in tears all the time, going out all over the place with anyone who came along?'

She said that she and Nicolas were both trying to re-establish a relationship. 'When he was small I found it strange having a child. I could not stand what was happening to me. I was always rather astonished and never really happy.' Now she saw him as grown up, 'solid, upright, healthy and very sweet'.

It wasn't to last, although Christine Gouze-Renal, who happens to be Nicolas's godmother, notes that there have been several times over the years when Brigitte tried to make everything all right.

'When he was 18, it seemed as if Brigitte was bringing him into her life, looking to make amends and rediscover her son. She tried to excuse herself, tried to make her son understand what kind of life she'd led, how she'd been carried away with this adventure that she called her life, how it all happened to her when she was his age and how she wasn't able to cope with every part of it. She begged him to forgive her. And, of course, he did. He told her he understood and wanted her to know that if it had happened to him at the same age, he might not have been able to cope with it either. It was very poignant.'

But it seems they couldn't keep their relationships going for more than a few months at a time. 'Then Brigitte was off again, back to being herself, rejecting him.'

Mijanou is very defensive of her sister and quick to point out that perhaps one of the reasons Brigitte couldn't raise her son was because of the agonizing conditions she'd been subjected to during her pregnancy.

'She had her child under exceptionally torturous circumstances. She wasn't happy. She wasn't feeling good about herself. Perhaps if she'd had her child under other circumstances, her relationship with Nicolas would have been different. She had to fill the need inside herself first and when she couldn't do that, there wasn't anything to give to Nicolas.'

She admits there's been a lot of hurt, although in recent years, Mijanou says, they've tried to put their relationship together. 'The truth is that Brigitte didn't so much abandon her son as agree with the boy's father that the child shouldn't be raised in the glare of the media, that Nicolas should have a normal childhood and not be exposed to the craziness of her world. Jacques Charrier also wanted his son to be raised as a normal child and not as a museum piece called Brigitte Bardot's son. She understood that and agreed.'

Olga Horstig-Primuz, like Mijanou, is equally defensive of Brigitte. 'She was more honest about it than many women. She admitted she wasn't capable of raising Nicolas and allowed Jacques to do it. It would have been dishonest of her to try to raise him. I'm afraid I know lots of other women who weren't honest enough to admit their failings, raised their children in spite of that and their children paid for it, just the same.'

Other people are not so kind. Some suggest that the conflict stems from the fact that, in French, 'BB' is pronounced '*bébé*,' which means baby. That somewhere in the depths of her psyche she would wonder, who is this '*bébé*,' when I am supposed to be 'BB'?

Nicolas studied economics at university in Paris, learned to play the piano – he's composed and arranged music – and, when he was 22, got a job modelling for Pierre Cardin. At six foot one, with parents as handsome as his, it's no wonder that he's a very good-looking man.

It was during his modelling days that he met a Norwegian girl who was also modelling in Paris, Anne-line Bjerkan, a diplomat's daughter, a year and a half younger than him. The couple were married in 1984 and moved to Oslo where he could live as Nicolas Charrier and not forever be referred to as Brigitte Bardot's son. He's in the computer business. They have two young daughters. And, while Anne-line speaks Norwegian to the children, she and Nicolas speak French together.

Brigitte had helped him buy his apartment in Paris and, on other occasions, tried to be there for him when he needed something. But the relationship had been so badly strained over the years, it was difficult to get through the bitterness on both sides. She, for instance, was hurt when Nicolas got married without telling her, without inviting her to the wedding. Then, too, he knew enough by now that he wanted to avoid the media circus that would have followed her to his wedding. At least during the early years of his marriage, contact between them was, at best, sporadic.

By 1989, Bardot still had not met her daughter-in-law. She said she was waiting for Nicolas to make the first move. As a matter of fact, she seemed genuinely miffed when she told friends that Nicolas didn't want to have anything to do with her. 'He hides himself away from me and the rest of the world somewhere in Scandinavia.'

Nicolas response was simply, 'My mother loves baby seals and I love a Norwegian.'

A few years later, when Nicolas sent Brigitte a picture of their first daughter, she sent it back.

Mijanou's daughter, Camille Bauchau, spent some time at La Madrague with her aunt when she was 16. That summer Nicolas was there too. He was 19. The cousins hung out together and he tried to teach her how to windsurf. At one point, Camille fell off the board, and landed in the algae bed, sitting there in 10 inches of water.

Brigitte, who'd been watching her son and niece from the shore, saw Camille fall, raced onto the small wooden dock in front of her beach and tried to get the attention of all the other windsurfers who were going back and forth in front of La Madrague. She signalled to them, as if she was hitchhiking, and yelled, 'Please go over there and save my niece.'

When the windsurfers realized it was Brigitte Bardot asking them to be a hero, Camille was saved by two dozen young men.

'Nicolas is a very sweet man,' Camille says. 'And it's sad that he and his mother have missed so many years when they could have spent time together. My aunt was very upset that Nicolas hadn't told her he was married. And she was upset when he didn't tell her about the birth of his first daughter, her first grandchild. But I think they're putting that behind them now.'

The breakthrough, if that's what it is, might have come in August 1992 when Brigitte and the man who would be her fourth husband went to Oslo.

Bernard d'Ormale says he felt that mother and son should get to know each other and encouraged the visit.

It was the first time Brigitte and Nicolas had seen each other in nearly ten years. It was also the first time Brigitte had met her granddaughters. So maybe it is a breakthrough because, the following summer, Nicolas, Anne-line and their two girls – Anna-Camilla and Thea-Josephine – came to Bazoches to spend a few weeks with Brigitte and Bernard.

*   *   *

Over the years, Brigitte turned down all sorts of big studio contracts because she didn't want to go to Hollywood. She was offered a fortune to play the lead in the film *The Story of O*. She refused. She was offered another fortune to work with Peter Sellers in *The Pink Panther*. She refused. The producers of *The Thomas Crown Affair* offered her nearly $500,000 to play the Faye Dunaway role with Steve McQueen. And she refused.

If she were a star today she could probably command upwards of $3 million. To draw her out of retirement, she might be able to command two or three times that. But it isn't going to happen. She believes that the cinema took the best of her and tossed it onto a large screen, like fodder for the public. She doesn't, even for an instant, miss anything about it. 'When I turn a page in life, it's forever. Before I turn a page, I think about it. But when I turn the page, that's it.'

Since her retirement, she has consistently refused to discuss her cinema career, and declines any and all requests to do so. Her excuse has always been, 'I never think about the cinema. Never. Those days are over. I live for the present.'

What's more, she's famous for saying, 'I never regret anything. It sometimes happens that I feel some remorse, but never regrets.'

Her answer was a firm no to a come-back film with Marlon Brando – whom she'd known and apparently liked when she and Vadim were first married – for which she was offered $2 million. And she supplied an equally firm no to an American producer who hoped to entice her back into films with a handsome offer to play Elena Ceauşescu, wife of the late Romanian dictator.

Another producer bandied her name about – and also talked of a $2 million fee – for a couple of weeks' work, playing the grandmother in *Three Men and a Little Lady*. But she was obstinate and wouldn't even discuss it.

Just after she retired, she picked up a handsome fee doing an ad for a men's toiletry company. In 1973, when her country asked her to help promote tourism for France, she lent her name and face to that campaign. And a few years ago, she allowed a photo of herself – taken by Philippe Halsman for his book *Jump* – to be used in a London-based campaign for Air France.

The British ad agency, Leagas-Shafron-Davis-Chick-Ayer wrote to her, asking if they could use the photo. To everyone's surprise, she said yes. She liked the picture – it depicted her beautifully – and also Air France wasn't asking her to endorse the airline. It was more that they wanted to represent her as one of the great symbols of France.

The agency sent her a mock-up, showing her what they intended to do, and offered, in lieu of a fee, to make a donation to the Brigitte Bardot Foundation. And, they admit to their surprise, they received a letter back granting them permission.

But those were all one-offs. Any attempts to lure her back into films continue to be met with a very resolute, no. It turns out to be difficult enough just to get her to go to see a movie. She watches them occasionally on television – and sometimes even sits through bits of her own when they show up – but she doesn't go to cinemas.

'What I look for in films is a little dream, some beauty. I hate vulgarity and I am horrified by violence,' she's noted. 'And when I see myself in a film, which is rare, I think I'm looking at someone else, someone who might look like me, someone who might be my daughter.'

In 1988, there was a major retrospective of her films in Paris. Entitled 'Images of a Myth', 22 films were shown, alongside an important exhibition of photos, posters and memorabilia. For many people, it was the first chance they'd really had to see her films in a cinema. For Bardot, it was a reminder of that other life. Constantly asked, will you ever make another movie again, she grew cross, saying that the cinema never pleased her and that when she made movies she was already bored with them.

At that point, not having made any films for 16 years, she lashed out, 'Just imagine to what point I'm interested in them now. To be very frank, I find that it's a job for idiots. I don't give a damn about movies.'

What's more, she told *Paris-Match* in no uncertain terms, 'There is no question whatsoever that I would go back to making films again, under any condition. To show my face no longer interests me. In any case, don't you think I've shown it enough?'

Just before the retrospective opened, she was invited to a private showing of *La Verité* and, not having seen it for nearly 30 years, she went. She said, of all her films, that was probably her favourite. But that's as far as they could draw her back into the past.

A year later, American film and theatrical producer Allan Carr felt it would be a terrific coup to get Brigitte Bardot as a guest presenter for the Oscar Awards in 1989. Originally he hoped to bring her to Hollywood. As a contingency plan, if she didn't want to go to the States, or her schedule was such that she couldn't afford the time, he figured there was always the possibility of a live satellite pick-up from Paris.

The trick was to get her on the show.

So he contacted her through a public relations woman in France and asked if she'd do it. Much to everyone's delight, the answer came back, yes. However, there were conditions. To secure her participation, Bardot insisted, furs would have to be banned from the evening – no one wearing furs could be permitted into the theatre – and then she would have to be given a few minutes of air-time to make a plea for animal rights.

Banning furs wouldn't necessarily be a problem. But Carr, together with the Academy of Motion Picture Arts and Sciences, had their doubts about allowing her to turn the ceremony into a forum for personal causes.

That sort of thing had happened in the past, most memorably the evening, several years before, when Marlon Brando made an impassioned defence of the rights of American Indians.

However, that wasn't something the Academy wanted to encourage. They felt that agreeing to Bardot's conditions might set a dangerous precedent. So Carr explained that such a speech would not be appropriate and Bardot responded, in that case, she was otherwise unavailable.

Carr recalls, 'It was a legitimate offer and a quick response' – although, by the time the press got a hold of the story, it was anything but. It was a 'walk out', they wrote. And described how Bardot had quit 'after a cat fight with the organizers'.

These days, the only connection she maintains with show business is the Brigitte Bardot International Award, given annually in Hollywood as part of the Genesis Awards by the Ark Trust.

President of the trust, actress Gretchen Wyler, approached Brigitte in 1992, asking if she would lend her name to honour a film dedicated to animals. Brigitte accepted on two conditions: that the award be given only to film-makers living outside the United States who have accomplished some remarkable strides via the major media that raise public consciousness of animal abuse and exploitation; and that she would always be advised before any award winner was finally selected so that she could have final approval.

The first award, in 1993, was made to a Moscow-based television news magazine programme that featured a major report on the Centre for the Ethical Treatment of Animals, the first animals rights' organization in Russia.

In a letter to Brigitte, Wyler asked if she would accept the Ark Trust's invitation to present the award herself. But that was a bit too much for her. Her response was the same when her husband tried to talk her into setting up a major fund-raising dinner for her own Foundation. 'Maybe, just maybe, if I could go dressed the way I always dress' – that means, in jeans and a sweater – 'and present an award or make a little speech and not have to do anything else, not have to have dinner with people or do my hair or meet people . . .'

Now she pauses, thinks about it, then shakes her head. 'No, maybe not. I don't care to put on airs for a bunch of people I don't know. I don't care to do that sort of thing any more.'

* * *

The sudden death of actress Romy Schneider in 1982 at the age of 44 was a great shock to many of Brigitte's closest friends. The German actress was reported to be the victim of a suicide. Except some people close to her say she never really intended to commit suicide. They say she was drinking and took some pills and the combination of drugs and alcohol killed her. It stunned Bardot's friends because they'd been worried for years that such a thing could happen to her.

Brigitte is very scared of dying, one of them notes, and she thinks about death a lot. But that's nothing new. Vadim noticed that as early as 1953.

'Death stops the clock,' he says she used to tell him. She would say things like, 'Death is the only banker who gets rich as he loses his capital.' And a few years later she confessed to him, 'Death drives me crazy. I sometimes feel like messing up his plans and arriving early, without warning, just to infuriate him, so that I can say, I got the best of you.'

Because of her suicide attempts, some people see her as a

victim of love or a martyr to success. But here Vadim has a different view.

'I see her more as someone who's devoured those she's loved. And I have to say that, when she was devouring, she was at her most beautiful.' Here he laughs. 'You understand, I trust, that being devoured by Brigitte is a unique culinary experience.'

In October 1983, shortly after she broke up with Allain Bougrain-Dubourg – and just about a week after her 49th birthday – Brigitte's gardener found her dazed, in the sea, late at night. She wound up at the Oasis Clinic in Gassin. Friends insisted she'd just been over-tired.

Two months later, Allain Bougrain-Dubourg produced a series of television shows with her.

He says, 'At first she didn't want to do it. And then, even when she'd agreed, it was still a delicate operation. She hates filming and she particularly detests all the paraphernalia that goes with it. So we used the very minimum of technicians, sound equipment and lights so as not to upset her. We had no make-up people, no hairdressers, no script.'

Some mornings, she'd see the crew arriving and she'd hide. More than once, the idea of going before the cameras made her physically ill. Yet she did it. And even if she didn't look at any of it until the day before it was shown on French television, and even if it is, in a way, a slightly soft-focus version of her life, it remains memorable for some of the sound bites:

On the cinema: 'I've given enough, good bye and thank you.'

On age: 'I don't see old age coming with anxiety or serenity. I just see it arriving. I won't have my skin stretched. I never use face cream. It's not amusing to watch oneself wrinkle, but with what I do now, it doesn't matter.'

On her retirement: 'If I had continued, the end would have been ugly because it's a rotten milieu.'

On love scenes in movies: 'I eventually became so uncomfortable I refused to address other actors during my most passionate scenes and insisted on staring at and speaking to a piece of cardboard instead. That way I could say what I had to say without being ashamed, whereas if I looked someone in the eye I froze. I was frightened.'

On animals: 'Sometimes I think it's impossible to keep on living in such a horrible world. But I won't have been useless on earth if I succeed in doing something for animals. My life is entirely devoted to them. They give me a reason to look forward.'

On romance: 'I think you wait for love all your life. Or you get blasé about it and that's unbearable. I wait for love, find it, take it, lose it. It goes away, it'll come back again.'

On her name: 'In the old days it didn't stand for anything positive. A movie star who made films, got married several times, got photographed. Now, more and more, people help me because I'm not the same woman.'

In the three days that followed the show, Bardot received 10,000 letters.

* * *

Alone and lonely, in 1986 she admitted to a friend in St Tropez, 'Someday I'd like to get married again. I failed the first few times, maybe because I wasn't ready. I want someone intelligent, good, who understands me, maybe a little wild but definitely funny.'

She said, 'Now that the entire world is getting divorced, I want the opposite, a real marriage.'

She believed she was still capable of abandoning everything for someone. 'Men only want to sleep with me. I'm not interested in that anymore. I want someone for me.'

But then, in the same breath, she advised, 'You can never count on a man.'

Her problem is simple, that friend in St Tropez believes. 'She had everything too young. Fame. Wealth. Hoards of men. Great beauty. International acclaim. Today she focuses on animals because they love her totally for herself and that's the one thing she's never had from humans.'

Brigitte once said pretty much the same thing to André Pousse. She told him, 'To find someone to sleep with is easy. I have more choice than I could ever make. But to find someone to live with me, why should that be so difficult?'

Knowing her as well as he did, Pousse claims that the usual image of her as a man-hunter is altogether untrue. 'She certainly has had her share of men, but most of her relationships lasted for a time. The thing about her is that there are more people who claim to have slept with her than actually spent the night with her. And then she often chose the wrong men. I think Gunter Sachs was probably the only man who could have been a match for her. But even he was little more than her Prince Consort. They'd arrive somewhere and everyone would look at her. She was the star. And living with a star can be very difficult.'

Of course, he says, the truly special one is Vadim, who will always have a place in her life. But Pousse isn't sure it's quite the same place that most people think.

'I met her just after she split up with Vadim. And I contend that, even if Bardot had never met Vadim, she would have had a great career anyway. It might have taken her a little longer but she had something very special and it would have come out eventually. Bardot was always Bardot. The thing about Vadim was, in those days, he was always interested in the sensational. I wouldn't say he was without scruples, but he was certainly interested in what people could do for him.'

Pousse sees her now as someone who succeeded in life as an actress but not necessarily as a woman who succeeded in life when looking for love.

'There's no doubt but that she could have had a much more brilliant career if she'd really wanted that. She could have gone further. But the rest of her life has hardly been a success. Too many men were probably afraid of her, afraid to become Monsieur Bardot, afraid of being totally submerged by a star of that magnitude and a woman with such a strong personality. And now, I don't know. In those days she loved to be with friends, to play games. These days she's another person. She's turned into a fortress. She doesn't want to see anyone. Possibly her deception quota had just filled up and her faith in the human race simply snapped off. In the end, animals can't replace people.'

* * *

Nearly ten years after they were divorced, she started getting messages that Gunter Sachs was trying to get in touch with her. She didn't return his calls, not because she didn't particularly want to speak to Gunter, but because she didn't want to speak to anyone from those years.

Yet he seemed insistent, and each time her housekeeper said, 'Madame is not in,' he dutifully promised to ring back. Eventually he wore her down and got her on the phone. He explained that he was calling because he wanted her to invite him for tea.

Brigitte has never been one to step back into the past, and except for Vadim, whom she used to see often, ex-lovers and ex-husbands were just that – ex. But Sachs wouldn't let her off the hook and so she gave in. She told him yes, fine, he could come for tea.

A few days later, at the appointed time, he showed up at La Madrague with his wife Mirja.

Although Brigitte was hospitable, she was slightly confused about his visit – why should he ring her after all this time? – and couldn't understand what this was all about.

The three made small-talk for a while, until Gunter handed her a tiny box.

She asked him what it was.

He said he'd just sold one of his businesses for a lot of money and had decided he would give a present to all the women who'd been nice to him. 'You never asked for alimony when we were divorced, so I want you to have this.'

At first she refused it. But he persisted. When she opened the box, what she found inside was an 8.76 carat, exceptional, white grade D, marquise-shaped diamond ring.

Flustered, she said she didn't want it. She said she couldn't keep it. She said he had to take it back.

Gunter declined to take it back. He wanted her to have it because he wanted to show her that, in his own way, he still cared.

So she accepted it.

And nearly ten years after that, when she needed to raise money for her Foundation, the ring Gunter gave her was the focal point of the auction, the single most beautiful object for sale.

*   *   *

In the early 1980s, while on a visit to Provence, Bardot discovered a lump in her breast. She had it removed at the Paul Brousse Hospital in Villejuif, near Paris, and the operation was followed by some radiation treatment that left her exhausted. Family and a few very close friends knew about it, but she never discussed it with anyone else, and she managed to keep it out of the papers.

Although, she was now telling friends who did not know about her operation, 'It's not only the end of youth which gets me. It's the beginning of all the problems with one's health.'

Her battle with breast cancer, now won, was not revealed until six years later. Brigitte heard that the German actor René Colldenhoff had been stricken with Parkinson's Disease and, very much out of the blue, she wrote him a letter.

She wanted to encourage him and she did that by revealing her secret. 'I have beaten it,' she wrote. 'I had an operation and came through, despite the agony.'

A few years later, Mijanou called Brigitte to say that her doctors had found a lump in her breast, were worried that it might be cancerous and said she would be going into hospital for three days of tests.

Brigitte's immediate response was, 'I'm on my way.'

She told her kid sister to get a room in the clinic with two beds, and, when Mijanou moved in, Brigitte moved in too. She installed herself in Mijanou's hospital room and spent those three days there with her.

Thankfully, the problem wasn't cancerous. Still, Mijanou's eyes redden as she tells the story. 'We were like little kids.'

Equally touching, Brigitte was there for her a couple of years ago when Mijanou was injured by two of her own dogs. They'd started to fight and Mijanou made the dangerous mistake of trying to pull them apart by stepping into the middle of it. She wound up in hospital. Again, Brigitte immediately came to her sister's bedside, making the trip every night from Bazoches to Paris to take her home-made soup for dinner.

When Mijanou was finally discharged, Brigitte changed the menu, sending her home-made clafouti along with bottles of champagne.

*   *   *

In his autobiography, Sacha Distel wrote that Brigitte was stingy.

Even now, among those people who have known her for many years, she has never been accused of being economically flamboyant.

She herself is fast to say, 'I don't throw money out the window, which is where my reputation for being stingy comes from.'

But, while no one denies she has always had a healthy respect for her money, stingy might not be the right word. It's perhaps more accurate to say that she was raised in a family where money was given a certain respect and where every penny was accounted for.

'When you talk about money,' Vadim says, 'you're talking about an area of Brigitte's character that is, like so much of her, paradoxical. When we were first married, she would spend so much time and energy going all the way across town to buy a product that was slightly cheaper than the one on sale next door. Or she'd scream at her maid for paying 14 francs for something in the market when someone told her it was on sale for only 12 francs in another shop.'

Instead of stingy, Vadim prefers to think of Brigitte as someone who is 'totally pragmatic' when it comes to money.

'She looks at every penny she spends and puts money aside so that she'll never go without. But the abstract value of money, the amount of money she could accumulate, is something she doesn't think about. It's not that she used to automatically say no when someone offered her a lot of money. But before she got to that, she'd think about her lifestyle and her comfort. It's not that money was or is unimportant to her. She's simply never been obsessed with making money or influenced by it in any way.'

As an aside, he says the same goes for her attitude towards people with money. She's never been impressed by them either. One night Aristotle Onassis invited them both to dinner. At the time, Onassis was probably the richest man in the world. And Brigitte refused to go.

'Money, wealth, power, famous names, none of that ever impressed her. When she turned down dinner with Onassis, she wasn't even 20 years old. So you can imagine how impressed she is by that sort of thing today.'

Brigitte was shrewd enough to seek sound advice when she was making a lot of money, and smart enough to listen to that advice. Most of her money was invested in property and today that provides her with a regular income. It isn't a great fortune, but it's enough to ensure that she can live well for the rest of her life.

She's all the more secure, where money is concerned, because she hardly ever spends any on herself. She has her two homes in St Tropez, her place at Bazoches and an apartment in Paris to maintain, but, even for someone with four homes, she doesn't live lavishly. There are no Picassos hanging on her walls. She doesn't throw parties for her 500 closest friends. She doesn't spend her money on clothes or jewels and she doesn't have a fleet of fancy cars.

'She holds onto her money,' notes Christian Brincourt. 'She has never lived like a Hollywood star. She's always does her own cooking. She's always done her own shopping. She's frugal. At the same time, she isn't impressed with money. She's never cared when someone dangled a big cheque in her face. She's only ever done what she wants to do. And money hasn't ever entered into it.'

Actually it turns out that she can be extremely generous.

As she's recently said, 'I give all my energy and all my time to my work with animals. I'm constantly being asked to do things. People write to me, as if I was God. To put an end to so many horrors, to find the master of a lost dog, to take charge of a badly run refuge. It's difficult to be everywhere at the same time. It costs me a lot of money. That's money I could spend on clothes. Instead I prefer to spend it on animals because they need it.'

Animals aren't the only recipients of her altruism. For years, family and close friends have known that Distel's description of her as stingy wasn't quite the case.

When her niece Camille went to spend time at her grandparents villa in St Tropez – she was six or seven – to keep the little girl happy, Brigitte bought a swing and jungle-gym set for their garden. As a gift to Pilou and Toty, Brigitte also put in a swimming pool.

To celebrate Philippe d'Exea's marriage, she sent him a home-made present. Within an oval frame, she'd spelled out his wedding date – 23 Juin 83 – using gold coins. Even though June has only four letters, it still took a lot of coins to write the date, so this wasn't an inexpensive gift. Attached to the frame was a small hammer to break the glass in case of a financial emergency. And attached to that came a little handwritten note, 'Thanks for not getting married in September.'

For Mama Olga's 81st birthday, she scoured antique dealers in the Paris area until she found a mirror that perfectly matched the one she'd given as a present to her own mother.

Although it's true that most of her money gets spent these days on animals, still, in very quiet ways, she has never been stingy when it comes to helping less fortunate people.

She read in the local papers one morning about a woman in the St Tropez area who'd been jailed for bouncing cheques. The article mentioned that the woman had seven children and, unless she paid the cheques, she'd have to stay in jail. The stupidity of the thing was that there was no way she could earn the money to keep her children and also somehow pay the cheques while she was still in jail. So very quietly, without saying anything to anyone, Brigitte picked up the phone, rang her local lawyer and arranged through him to pay the woman's way out.

Without saying anything to anyone, Brigitte Bardot has been doing this sort of thing throughout her life.

While filming *Les Repos du Guerrier* with Vadim in Florence in early 1962, they were staying at the Villa San Michele, just above the city in nearby Fiesole, when one night a man broke into her room. In his early 60s, with a scrawny face and almost no teeth, he was – menacingly – carrying a crossbow.

Her first thought was, he's going to kill me.

When she demanded to know what he was doing there, the man handed her a notebook.

She wanted to know what it was.

He said he'd written a poem for her and instructed her to read it.

Confronted by a man who was clearly crazy, she tried to do what he told her. But she couldn't read his handwriting and when she faltered he started screaming that he was going to cut his own throat.

Somehow, she had the presence of mind to ask him if it would be all right if she summoned her drama coach. He said that was all right, as long as she was going to read his poem, so she rang Vadim and told him to come right away because there was a man with a crossbow who was about to kill her.

First, Vadim phoned Francis Cosne, who was producing the picture, and told him to call the police. Then he raced down to Brigitte's room.

The man with the crossbow allowed him to come inside but, before Vadim could do anything, the man with the crossbow collapsed into a chair and started weeping.

The police soon arrived to take him away. However, something about this desperate old man touched her. A few days later, she dragged Vadim along with her when she went to visit him where he was under police guard in a hospital. His book of poems had been confiscated as evidence, so she never really got to study the poem he'd written about her. But when it came time to charge him, she refused. She even sent him some money so that he could try to put his life back in order.

Like most well-known people, she is bombarded with requests for help from strangers. Letters come in daily. In fact, for more than 35 years, the St Tropez post office reports, Brigitte Bardot has been their single largest private customer. Over three and a half decades, they have delivered more mail to her than anyone else in town.

For years, her local postman in St Tropez, Pierrot Bonnet, had her permission to sort through her mail to see what should be delivered to her, what should be sent to her secretary or what should be returned to the sender. Registered mail, for example – except something official – was almost always returned unopened. She wouldn't sign for anything. Not because she was afraid of what she might receive, but because that's a very typically French attitude. Never sign your name if you don't have to.

In the overwhelming majority of cases, she doesn't get involved when people write asking for help, mainly because there are just too many requests coming in all the time. Most famous people find they have no choice but to ignore the bulk of their own mail. They simply can't afford to help everyone.

But certain letters, for whatever reason, touch a chord.

One day, she received a note from a young man saying that he was ill and confined to a wheelchair. He wrote that his one dream in life was to learn to play the accordion but, as neither he nor his mother had any money, there didn't seem to be any way that he could fulfil that dream. He wondered, would you please buy me an accordion?

She asked her secretary to look into the boy's story and, once she confirmed it was genuine, Brigitte went shopping for an accordion. As it turned out, new accordions were very expensive. Yet a second-hand accordion could be purchased at a reasonable price. So she bought her young admirer a fine, second-hand accordion from a reputable dealer, and duly sent it to him with her compliments.

For nearly two months, she waited for a response.

Irked that he 'hadn't taken the time to say thank you, she'd just about pushed the incident out of her mind when a letter arrived from him. The young man told her, 'I am not in the habit of getting used gifts from people. If you want me to keep this out of the papers, you'd better send my mother a washing machine.'

The boy's mother is still doing his shirts by hand.

One day, while she was still acting, she got a letter from a woman in a clinic – a total stranger – saying she needed an operation, was desperate and didn't know who else she could turn to. Brigitte sent her a modest but nevertheless reasonable cheque. The woman cashed it, then wrote back, insulting Brigitte that, for a woman of means, she certainly didn't send very much.

Another woman – this one only 18 years old – wrote to her some time afterwards, explaining that she badly needed to have her nose fixed, had saved some money for the operation, but was still a few thousand francs short. Bardot sent the money.

In a similar vein, there was a girl working on one of her films who had a nose that was anything but beautiful. The girl confided in Brigitte that she was hoping to have a career in the movies. Knowing how much that meant to the girl, Brigitte also paid for her nose job.

Without saying anything, or attracting any attention to herself, Brigitte regularly sends flowers and confectionery to homes for the aged. There are times, like at Christmas and on Mother's Day, when she even shows up and spends the afternoon visiting these people who are, after all, total strangers.

But the classic story is the one about the ring.

In the mid 1960s, Brigitte received a letter in the mail from a total stranger – the woman's name was Suzanne Penière – explaining that she was suffering from throat cancer. She said that the doctors had cut her vocal chords and that she was going to die.

Along with the letter came an antique engagement ring – a band with a small circle of diamonds.

Madame Penière wrote that it had been hers and, as she had no children, there was no one to leave it to. She told Brigitte she found her sweet and wanted her to have some of the happiness that she'd found in her own life, as signified by the ring.

Instantly reduced to tears, Brigitte had her secretary establish that the story was true. And when the secretary confirmed that it was, Brigitte went to see the woman in a Parisian clinic.

It was Christmas. She walked into the woman's hospital room carrying a Christmas tree, a television set and some other presents. And the moment Madame Penière spotted Brigitte Bardot standing there, she passed out.

Brigitte spent the rest of that day at the woman's bedside. Before she left that evening, she told Madame Penière, 'I don't have any grandmothers any more, so you have to live for me.'

She began visiting the woman regularly – 'I wasn't Brigitte Bardot when I what to see her, I was her granddaughter' – and, when the woman was able to leave the hospital, Bardot rented a small house for her. The woman couldn't speak so she wrote to Brigitte.

They spent almost every Christmas together for the rest of Suzanne Penière's life.

Given up for dead by her doctors, Suzanne Penière was literally loved back to health by Brigitte.

The woman died at the age of 84 in 1981.

Today Brigitte still wears her ring.

Chapter Fifteen

BUILDING A LEGACY

S he arrived at the derelict property that Saturday afternoon, only a few minutes after the police had secured the scene.

It looked like a battleground.

Dressed in tight jeans, a sweatshirt and a leather jacket – still wearing her long blonde hair the way she did 35 years before – large sunglasses now hid her still remarkable face.

She'd been crying.

The shepherd, who'd been squatting here – amongst the ruins of the abandoned Saint-Ame castle, between St Tropez and Ramatuelle – insisted that neighbours had allowed his animals to get out at night and that their dogs had ripped them apart.

But that didn't explain the lamb she found drowned in a small basin. Or the badly decomposed body of a sheep she spotted nearby. Or nine more sheep she saw, their corpses piled one on top of the other, hidden in brush behind a wall. Or the goat's head she discovered, nailed to a tree.

Utterly horrified, she lashed out at the scruffy, bearded vagrant, calling him a savage, accusing him of this carnage, blaming him for deliberately massacring his animals.

The man had been there for almost for a year, living without electricity, without water and obviously without enough food to feed either himself or his flock. Now, at the end of October 1992,

307

the remainder of his animals – 30 sheep, 10 goats and one donkey – were corralled in a small pen, starving and near death.

Her tirade continued.

And the police had all they could do to keep what was already an ugly scene from becoming violent.

A veterinarian arrived, summoned by the police, but after examining the animals, he said he couldn't determine the cause of their death. She argued vehemently that the cause of their death was obvious – the shepherd had murdered his own animals. And now she demanded that the police arrest him.

When the senior officer asked her if she would file a formal complaint, she didn't hesitate to say she would.

The shepherd was taken away for questioning.

The moment he was gone, she swung into action. She fetched food for the remaining animals, lugged bales of hay from her car, and comforted the ones that were too sick to eat. Later that day – but only after she was convinced the animals were safe – she went to the police station and brought charges against the shepherd. She also had her local attorney obtain a court order that allowed her personally to take the animals into care.

However, before the evening was out, the police released the shepherd. Their excuse was that, based on the evidence, they were unable to make a satisfactory case against him.

She was livid.

Having seen the intensity of her celebrated temper several times in the past, the police decided to charge the shepherd with the misdemeanour of having failed to notify the proper authorities within 24 hours of the animals' deaths.

Not at all satisfied, she let loose with the power of her fame. She publicized the affair throughout the country, enraging people who shared her horror that such an awful thing could happen and that, for whatever reason, the police appeared so apathetic about seeking justice.

Four nights later, the shepherd was brutally beaten by three cloaked men carrying baseball bats.

There has never been any insinuation that she was in any way involved with that. But around St Tropez they don't hesitate to label it a *règlement de comptes* – the gangster term for revenge.

Except that wasn't what she wanted. She didn't give a damn about the shepherd. She cared only about the animals and the extreme cruelty she'd witnessed and about stopping it from ever happening again. She wrote a scathing letter to the mayor of Ramatuelle, partially blaming him for not having done everything in his power to prevent it. He answered, feebly, that there was no provision in law that would have permitted him to remove the squatter from the property.

She kept the heat on, writing to some people and phoning others, letting everyone know how disgusted she was. There was no hiding her fiery emotional involvement. And when confronted with the indifference of the various authorities, there was no hiding her frustration.

At around 8 pm, on Saturday 14 November, exactly two weeks after she'd seen the carnage at the Chateau Saint-Ame, she mixed her regular tranquillizers with a glass of wine. Moments later, she collapsed.

Her husband of three months called for help. She was rushed by ambulance to the Oasis Clinic, where her stomach was pumped.

As soon as she was out of danger, Bernard d'Ormale issued a statement. He said she'd been suffering from extreme fatigue, having been traumatized by the massacre of those animals. He denied that this was a suicide attempt.

'She bottles these things up inside her,' he notes, 'until she explodes. These things always take their toll.'

*   *   *

'I lived a paradox with her,' says Allain Bougrain-Dubourg.

When he was 10 years old – much too young to get into a movie house to see the just released *Et Dieu Créa la Femme* –

he started a club for animal lovers. This was at a time when no one in France was doing that. When he grew up, he studied natural history, started speaking to school groups about protecting the environment and endangered species and somehow, through that, drifted into television.

Today his programmes about animals are among the most watched in France.

He met Brigitte when she went to the ice flow to campaign for the baby seals. They became friends and, when she split up with Mirko, they moved from friendship into a love affair. The strength of their common interest in animals has always been such that Bougrain-Dubourg is one of the very few ex-lovers in her life with whom she still maintains some sort of contact.

'In the beginning,' he explains, 'people said she was only working to protect animals for the publicity it brought her. They said, she no longer makes movies, so she does this to keep the public talking about her. At the same time, dozens of requests came in every day for interviews from all around the world. Every day there were people asking to interview her. And she refused them all. So there she was, saying no to publicity because she hates that and here were people saying that the only reason she was doing all this work for the protection of animals was for the publicity. Those people didn't understand a thing about her.'

In many ways, when Brigitte and Bougrain-Dubourg found each other, they both needed someone to help them move onto the next level in their work as animal rights activists. She helped nurture in him a deep passion for this work. He helped her to understand that, to succeed, it would take more than just passion.

He maintains, 'Brigitte always fought with her heart and soul. In the beginning, when she came across some horror story, she thought it was enough simply to speak out. She believed that by telling the world about it she could solve the problem. She never liked reading dossiers. All the paperwork and background material bored her. Over the course of time, she's learned enough

310

about the subject to fight with her head as well. Little by little, she's become very knowledgeable about animal protection. She is still as combative as ever but now she understands that simply by screaming and pointing to these horrors she cannot put an end to them. She is more prone to use her expertise and create a dialogue.'

Because she is so knowledgeable, she carries with her today a personal credibility that she never had when she was an actress.

He says, 'In those days she was a myth. Today she is a reality.'

One of her strongest points, he feels, is her good common sense. 'People are sometimes quite amazed that when she says something, especially something shocking or something that seems incredible at the time, she makes sense. She's a very logical woman. And that sometimes startles people who think of her as nothing more than an ageing actress. To her great credit, where the public is concerned, people recognize her enormous honesty. There are people who might not appreciate what she says, and there are people who believe she should take care of human beings instead of animals. But even the people who criticize her are eventually forced to admit that she is completely honest in what she does and entirely honest in what she says.'

Trying to press home the need for support from the top, in October 1984, Brigitte and Bougrain-Dubourg went to see French President François Mitterand.

Under normal circumstances, it is not a foregone conclusion that the President of the Republic would have received an animal rights activist. At least, he wasn't prone to in the past. The fact that this particular animal rights activist happened to be best friends with Christine Gouze-Renal, whose sister Daniele was married to the President, didn't hurt. But the real reason he saw her was because this particular animal rights activist was Brigitte Bardot, and he couldn't afford to refuse to see her. After all, she is still probably the only person in France

311

who can, if she wants, grab more media attention than the President.

For his own part, he seemed quite content to meet her, and led his guests to believe that he was indeed interested in animal welfare. She and Bougrain-Dubourg handed him a list of 30 urgent measures they hoped he would implement to further the cause of animal protection in the country, and he promised to study the list.

It was obvious that he had a certain affection for her. Not only because of her friendship with his sister-in-law, but because, for people of Mitterand's generation, Brigitte will always be a myth.

At the same time, he realized, by doing something for animals — a decidedly neutral gesture politically — he could associate his name with hers. And, given her popularity in France, being associated with her, at no political cost, was a pretty astute move.

Pictures of Brigitte, Mitterand and Bougrain-Dubourg leaving the Elysée ran in all of the French dailies. More than 10 years later, none of the 30 measures have been enacted.

Among the things they'd campaigned for was repeal of the Verduil Law. Unique to France, it was originally framed to give pheasant hunters the right to follow their prey onto private property. Due to the loose interpretation of this legislation, hunters of all animals believe they have the right to enter private property in pursuit of game. And if hunters come onto your property, even if you don't want them there, you cannot stop them from trespassing.

The classic argument against the law cites a case near Toulon, some years ago, when a man refused to allow hunters access and, in their anger, they shot and killed him.

Bardot has always been outraged by the Verduil Law and, along with Bougrain-Dubourg, she continues to be very vocal in fighting for its repeal. As a result, both she and Bougrain-Dubourg have received threats and obscene phone calls from hunters. Once, they even found themselves facing hunters' guns.

There used to be wild boar in the woods surrounding La Garrigue and one afternoon a party of 15 hunters came past her house chasing one of the animals. Bougrain-Dubourg jumped up from the table where he was having lunch with Brigitte and announced that he was going to stop them. He caught up with the hunters and did his best to obstruct them. But the hunters were drunk and they warned him that if he continued to interfere, there would be an accident.

Terrified that they would in fact shoot Allain, Brigitte phoned for the police. She too then waded into the fracas, cursing at the hunters for being such cretins.

The wild boar escaped – which was precisely what Brigitte and Allain intended to happen – but the confrontation quickly turned into a very nasty showdown. The 15 macho Frenchmen with guns weren't going to let this kid and his ageing actress girlfriend stop them from killing anything they wanted to. And the 15 macho Frenchmen with guns were just drunk enough to prove that point.

The gendarmes didn't get there a minute too soon. But when they arrived, there was another problem. They warned Brigitte that they might not be as effective as they'd originally hoped because among the 15 hunters were a number of gendarmes, including their chief.

'It was very tense,' Bougrain-Dubourg recalls. 'We stood there for an hour, trying to negotiate with them. We wanted them off her property. As a matter of fact, they were in violation of the law because Verduil forbids hunting within 150 metres of a residence. The gendarmes eventually got rid of them for us.'

The problem in trying to revoke such laws, as she has repeatedly found out, is that in France hunting is a traditional sport. What's more, the season runs for seven months of the year, whereas most other countries limit hunting to as few as half that.

Alone, or even with the support of someone like Allain Bougrain-Dubourg, Brigitte found she simply couldn't be as effective as she might otherwise be with the weight of a group behind her. So, 10 years after suffering an embarrassing defeat with the first Brigitte Bardot Foundation, she picked up courage to try again. She knew she was possibly exposing herself to more embarrassment, but this time she was 10 years older and, she hoped, 10 years wiser.

.   .   .

To finance the Brigitte Bardot Foundation, Mark II, she put together the world's swankiest garage sale.

After incorporating an association in St Tropez in 1986, she set out to raise a minimum of three million francs ($358,000), as required by French law for official status as a non-profit-making charitable foundation. She literally cleaned out her closets, gathered up everything she could find that might have some interest and put it all up for sale.

The Parisian auctioneers Ader Picard Tajan scheduled the event for 17 June 1987. Originally, they'd planned to hold it in two rooms at the Nouveau Drouot, where most auctioneers have their usual sales. But this one was anything but usual. Interest was so intense, they had to move it to the considerably larger International Congress Centre – ironically, a ten-minute stroll from the apartment on the Place Violet where Brigitte was born.

The moment she stepped into the big room at the conference centre, that night, the 1,100 people who were crammed into it all stood up and started applauding.

Tears welled up in her eyes.

They continued to applaud.

She told them, 'I gave my beauty and my youth to men. I am now giving my wisdom and my experience, the best of me, to animals.'

314

Listed for sale were 116 lots. They included: books; photographs; lithographs by Carzou, César, Chagall, Clavé, Dali, Fini and Folon; watercolours by Clavé and Laurençin; gouaches; drawings; paintings; sculpture by Arman and Aslan, which was a bust of Brigitte as Marianne; costumes from *Shalako*, *La Femme et le Pantin* and *Boulevard du Rhum*, and the wedding dress she wore when she married Roger Vadim; various personal items, such as Baccarat crystal champagne flutes, a make-up kit, a guitar, a slot machine; and jewellery, including the tri-colour Cartier bracelets Gunter Sachs had given her as a wedding present, and the 8.76 carat diamond ring he'd given her 10 years after they divorced.

The ring was sold for 1.3 million francs ($162,000), just slightly less than it cost Roger Vadim to make *Et Dieu Crea la Femme*.

The tri-colour bracelets went for a total of 210,000 francs ($26,190), knocked down to a mystery buyer.

It turned out to have been an agent acting for Gunter Sachs.

'She's only interested in animals,' he smiles, 'which is why I had to buy my jewels twice. You know, it's very rare when a man has to do that. I sent someone into the auction house to get them for me. And at one point, after I bought them, I considered giving them back to her. I thought about it, but then I convinced myself it would be endless. She'd sell them, I'd buy them, she'd sell them, I'd buy them. It would be perpetual motion.'

*   *   *

The Brigitte Bardot Foundation remained in St Tropez for its first three years. In 1989, she moved the headquarters to Paris because, by then, it had grown too big to be administered from her kitchen table. Today it boasts 27,000 members in 42 different countries, including the United States, Great Britain and Germany.

Her philosophy is simple – to relieve animal suffering wherever it exists. And, when she takes up a cause, it doesn't matter if there are thousands of animals involved, or only a few. It's the animals that count.

When 30,000 seals were scheduled to be clubbed in South Africa, Brigitte wrote direct to President F.W. de Klerk, offering to buy all of them. It was her personal intervention that provoked the South African government into having second thoughts about this planned slaughter, and eventually to cancelling it.

Shocked that the city of Toulouse had granted a permit for a rodeo to take place, she immediately petitioned the mayor to ban it.

'Rodeo', she claimed, 'is to the United States what bullfighting is to Europe. It is a ludicrous and cruel exploitation of animals which honours neither those who watch nor those who take part in such buffoonery.'

When two pregnant female dolphins died in captivity of a liver infection, she used those headlines to condemn the keeping of dolphins in captivity for public entertainment.

'The capture of dolphins, the distress and suffering it entails, must be formally banned. The imprisonment for life of an innocent, sensitive animal just to amuse a few visitors should no longer be tolerated.'

When she heard that the Beachcomber Hotel in Nouméa, New Caledonia, planned to display up to a dozen dolphins in an aquarium, she attacked the hotel, pointing out that it was barbarous to put dolphins in a tank like goldfish.

The Foundation urgently sought action by France's Environment Minister, Michel Barnier, to apply a French law on animal protection which would put a halt to the hotel's plans. Initially, Barnier tried to pass the buck by saying that French law on animal protection doesn't apply to overseas territories. But Barnier underestimated Brigitte's determination.

She reminded him that, in fact, under international treaties signed by France – which do apply to French territories – the capture of dolphins is permitted only for scientific purposes.

As a result of the Foundation's intervention, the authorities in New Caledonia were able to use that treaty to reject a permit application by a business called Dolphin Quest to capture dolphins for the hotel aquarium.

The French government held that up as a victory for themselves.

But Brigitte considered it nothing more than a first step and set out to muster enough public support to thwart the building of the aquarium itself.

When she heard that a panther had been smuggled into France and was being kept in a cage in a restaurant, the Foundation rescued it. But someone had cruelly pulled out its claws, meaning that it could never again survive in the wild, so the Foundation took charge of it and is supporting it for the rest of its life.

When a man in the south of France locked his dog in a cupboard, then nailed his muzzle shut to keep him from barking, Bardot not only rescued the dog, she pressed criminal charges against the owner and saw the courts hand down a prison sentence for cruelty to animals, the first time that had happened in those circumstances.

When she learned that the Argentine seaside resort of Mar del Plata planned a bull run, mirroring the famous running of the bulls in Pamplona, Spain, Bardot appealed directly to President Carlos Menem, urging him to stop this 'archaic and cruel show'.

When French farmers marched on the Champs-Elysée, with chickens on leashes to protest against the Maastricht Treaty, the Foundation came along and gathered up all the chickens to save them from the farmers' torture.

When she found a cow in a shopping mall chained to a nativity scene, she bought it, put it in her car and drove it back to La Garrigue.

When a magazine in France published a lead story suggesting that 30 per cent of all cats in France carried the AIDS virus – creating a panic in the country, with cat owners abandoning their animals – she joined with several other animal welfare associations and took the magazine to court. There, judges ruled that the magazine didn't have a case to answer. The group then appealed to the magazine, asking for equal space to reply. The magazine refused. So Brigitte took the matter into her own hands, approached the magazine *Jours de France* and traded a photo session for an article. Brigitte appeared on the cover, cuddling a cat, and inside the story ran that cats, in fact, do not carry the AIDS virus.

When students at a Catholic school just next door to the Foundation's former offices on the Rue Franklin in Paris celebrated what they claimed to be an annual tradition of squashing live birds into each other's faces, staff members from the Foundation showed up to put an end to it. Bizarrely, they were ill treated by both the students and their teachers for doing so. But that lasted only until the Foundation brought the press along to show the country how men of religion allowed their charges to act. And the annual tradition has now been permanently cancelled.

When the State of New Jersey condemned a 110 pound Akita dog to death for biting a child, Brigitte petitioned Governor Jim Florio to spare the animal. She even agreed to fetch the dog herself if that meant it would be permitted to live. Her interest in the animal's fate helped other animal rights' activists in the US to make the dog an election issue in the 1993 campaign. When Florio was defeated by Christie Whitman, the dog was reprieved.

And when the Vendeuil Zoo in France went out of business, she used the Foundation to buy the animals, and placed them in parks where they could live almost normal lives.

*   *   *

In May 1989, the first of nearly a dozen television specials that she would do for the Foundation was aired in France. Under the title 'SOS Elephants', she opened the series with a grisly exposé of the ivory trade.

She went before the cameras – something she would not do for any other cause – to make a series of television shows that refused to bow to politics or vested interests.

In 'SOS Elephants', she forced the nation to confront some truly shocking footage of elephant slaughter along the ivory trails of Africa.

'One African elephant is killed every four and a half minutes,' she explained, lighting the spark that would fire public opinion in France, to the point where the government could no longer ignore the problem. And, although she wasn't alone in this fight, Brigitte Bardot was a major catalyst making France the first nation in Europe to ban the importation of ivory.

That programme was quickly followed by others in the SOS series, covering animal experimentation, hunting, slaughter-houses, illegal animal traffic, the plight of marine mammals, fighting animals, fur, cats and dogs, horses, and large apes.

Never pulling her punches, the scenes she showed have been, at times, absolutely brutal. But little by little she's forced her fellow countrymen to confront the plight of animals.

In one of her SOS programmes, Brigitte created a minor *cause célèbre* by alerting the nation to the fact that 60,000 dogs disappear in France each year, half of them stolen for use in medical research. Thanks in part to her campaign, 20 people were arrested and sent to trial, accused of providing medical laboratories with thousands of stolen dogs for vivisection research. The defendants included a university professor, two veterinarians and a bunch of small-time gangsters. One of the middlemen for the gang had already publicly admitted to selling 5,000 dogs to just one laboratory in southwestern France.

She went from dogs to bears, appealing to the Chinese leadership to end the practice of raising Asiatic black bears in cages for their bile, which is the basis for a Chinese medicine.

Using her favourite 'open letter' technique, she reminded Communist party leader Jiang Zemin that the bears are an internationally recognized endangered species and that there were more than 30 farms in China raising them in atrocious conditions. She pointed out that they were confined to minuscule cages, with a catheter tube inserted in their gall bladder to drain them of fluid.

'No medicinal property can justify such cruelty,' Bardot insisted. 'The lucrative industry in oriental remedies is the shame of our times, it respects nothing and decimates endangered animals in a revolting manner.' She added that many of the bears are further subjected to heartless amputation of their limbs to supply the restaurant trade with a so-called delicacy, bear's paw.

She also lobbied the mayors of France to put a tax on cats and dogs – as a measure to help reduce births of unwanted pets – to initiate a nationwide ban on bullfights and cockfights, to create special areas for animals in parks, to sterilize stray cats and to distribute granules that would sterilize pigeons and reduce their population in urban areas.

'The surplus population of dogs and cats can be regulated,' she says. 'Every birth should be registered, with every animal being given a number. We do it for cars! Then there would be compulsory castration for males and compulsory sterilization for females. That would stop the soaring rate of reproduction in the kennels. Instead of rounding up strays and sending them to the gas chamber, why not vaccinate them and sterilize them. It wouldn't be more expensive.'

She knows, all too well, that as she and her Foundation go into battle, they are bound to lose more than they ever could possibly hope to win. But that doesn't deter her. She knows when she protests against bullfighting in Spain – 'That country is among the worst when it comes to cruelty towards animals' – that the people of Spain are not going to rise up, cry '*Brigitte si, corrida no*', and wipe away several centuries of tradition.

However, she believes she must take that first step. She's convinced that, in the case of bullfighting for instance, there are a lot of like-minded people in Spain who share her concerns but do not necessarily have the opportunity to express themselves. When they see her speaking up, it greatly encourages those people inside who are sometimes not prepared to speak up.

And every now and then, victory comes when she least expects it.

To her own surprise, she was recently successful in stopping a traditional festival in Spain where priests would climb to the top of their church and throw live goats off the roof. It's a small concession that now, instead of being killed, the animals are caught in nets.

*   *   *

When her dog Douce was ill and the vet said he didn't think she'd last the night, Brigitte stayed with her and in some sort of pact with God—the way we all bargain with Him from time to time—she promised not to smoke or touch a drop of alcohol if the dog lived.

Douce survived for another five weeks and Brigitte kept her end of the bargain too.

*   *   *

A very strange woman named Françoise Capblancq-Bégue ran an animal refuge outside Paris in the village of Mureaux.

It was a pretty marginal operation, designed around a questionable philosophy, where animals were never put in cages and were allowed to continue breeding. She had no running water or electricity at her refuge. Her animals were well fed with leftover food that she collected from restaurants, schools and canteens. The animals were dirty and not cared for medically, but they were warm and loved.

The woman was criticized by most of the animal protection societies, but in dedicating herself to her animals – dogs and cats – and allowing them to live without human restriction, her voice was heard. One of the French television channels decided to do a programme on her, and give her the chance to explain her beliefs. Someone phoned to tell her and Capblancq-Bégue was so thrilled and so moved that she suffered a heart attack and died.

In creating an environment for her animals, at just 46 years old she'd been completely used up.

The village had always looked on the refuge as an eyesore and now, without her to carry on, they reclaimed the small tract of land and announced that, if no one claimed the animals, they would all be put down.

That is precisely the kind of insensitivity and cruelty that is guaranteed to mobilize Brigitte.

She and her staff of about a dozen, working out of the Paris offices, mobilized immediately. First, the Foundation entered into negotiations with the local authorities to convince them to relinquish control of the animals. Once they managed that — guaranteeing that the animals' lives would be spared — Brigitte and her staff had to figure out what to do with them.

The Foundation was never intended to be an annex of the Society for the Prevention of Cruelty to Animals. In most countries, France included, there is a well-established infrastructure for these types of things and organizations already equipped to take in animals.

Brigitte always envisaged her Foundation as more of an umbrella group, an association that could influence legislation, educate, and in particular cases, lend support to other associations, such as those that have facilities to take in and care for animals. But she was moved by Capblancq-Bégue's story — although they'd never met — and would not allow those animals to be killed. With no place to send them, she had the Foundation buy an old house in Normandy, with enough ground that these animals could be properly looked after and live out their final days in peace.

Saving a few hundred dogs and cat turned out to be a fairly straightforward operation.

Saving 80 wolves that had been smuggled into Hungary was a lot more complicated.

She'd given an interview to a Hungarian television station in which she spoke about her work with animals, and that prompted the mayor of Budapest to contact her. He explained that 80 wolves had been brought illegally into Hungary from Mongolia, intended to become victims of the fur trade. The police had seized the animals, but the city didn't know what to do with them. He said if she couldn't help, they would have to be destroyed.

Again, it was her kind of challenge.

Of course, she said yes. But between saying yes and actually being able to save the wolves, a lot of time, effort and money had to be spent. It took the Foundation nearly three months simply to get through the red tape that would have prevented them from transporting 80 wolves across five national boundaries. They had to meet five different sets of requirements and fill out five different sets of paperwork. Today, the 80 wolves and their offspring live in liberty at the Gevaudan Nature Park in Lozère, France.

*　　*　　*

Deciding one day to empty some closets she took a stall at the Saturday morning market in St Tropez and stood there – barefoot – selling robes, shawls, dresses, one bicycle and signed postcards. The money went straight into the Foundation's bank account.

That worked so well she also set up a Foundation shop. She found a store front, rented it for a couple of seasons, stocked it with stuff and sold Brigitte Bardot Foundation souvenirs to tourists.

As she used to tell Vadim, there's no such thing as a little profit.

*　　*　　*

Brigitte and Alain Spada called a truce in early 1993 when, as mayor, he presented her with a permanent location in St Tropez for her Foundation.

She'd been hoping to find somewhere to put a regional office, so Spada gave her a small, hexagonal kiosk on the Place Blanqui, near the gendarmerie.

Inside it's one small room, with a glass-topped desk and three white cane chairs with blue cushion seats. The windows are

323

decorated with index card announcements – dogs and cats that are lost, dogs and cats that have been found. They sell leashes inscribed 'Brigitte Bardot Foundation', and t-shirts that say the same thing. There is one colour photo hanging just inside the door – of Brigitte – looking absolutely gorgeous, next to a baby seal, looking extremely helpless.

Spada is the first to admit that she's had some success with her campaign for animal rights. 'She has two very important things going for her. The first is that, in many cases, the stands she makes are based on sound reasoning and are morally right. The second is that her celebrity status still commands attention.'

.   *   •

'Animals are the last minority,' Brigitte says. 'And we judge the quality of a culture, the quality of a society by the way we treat animals.'

Many people understand that. Other's don't.

The reaction to her work as an animal activist – she insists, 'It's not a job, it's a religion' – has brought her more mail from strangers than she ever got as an actress.

Much of it is from children, who see her as 'the fairy godmother of animals'. That pleases her enormously. These are fans who are too young to remember her as a sex kitten on screen. These are children who share her love for animals. And she knows that, if she can nourish that love in them now, they will follow her example for the rest of their lives.

Then there are those people who criticize her, saying it would be better if she took care of people instead of animals.

'If I could do something about all the human horrors, about war and famine and crime and despair, if I could do something about the rest of the world, I would,' she insists. 'But I've been fighting for animals since 1973 and I haven't yet solved all those problems. I would be even less effective with those human horrors.

324

I don't ignore the rest. But I try to do the best I can in the area I've chosen.'

Anyway, she points to those people who criticize her, 'They are the same people who do nothing for anyone. At least I do this.'

.   .   .

It's no secret that Brigitte used to wear fur. Except, of course, it was a very long time ago. She gave it up as soon as she understood how animals were tortured by the fur trade, and has never worn fur since.

Thanks to Brigitte Bardot's campaign against fur, there are teenagers in France today who have stopped their mothers from wearing furs. She has, through the sheer force of her convictions, helped to turn what once was a status symbol into a political statement.

'Anyone who wears fur', she says categorically, 'is wearing a cemetery on their backs.'

She has also made it her business to try to stop the Palio – the 800-year-old horse race through the cobbled streets of Siena. It invariably results in serious injuries to the animals, and frequently results in their death.

Just as she has made it her business to intervene, interfere and disrupt in any way she can the so-called traditional hunting of turtle doves in the French Médoc region.

Each year, over a three-week period, as the birds are migrating back from North Africa to lay their eggs – and despite the fact that the hunting season is officially closed – approximately 1,000 hunters line the hills like infantry soldiers and massacre up to 30,000 birds as they fly overhead.

Brigitte goes to the Médoc when she can, and physically tries to restrain the hunters. And although police are sent to protect her – each year she receives death threats – the government simply refuses to send in the police against the hunters.

'With politicians,' says Dominique Jacob, a leading force at the Foundation, 'it doesn't seem to matter. If they're right wing or if they're left wing, the government will always do as little as possible. There are so many laws that are supposed to protect animals against cruelty but almost never get implemented. If people are starting to complain about cruelty, that's thanks entirely to Brigitte who has forced people to face up to these horrors.'

Her name is such that she's always being solicited to lend her weight to causes in other parts of the world.

A request came from Uruguay to join with animal rights activists there in condemning the torture of animals in experiments at the National University's School of Medicine. She did.

A request came from a Russian group, alerting her to the massacre of baby seals in northern Russia. She appealed directly to President Boris Yeltsin. Referring to the seal pens at Koyda, north of Arkhangel'sk on the White Sea, where pups were kept tied up until they were killed, she wrote, 'There are words that terrify and I had hoped never again to hear of death camps or gulags.'

Interestingly enough, her message had obviously somehow got through the Iron Curtain because, with the fall of the communist bloc in Eastern Europe, letters cascaded in asking her to do something about the appalling conditions at places like the Moscow and Belgrade zoos, among others. She didn't think there was much she could do, but that didn't stop her from writing letters and at least trying to mobilize animals rights groups and politicians in those places.

On the other hand, she was able to speak out loudly in aid of the red tuna. She was informed that Japanese and South Korean fishing boats were regularly coming into the Mediterranean and, illegally, using nets that stretched for as many as 40 nautical miles to catch their fish. Because this was a direct violation of EC regulations, she brought it to the attention of the law-makers in Brussels and demanded that action be taken.

Doing battle with the Japanese is something she's getting used to. 'They have no respect for anything. In an attempt to find all the aphrodisiacs in the world they mutilate animals, using seal penises and rhino horns and all sorts of things. It's scandalous. Look at their whaling industry. The Japanese should stop haunting the world and leave those animals alone.'

Jacob insists, 'It's an understatement to say that Brigitte isn't afraid of annoying someone. She'll annoy anyone when she wants something. She goes all the way. There are times when her persistence can even appear to be excessive. She bothers people until she gets what she wants. And politicians don't like that. It's one thing for a government to pay lip-service to any foundation that bears a famous name, but she doesn't want lip-service.'

Furthermore, she says, Brigitte has never been known to mince her words. 'Not at all. She says what she means to say and she doesn't care to whom she says it. She talks to politicians and ministers the same way she talks to every-body and they don't like that. I think a lot of that comes from the fact that she is profoundly sensitive, that she takes in so much and feels so strongly about her cause that she refuses to let anyone get in the way of it. But don't for-get that she doesn't do this for herself, she does it for the animals.'

Mijanou recognizes that her sister's determination, once she gets onto a cause, knows no bounds.

'She isn't afraid to get into a fight because she's a fighter. She fights for things she believes in. When she sees injustice towards animals, she dives in and is willing to take on the world. She sees the horrors first hand, every day, and doesn't shy away from them. I know what she feels because sometimes at night, when she's alone, she phones me and tells me. I know how deeply she suffers.'

For the cause, Brigitte has willingly locked horns with medical laboratories, politicians, governments, it doesn't matter who gets in her way. She isn't afraid to get her own nose bloodied. She fights for what she believes.

'Public opinion is not a simple thing to change,' Mijanou says. 'But it's not only big fights. She also does all sorts of little things that nobody notices. There was an old lady she knew who had a bunch of cats and dogs, and she died just before Christmas a few years ago, so Brigitte adopted all her animals and took them all to Bazoches. No one talks about it, but when the Foundation is strapped for funds and a project comes along, Brigitte pays for things out of her own pocket. She pretends to be very strong. But that's only to hide how extremely fragile she is.'

For Brigitte, these days, every day brings new horrors. 'It's very demoralizing,' she admits. 'I fight and fight and maybe do a little. But things seem to get worse and worse. Maybe if I go on fighting as long as I can, someone will come after me who will achieve something. The legacy I want to leave is the Foundation. If I was hit by a bus tomorrow, it's for my work with animals and for the Foundation that I would wish to be remembered.'

There are some people who feel that, given time, that's exactly how she will be remembered – not for the name she made famous in her first life, but for the work she is determined to see through in her second life.

'Just look at what she's accomplished,' says Allain Bougrain-Dubourg. 'There's been so much. Her biggest single success has to have been her campaign for the baby seals. But when I told her that she'd won, when I said that Europe was going to boycott the importation of seal fur and suggested that we open a bottle of champagne, she didn't seem very enthusiastic. I said, "But we fought so hard for so long." She answered, "It's so elementary. It's only logical that we should win." That's the way she is. And when she can save the lives of 30 dogs in a refuge, she sees that as a great success too.'

•   •   •

After she auctioned her possessions to set up the Foundation, she explained, 'I don't attach any importance to material objects. For me, the most important thing is the value of life. To fight on requires money. The aim of my campaign is the survival and the respect that we owe animals. That's worth all the jewels in the world.'

She soon came to realize that, in order to continue her work, the Foundation required a continuous flow of funding and that subscription contributions would never be enough. The next step up from non-profit charity status in France is the very valuable title, public utility. This gives selected charities the right to be named as beneficiaries of wills without having to pay inheritance tax.

If people could bequeath their worldly goods to the Foundation, she believed, it would guarantee that her work could go on long after she was gone. So, with her lawyers, she made the proper applications. She asked the government to award the Brigitte Bardot Foundation public utility status and, in 1991, the government turned her down.

Their argument was that, as a charity, the Foundation didn't have enough capital to merit the worthier title.

She'd already sold just about everything she owned of any value, and the government seemed very vague about how much more she'd have to put into the coffers. Looking around, there didn't appear to be all that much left.

Except one thing – La Madrague.

In December 1992, she signed the paperwork, ceding her ownership of the property to the Brigitte Bardot Foundation. She had it valued at 20 million francs ($3,375,000) and the government accepted that valuation.

With an asset like La Madrague on the Foundation's books, she was encouraged to reapply for the public utility charter. And, a few months later, it was accorded.

Now, in keeping with that charter, three government ministers – Environment, Culture and Interior – sit on the Foundation's board, overseeing the accounts.

And now, as a Public Utility, the future of the Foundation seems secure.

Under the terms of the agreement, she is allowed to live at La Madrague for the rest of her days. On her death, it will become the Brigitte Bardot Museum, owned and run by the Foundation.

'I gave my house to the animals.' She shrugs with a smile. 'Now I live at their place.'

Chapter Sixteen

D'ORMALE

I t was raining that Sunday when they spotted a tiny church at the end of the fjord, lost in the Norwegian countryside.

And just like that they decided to get married.

The front door of the church was locked, so they went in search of the preacher. They found him in the village and he was quite taken aback when they told him what they wanted to do. But they convinced him that they were serious about this and he said, all right, you'll need two witnesses, so they asked the only other people they saw – the taxi driver who'd brought them there and the person cleaning the church.

On 16 August 1992, after a simple religious ceremony to consecrate their love for each other, Brigitte Bardot became Mme Bernard d'Ormale.

* * *

His real name is Bernard di Chiara-d'Ormale.

Born in Marseilles in 1941, he moved around for most of his childhood, living first in Paris, then for a time in South America.

At the beginning of the 1960s – now bouncing around French-speaking Africa, trying to earn a living in import and export – he found himself stranded in Monrovia, Liberia, unable to get a plane out for eight days.

331

An awful place with absolutely nothing to do – except hang out at the hotel bar – there he met a Lebanese fellow one evening who was also trying to get out of Monrovia. The two got to talking and the Lebanese chap – who was living in Brazil at the time – told Bernard that he sort of had some interests in the film business. Bernard asked what he meant and the man explained that he happened to own the rights to a black and white film about the Brazilian soccer star Pelé.

As Brazil had won the World Cup just a few years before, Pelé was probably then the most famous athlete on earth. What made this film different, the man went on, was that it had been shot when Pelé was just 13 or 14 years old.

D'Ormale pondered that for a while and, with an eye for a deal, thought to himself that he could probably sell this film throughout Africa. So in the bar of a hotel in downtown Monrovia, stuck there until he could get a flight out for Europe, he bought the rights to this fellow's film.

Over the next year or so he travelled Africa, selling it to cinemas, netting for himself the then handsome profit of $50,000.

'It was a lot of money in those days,' d'Ormale says. 'But it didn't last long. I came to Paris with it and had a very good time.'

However, that film opened the door to a couple of opportunities. He set himself up as a cinema distributor in Africa and also did a brief stint in Rome, working in feature film production and on films for American television. It was there he discovered that having a double-barrelled name confused people, so he dropped the di Chiara part and started calling himself simply, Bernard d'Ormale.

'Because it was easier to pronounce.'

Many years later the French press would uncover people who recalled that his name was di Chiara and insinuate that if he was now suddenly calling himself d'Ormale it must be because he had some deep dark past.

These days, when he hears that, he merely raises his eyes and shakes his head. Since his name has been linked to Brigitte's, he's never ceased to be amazed at the lengths to which some people will go to cast aspersions.

Back in Africa by the beginning of the 1970s, a friend offered Bernard the chance to join him in the south Pacific and launch a business cultivating black pearls. But d'Ormale decided he was doing fine with film distribution – that's where he thought the money was – and anyway, there was a lady he was seeing in France, and the south Pacific seemed very far away. So, after considering it for a while, he begged off and stayed in Africa.

It is, of course, the story of the fish that got away. His friend went to the south Pacific, started the business with just about five francs and sold it a few years later for $5 million.

'My timing', he admits, 'was very badly off.'

His timing was off again 10 years later, when he heard that the Victorine Studios in Nice were up for sale.

Seeing an opportunity, he studied the operations of 60 film studios around the world before putting together a consortium of investors to buy the Victorine, with an eye towards turning Nice into the Hollywood of Europe.

He raised $25 million, some of it in the Gulf – mainly in Saudi Arabia and the Emirates – and the rest in the States. He also collected a bunch of loan guarantees from the city of Nice and all the necessary building permits that would allow his group to modernize the studio facilities so that they could compete properly. Everything seemed to be falling into place until May 1981. That's when the French elected François Mitterand, a socialist President, and Mitterand made good on an election promise by putting four communists into his cabinet.

'That was the end of that. As soon as the Americans heard there were communists running four French ministries, they pulled out and, when they went away, so did the rest of my investors.'

Some 10 years after that, he finally got his timing right.

On 7 June 1992, his friend Jean-Louis Bougureau, a lawyer in St Tropez, invited him to a dinner party. It was a rainy Sunday night and at least one of the guests almost didn't come. She was a friend and client of Bougureau's, a local girl who first said no, she didn't want to go a party, then said okay she'd be there. Then she changed her mind again – because it was raining and that depressed her, so she didn't feel like getting all dressed up or talking to people – except that in the end she did show up.

That night, Bernard d'Ormale – who'd never been married before – knew something important had happened to him.

'The moment I saw Brigitte I realized I'd been looking for her all my life without ever knowing it.'

At the end of the evening he walked up to her and asked gently, may I kiss you?

They started seeing each other, and two months later had reached the point that, when they saw the tiny church at the end of the fjord, lost in the Norwegian countryside, on that rainy Sunday, they knew exactly what they wanted to do.

After the ceremony, the bride and groom invited the preacher and their two witnesses to join them at a little restaurant in the village. They never bothered to announce their marriage officially, because this wasn't a marriage for the sake of official announcements. This was something private – and very romantic – that they'd done only for themselves.

The press didn't hear about it until 20 September, when Bardot and d'Ormale arrived at the voting booth in St Tropez to cast their ballots in the referendum over the Maastricht Treaty. Brigitte casually confirmed to some friends that she and Bernard had recently got married. The next day it was front-page news.

One journalist tried to confirm the story by ringing Gilles Dreyfus, who hadn't been aware of it at all.

'I have sometimes been asked to plead in divorce cases,' he said, 'but this is the first time anyone's asked me to plead in a marriage case.'

When another journalist checked to see if there was any record of the marriage at the town hall in St Tropez – there isn't – he questioned whether or not they were legally married under French law.

334

'We were married in front of God,' Brigitte answered, 'in front of us, not necessarily in front of other people.'

Bernard contends, 'That we weren't married under French law doesn't matter. We did what we wanted to do, which was to be married in a church, in the eyes of God. That's what matters to Brigitte and to me.'

Word also soon got into the papers that for seven years, until she met d'Ormale, she'd been living like a nun. Actually, she can be very funny about it and used to tell friends, 'I haven't seen the wolf for seven years.'

During that time, some of her friends say, she changed.

Before, there were always dozens of people hanging around. She was always going out, to restaurants and to clubs. When she was invited somewhere that she didn't know people, she always arrived with three or four of her own friends because in those days, if she wasn't surrounded by people, she felt vulnerable.

Now, seeing practically no one, completely disillusioned by humans, she sought fidelity and friendship with animals.

She loved to hear birds singing in the morning and when they sang for her she would feed them, leaving grain wherever they'd find it. She filled her farm with goats, sheep, donkeys, horses, dogs, cats and ducks, whose wings were not cut so that they can fly if they want to.

'I have been disappointed in love,' she used to say, 'severely disappointed, because it always turns out to be a one-way street.'

Settling into this long period of solitude, which would characterize much of her second life, everything about her seemed to take on a calmer air. 'I was the way I was because, in those days, I wanted to be that way. Now, if I had to relive that life, I'd be sick. I am much more at ease with myself today.'

In this, her second life, she found time to read. For so long, all she ever read were scripts. There were always lines to memorize for the next morning. Now she could devour books. 'When I find a book I like it's as if I've found a friend just when I'm about to go to bed or curl up in front of a fire. With some books, when I know there isn't a sequel, I make the last few pages last as long as I can and when they're finished, it's as if I've lost a friend.'

There was time for music too. She has a large classical record collection, and listens to nothing else because, she says, it relaxes her and raises her spirits. 'It makes me think of ethereal things, rather than earthly things.'

Music has always made her dance – 'It's my body speaking' – but her disco days are part of that first life, long gone. She wouldn't even think of going to a disco today, any more than she would think of getting on the Paris Métro during rush hour.

As she often says, 'I want simplicity. I try to live a healthy life. I walk in the country with my animals. I eat very little. No sauces. Very little meat. I like vegetables and fish and eggs from my own chickens. I take very little or no medication at all. People abuse medicines. Chemical products aren't good for you and can have bad effects on the human system. I stay away from all these kinds of things because I see them as poison.'

She still likes a little champagne – 'Because it's happy' – but drinks a lot of exotic teas these days because that's more in keeping with her lifestyle, more in keeping with someone who wants to take the time to live.

She also surrounds herself with exotic odours – sandalwood, rosemary, thyme, lavender, all sorts of dried plants.

She doesn't travel much any more. But then she never much liked to travel and every time she went some place she was always glad to come home.

While she was going through those seven years of solitude, the few people she still saw came to realize that Brigitte was growing up, that, among other things, she was finally learning one of the great virtues – patience.

Mijanou is among them. 'When we were children, Brigitte was not a particularly patient young girl. Now, she seems to understand that you can't always demand perfection. And that sometimes, at least, there must be concessions.'

Insists Bernard d'Ormale, 'All you have to know to understand Brigitte is that she is a peasant at heart. She loves things that are simple. She loves things that are rustic. She never does things for effect. She does things because she wants to do them. It's been like that all her life, but people never accepted that. They thought that when she started wearing gingham dresses, she was trying to create a new fashion. No, that's not the way she is. She wore gingham because that's what women who lived in the country wore a hundred years ago. After the life she used to lead, which she hated, she's come back to nature because that's what she really likes. That's really her taste. That's really who she is.'

*   *   *

During the French regional elections in March 1992, d'Ormale helped to organize Jean-Marie Le Pen's personal office in Nice.

Le Pen is the controversial right-wing leader of France's *Front National* (FN).

But d'Ormale is quite adamant that his relationship with Le Pen does not extend to the FN. 'I am not a member of the FN. I am simply an old friend of Jean-Marie. And it's not fair that people confuse the two. I ran his private election campaign office, not the FN's election campaign office.'

Despite his pleas, that confusion has haunted d'Ormale since his name was first tied to Brigitte's. In turn, it has haunted her, as some people in France have decided that, if her husband is involved with the FN, they no longer want to be associated with her Foundation.

'I am apolitical,' she insists. And her friends confirm that politics have never interested her. She has little regard for politicians and even less patience for political arguments. Bernard enjoys discussing politics but she doesn't. Going to a small luncheon one day at her neighbour's house, Bardot felt the need to ring her hosts in advance and beg them, 'Please, no discussion of politics.' And as long as the conversation steered clear of politics, her neighbours say, she spent the whole meal holding d'Ormale's hand, like a teenage girl, in total awe of him.

There have, in fact, been the odd times when she's appeared slightly less apolitical than she is now. In 1974, she supported Valéry Giscard d'Estaing's campaign for the French presidency, and even wore a t-shirt around St Tropez that heralded, 'Giscard at the Helm'.

She thought well of him, in general, but never liked his taste for hunting. And every time they met, she harped on that subject, asking him to denounce blood sports. She reminded him on several occasions that not only was it distastefully aggressive behaviour, it also set a bad example. She chastised him, 'At your age, you still haven't understood that you've got to put down your guns.'

The best he would ever answer was, 'Yes, yes,' and take on evasive airs.

She got especially defiant with him once on a television programme, prompting him to ask, 'Is it in your nature to show tolerance to your enemies?'

But she cut him down to size, responding, 'I am, for the most part, tolerant, but I can't accept barbarism.'

Like Mitterand all those years ago, French politicians are usually receptive to her – it's the price they pay for the photo opportunity – because many of them, especially the generation now in power who grew up with her films, still think of her as 'BB.'

Needless to say, she is quick to set them straight on that point. They are all quickly put in their place, told in no uncertain terms that she is Brigitte Bardot and that the only subject she'll discuss with them is animal welfare.

In real terms, she presents problems for politicians because she puts their backs up. She gets under their skin, and it doesn't matter which political party is in power. She bothers them all. She attracts them as 'BB', then turns on them and bothers them as Brigitte Bardot.

She has very definite priorities, and politicians – even those she may admire – clearly aren't high on her list.

D'Ormale

When Polish President Lech Walesa visited France in 1988, he announced that the two things he truly wanted to do were to see the Eiffel Tower and to meet Brigitte Bardot. A request came down to her from President Mitterand's office and, as she'd respected how Walesa had breathed oxygen into his country, she agreed to meet him privately. No press. No photographs. No political statements issued afterwards. Just the two of them. So a meeting was arranged. But that morning, in St Tropez, one of her dogs took ill. She sent word of apology, politely excusing herself, and stayed home with the dog.

She'd even met Jean-Marie Le Pen before.

In 1962, she was visiting soldiers in a hospital who'd come back to France after having been wounded in the war in Algeria. Le Pen was visiting the hospital the same day. They didn't know each other, but he knew who she was and arranged to be photographed with her.

Thirty years later, when d'Ormale came into her life, some photo researcher managed to find that old picture and published it, suggesting that Bardot had once been directly associated with Le Pen.

It is precisely that kind of journalism that Brigitte has always resented.

It is precisely the sort of thing that has, since 1957, created in her a huge well of suspicion and indignation for the press.

* * *

Like many well-known, successful people in France, Brigitte has been awarded the Légion d'Honneur. She was nominated for it by Christine Gouze-Renal. And even if there are political overtones that come with the award, she seemed happy to receive it. Brigitte is, after all, quintessentially French and the Légion d'Honneur is quintessentially part of her French heritage.

But Gouze-Renal re-emphasizes Bardot's apolitical tendencies. 'Her upbringing was probably on the right of the political spectrum. Conservative or Republican. That's the kind of family she came from. That was part of her bourgeois upbringing. But she herself isn't political. When François Mitterand does something to help her cause for animals, she's in favour of François Mitterand. When Jacques Chirac or Valéry Giscard d'Estaing does something to help animals, then she's in favour of them. The truth of the matter is, she doesn't have any real political opinions.'

Her genuine friends know that. Yet many of them were still quite shocked when she announced that she was married to Bernard d'Ormale and that he was connected to Jean-Marie Le Pen. They couldn't forgive her for getting involved with someone who could somehow associate her name with the FN.

Gouze-Renal was particularly horrified. Married to the actor Roger Hanin, who happens to be Jewish, Gouze-Renal says she couldn't have imagined anyone less suitable for Brigitte than someone who might be friendly with Le Pen. In fact, she was so turned off by the whole idea of such a union that she refused to phone Brigitte, refused to have anything to do with her, for several months. Then, one night, turning the dials on her television set, she stumbled across one of the films they did together and gave in to the urge to ring Brigitte.

'The moment she heard my voice on the other end she started crying. She said, "I know why you haven't phoned me. I understand. I'm so embarrassed about all the publicity that surrounds us. But don't worry. *Ma Cri-Cri*, thank you for calling me." Anyone who knows Brigitte knows that she can be extremely rude and at times very cruel, even to friends. And sometimes her behaviour is indefensible. But she also has such an irresistible side. She can be so deep, and yet she can also be so superficial. She can be so grown up and yet she can be such a child. It's amazing how people can get so angry with her, and want to stay angry with her, but eventually give in and are willing to forgive her because she can be so alluring.'

Alluring, indeed. But rude and sometimes cruel, as well. It is the major contradiction in her life.

'There are two women inside her,' says Madeleine Venant, who worked as her housekeeper for nearly 18 years. 'There is one who can be adorable, wonderful and generous, and there is the other who is awful and terrorizing. She changes from one second to another. I don't know why. She can be so marvellous. And one second later she can be so nasty. She is someone no one can really understand but she's also someone you can never forget.'

Vadim knows it all too well. 'When we were together I noticed that she had a natural gift for lying. Not in a malicious way, but in a simple and logical way, like a child, which was designed to make life correspond to her wishes. That part of her which is a child is another example of her total egoism. But it's the innocent ego of an infant. Children never realize the demands they make.'

Mijanou knows it too. 'She doesn't know when she hurts someone. She doesn't see it. Doesn't understand it. She lives very much for the moment. She's not able to understand someone's reaction when they show how hurt they are. She doesn't even understand that she's capable of hurting other people.'

* * *

Their first summer together, a few weeks after Brigitte and Bernard met, the story hit the papers that they'd gone sailing on Jean-Marie Le Pen's yacht.

In fact, the paparazzi even got a photo of them lunching on the deck.

D'Ormale contends, 'Like so much of the commotion that surrounds Brigitte, the truth was taken totally out of context. It was not Jean-Marie's yacht. It belonged to some mutual friends in St Tropez. And we didn't sail on it. At least, we didn't go very far. Jean-Marie had been invited for lunch and our mutual friends invited us to come along. That was the whole thing. Those friends asked us to join them for lunch because they knew Jean-Marie was a friend of mine. And I'll tell you something else. At no point during that lunch did anyone discuss politics. We were just a bunch of people having lunch on a boat. It never was any sort of endorsement by Brigitte for the FN, as the papers tried to suggest.'

The next thing Brigitte and Bernard knew, the papers were quoting her as saying that, for the cantonal elections, she voted for the FN's candidate. Much of France was outraged.

'If she had said that,' d'Ormale notes, 'they might have been right to be outraged. But she didn't say it. She doesn't tell people how she votes. The only time that I know she's ever discussed such things in public was when she said she voted no on the Maastricht Treaty. But that's all.'

Still, sensing the dangers, she's steered a careful course clear of politics, and especially clear of the FN, ever since – although she has found the need to remark, on several occasions, 'I married Bernard, not the *Front National.*'

In the meantime, Bernard has tried to bring some order to their lives. Admitting that she's 'looking for simplicity, but is not necessarily a simple woman,' he started out by making a few changes in their household. Now there are no more cats crawling all over the table when they eat, and no more dogs sleeping in bed with them.

D'Ormale says that Brigitte has been so badly exploited by so many people over the years that he's trying, slowly and quietly, to put that right to some extent. In doing that, he's made some enemies. For example, he's stepped on some egos at the Foundation because he felt they had to be more businesslike. And he convinced Brigitte that their old rambling offices – which had been spread out on several floors of an old building – were inefficient. Some people at the Foundation thought he was meddling in their affairs, but he helped to find them new office space – more businesslike office space – and they've since moved.

He has also been reviewing a large pile of her old contracts, discovering payments that were never made to her, rights that are due to her. She is not a businesswoman and has never pretended to be one. So he's stepped in to try and put some order in her business affairs as well.

At the same time, Bernard has tried to encourage her to get out more, to make public appearances for the Foundation, to meet people and rally their participation in her projects.

Until the end of 1993, she seemed reluctant. Then things started to change. She started to see how public opinion was affecting the Foundation's finances. A number of wealthy French people had withdrawn their support in protest at d'Ormale's affection for Jean-Marie Le Pen. French Jewish donors were among the most vocal, objecting to any link, however slight, between Brigitte Bardot and Le Pen because of what they see as the FN's anti-Semitic and racist views. Legacies that had previously been promised were taken back. Membership subscriptions and donations dropped by a third, costing the Foundation some two million francs ($360,000) and creating a cash crisis.

Hoping at least to stop the bleeding – with Bernard's encouragement – Brigitte made a rare live television appearance on the French national evening news. She was there to reason with her former supporters, hoping to make them understand that her husband's political views and her own work were two completely separate issues and that it was unfair to mix them together.

'If all this does me too much harm, we will be forced to separate,' she said. 'But I think it would be unfair for me to have to end my life alone.'

Then, in an aside, she confessed that she'd spent seven years alone and miserable before meeting Bernard. 'He deals with politics, I deal with animals. Perhaps I would have been better off falling in love with a shoe salesman.'

The response, in just the first fortnight, was an overwhelming show of support, making up the two million francs shortfall.

She is willing to acknowledge that her husband's political links have tarnished the Foundation's image. But she reminds her critics that she has given everything she has to her cause. 'I've given everything I've got to animals. I've given them my health, my jewels, my home. The Foundation is my life, my child.'

Never one to hide her feelings, she says she finds the FN too extremist and once even tried to convince Bernard to join the Gaullist RPR party led by Paris mayor Jacques Chirac. He wouldn't go that far, but constantly reminds his critics that he is not a member of the FN, nor has he ever been. 'This whole thing has happened because I've known Jean-Marie Le Pen for many years. We're friends. That's all.'

While his friendship with Le Pen and her work with animals should be mutually exclusive, that appears to be a difficult concept for some people to grasp.

Part of the problem clearly stems from the fact that, while the FN is very much in evidence in France, the French are, by nature, very Cartesian. Their language may be full of nuance, but there is not a lot of room for nuance in the French political psyche. They have a long memory when it comes to the damage done to their country by political extremists, and even 50 years after World War II it still grates on some people there that French soldiers might someday serve alongside German soldiers in a European alliance.

It's difficult for them to accept the idea that where people may have good points and bad points — especially where political philosophies enter into the picture — it's possible to reject a bad quality and still accept a good quality.

That's not the way the French behave. They either like someone or dislike someone and there isn't much room in between.

So, as soon as Brigitte's name was somehow associated with something as easy to dislike as the FN, she was condemned by association.

And the fall-out has been harmful.

For example, she was the object of scorn at a news conference in Strasbourg in 1993 when certain members of the European

Parliament refused to sit at the same table with her because of her marriage to d'Ormale.

Also, her views reproaching Muslim sheep-slaughtering rituals were immediately overshadowed by the fact that she'd expressed them in a newspaper with far-right sentiments.

Each year for the past several years, she has criticized the Muslim world for its celebration of Aid-el-Kebir, the feast of the sacrifice. And each year, she gets their dander up.

But in May 1993, just before the festival, Bardot issued a statement condemning the traditional sacrificing of sheep, saying she was 'Revolted and outraged by this barbarous custom from the dark ages. The blood of thousands of sheep will flow on Monday as these celebrations take place on the day of the Catholic Pentecost feast, which has been dethroned since France is now an elder daughter of the Muslim religion. What would Muslim countries say if we pushed aside their religious celebrations with Catholic processions?'

Coming from a woman who was now married to a man who was often – albeit mistakenly – described as 'Jean-Marie Le Pen's right-hand man', her protest was immediately considered a racist affront to France's two million-strong Muslim population.

The president of the Islamic Centre of Nice demanded to know, 'Since when has Brigitte Bardot taken up politics? Her statement is a political one. What is more serious? Cutting an animal's throat or a man's? Why doesn't she react when villages are burned in ex-Yugoslavia or when Muslims have their throats cut in Kashmir?'

Because two major themes of Jean-Marie Le Pen's FN platform are to restrict Arab immigration to France and to outlaw the public sacrifice of sheep in immigrant neighbourhoods, leaders of the Muslim community in Marseilles issued a statement reminding her, 'Muslims are not criminals and we hope God will show Brigitte Bardot the right path so she continues her days in peace.'

Retorting that an estimated 10,000 sheep were to be slaughtered under official supervision in the Marseilles area alone, Bardot lashed out, 'If you know anything about my personality, you'll know that my opinions are my own. I didn't wait until now to criticize this disgusting practice. No one called me a racist when I criticized the Canadians for killing baby seals or the Africans for slaughtering elephants.'

* * *

Just after their marriage was announced – coinciding with a politically troublesome period for St Tropez's mayor, Alain Spada – Bernard d'Ormale began making regular visits to the town hall.

He wanted the Mayor to know that he and Brigitte both supported what he was trying to do. Spada told d'Ormale that he appreciated their endorsement. But if it ever was an endorsement, it was short lived. Spada got into a fight with the town council, they resigned and the Prefect of the Var, who oversees political control of the region, ordered new municipal elections.

Now d'Ormale said that he intended to run for mayor.

The French system requires candidates to submit an electoral list that will comprise the entire local council. In other words, the mayor comes along with an entire team already in place. Voters then choose the team they want. With Spada locked into a bitter fight against Jean-Michel Couve – the man he'd replaced as mayor – d'Ormale's candidature was seen by many as disruptive and nothing more than a way of making a name for himself locally.

Possibly because his friendship with Le Pen was so well known, he appeared to be having trouble getting enough other candidates onto his list. He openly distanced himself from Le Pen, insisting that he wanted to wage an apolitical campaign. 'I wanted to restore St Tropez to the festive mood it had in the sixties. This had nothing to do with Brigitte. I wanted to leave her out of all this fuss.'

But it's impossible to be Brigitte Bardot's husband and run for office in St Tropez and think that she wouldn't be inadvertently dragged into the campaign. Brigitte dug her heels firmly in her apolitical stance, and without her direct support he never stood a chance. He was forced to drop out. Then again, even with her support he couldn't have won. The Le Pen connection simply bothers too many people.

'Come on,' Bernard says in his own defence, 'it's not being a fascist to want to install a music kiosk and bring in a few minstrels. The detestable political climate here has caused Brigitte a lot of suffering, and harmed her animal welfare foundation.'

And then, to explain why he resigned from the campaign, he states simply, 'Because Brigitte comes first'.

In the end Spada lost to Couve by only 52 votes – out of a total 3,878.

*   *   *

Bernard says he's the sort of man who likes to move around, while Brigitte is the sort of woman who likes to stay put. He loves to travel, she doesn't. He wants her to get out and fund-raise for the Foundation, she doesn't want to do any of that sort of thing.

When the opportunity to appear on a major variety show came along, early in 1994, he encouraged her. And, for the sake of the Foundation, she did it.

On Wednesday evening, 26 January 1994 some eight million French people tuned into a very special edition of television station TF1's regular weekly variety show *Sacre Soirée*.

As the guest of honour, Brigitte Bardot was making her first live, prime-time variety show appearance in more than 20 years.

The show's host, an amiable, former disc jockey named Jean-Pierre Foucault, had invited her to talk about her work with animals, and had invited the studio audience to prepare questions in advance that would then be posed to her.

Originally, the show's producers had hoped Brigitte would be there with Foucault, in front of the studio audience. But Brigitte was making movies before Foucault was going to school and she knew better than anybody how to come across at her best. She was too experienced to expose herself to bad lighting, unflattering camera angles and the whims of an ambitious young host. No, she said, if you want me on the programme, you have to agree to my rules. Of course they wanted her, so of course they agreed to her rules.

First, she said, she wouldn't go to the studio. They'd have to set up an outside unit in her Parisian apartment. That way, she could wear a black bolero waistcoat, sit in front of her red fabric walls, keep the camera at a respectable distance and light herself in pinks, which are softer and kinder than a big studio's bluish tones.

Then, she wanted it made perfectly clear that this was about animal welfare, that there would be no questions and no discussion about either her film career of her private life.

As she wasn't in the studio with him, Foucault knew there was absolutely no way he could control her, that if he upset her in any way, she could quite easily get up from her chair and leave him with no show. So he complied with her conditions, and trod softly throughout the 90 minutes.

At one point, thinking they were being cute, the producers showed a report from Arizona about a man who kept a large collection of iguanas at home and earned his living by photographing them in quaint poses for postcards. After the tape ran, Foucault – hoping that Brigitte would say, isn't that sweet – asked her what she thought.

Without hesitation, she lashed out at people who took pets out of their natural environment. She accused the man in Arizona of torturing his iguanas by keeping them in his apartment where they would be disoriented. She reminded the audience that pets aren't toys, that they are living beings.

The first thing Foucault did was back down, agreeing with her, and quickly going on to the next part of the show.

When he mentioned the cinema, she put him firmly in

his place. 'I never regret anything,' she said, 'and certainly not that.'

He quickly got the topic back onto animals.

She was there that evening to make three main points, hoping that the nation would join her in her campaign.

She condemned women who still wore fur.

She spoke about abandoned animals and begged people who were looking for pets to find them in refuges – which were teeming with them – rather than going to breeders who merely added to the overpopulation of dogs and cats, which invariably led to more animals being abandoned. She advocated tattooing, vaccination and sterilization of all household pets – and castigated people who accept pets into their home, grow bored with them and discard them.

But when she spoke about the cruelty of the horse butchers of France, she was at her best.

In a frank, straight to camera appeal, she begged the nation to stop eating horse meat. She said that more than 300,000 horses were butchered each year in France and beseeched the nation to realize that there are plenty of other things to eat, and to realize that horses were not cattle. That horses were noble animals, who suffered terribly, and who understood death.

Instantly, the TF1 switchboard lit up, saturated with calls as thousands of people rang to support her, and hundreds of horse meat butchers rang to condemn her. The passion she evoked was extraordinary. Unfortunately, among the calls were several death threats.

Before the evening was out, she was given police protection.

Two days later, in an open letter to the Minister of Agriculture, she reiterated her position, that horse meat was dangerous to eat and also led to immoral slaughter. She urged he ban horse meat. 'It shouldn't be on our plates.'

The death threats continued.

Bernard was duly concerned.

349

But she shrugged them all off. 'I couldn't give a damn about them. It shows just how inhuman these men are.'

Fearlessly, she'd taken on a profession with roots deep in French society and struggling to survive. And she was having some effect. Two months later horse meat sales had dropped a reported 30-50 per cent.

A spokeswoman for the French meat information centre, noting that Bardot owned cats, stated, 'Cats are carnivorous,' and wondered, 'Just what does she feed hers?'

But the silliest response came from a butcher who threatened that, if she were allowed to continue like this, Bardot would next be taking on snails and oysters. He wanted to know, 'What does she eat, grass?'

.   .   .

No one can doubt Brigitte's courage.

Bernard sees it every day, as she goes through her morning mail.

He says she reads about such horrors, such awful things, and is deeply moved by it all. 'She takes it all in. She bottles it all up inside. It's very difficult for her. That's why she sometimes gets very depressed. She tries to do too much. She gets a letter about something horrible being done to an animal and she wants to go there right away and save the animal. It takes its toll on her.'

In the beginning, when she started all of this, the French seemed a bit circumspect. It seemed easy to put her down. It was troubling for many people to watch her getting old. But that has more to do with them than it does with her. It's comforting to remember her the way she was, because that's the way we were. So it took some time for people to accept her in this new life. She wasn't some crazy old lady with 50 cats. She was someone who had, like Allain Bougrain-Dubourg said, gone from myth to reality.

Anyway, the French are really only now learning how to deal

with special action groups. They like animals but they don't have the same kind of spirit to demonstrate on behalf of animals the way they do in other countries. In Britain, for instance, there probably isn't a Member of Parliament who doesn't have a small bird-feeder in his garden. In France, it's something very new.

Her hope for the future, then, lies in the younger generation, in the ones who don't see her as a movie star, in the ones who think of her as the 'animals' fairy godmother'.

And that, she says, is the way she would like to be remembered.

His Highness Prince Sadruddin Aga Khan, whose own Bellerive Foundation frequently works in the areas of animal rights, sees that image of her as a terrific inspiration to others.

Brigitte and the Aga Khan joined forces in September 1993, to try to establish a set of guidelines for the more human transportation of animals on their way to slaughter. They were two loud voices among many who have protested against cattle, sheep and other animals being crammed into trucks and boats for journeys of several days with little water, food or rest.

The day they were supposed to present a manifesto to the European Commission, Brigitte had the flu and was running a temperature. But she felt so strongly about this cause that she got out of her sick bed and went to Brussels for the day.

And the Prince says that's typical of her dedication.

'The amazing thing about her is that she doesn't get discouraged. She has this extraordinary, unstinting energy. She's very resilient. And she understands that what's important is the fight itself. She makes sense and has this extraordinary determination. Unfortunately, she is still seen by some people as an old actress who used to be a beautiful starlet. People are very unfair, very mean, and they should know that she has made an enormous contribution.'

Part of that contribution has been in establishing a thread that clearly runs through many different problems.

'She helps people see the link between, say, trapping and animal transport or animal transport and vivisection. At first, some people think, why is she dealing one day with bullfights and the next day with pounds where dogs are ultimately put to sleep? They can't, on their own, see the link. Well, she shows it to them, and it is that we must change our attitude towards other living beings, including animals. Our whole approach needs to be reviewed. This is the message she drives home so effectively. That's why I think that what she has done is so terribly important. She's not just a do-gooder who's concerned with fluffy, loving animals. She's somebody who has a vision and who is not afraid to express it. The problem is, most people haven't yet got the message.'

Epilogue

'Some day,' she said in 1971, 'I'll be 60. But I'll still be a little girl. A little girl who's 60 years old.'

*   *   *

Garrigue means scrub land.

And La Garrigue is her French version of a ranch. She's built a tiny house there – very rustic – and added all sorts of little decorative touches that leave no doubt about her well-defined but simple taste.

You walk in through a low door, and find yourself in the kitchen. There's a table and chairs under the windows on the right where she and Bernard eat most of their meals when they have to eat inside. The rest of the time, they eat in the garden.

Beyond that is the living room, with a few couches and a television set and a stereo with classical CDs scattered around it. On one wall there is a portrait of an ancestor on her mother's side – a man who'd once been a Prefect in Corsica. At the far end of the living room is her bedroom.

To the side of it, down a step, is a tiny study where she sometimes works – a room with a desk and a chair, lined with bookshelves. Many of the books that fill them are stories about life in Provence around the turn of the century, when people lived a simpler, less complicated existence and were more in touch with nature.

Those are her favourites.

She is a letter writer – it's her way of keeping in touch – because for her that's more personal than picking up the phone. Her handwriting is forceful and deliberate, with very rounded letters, as if some teacher in school, all those years ago, made her sit at her desk and practise each letter until she got it perfect. But then her spelling is also perfect and so is her grammar. Her vocabulary is rich, a hearty mixture of words bordering on the intellectual – what might be called good Scrabble words – together with street slang.

A few years ago – she must have been cleaning out a drawer – she sent photos to a lot of people. Snapshots. Stuff taken years ago. She just stuck them in an envelope and posted them.

La Garrigue epitomizes her clean break with her past.

And when she's here, there are rules.

The first is that no one is permitted to phone her at La Garrigue. It is a place for her to escape everybody, even friends, and when the phone rings there she can be vile. One very close friend made that mistake recently – he merely rang to say hello – and she gave him absolute hell. She yelled that he was never ever to ring her there and slammed the phone down before he even had a chance to say anything more than how are you.

Even when she's at a place where she will accept calls – like La Madrague – friends know not to ring in the morning before 11 or so. Not that she's still asleep. Sometimes she gets up very early and spends the entire morning with her animals. It's that she thinks of mornings as a quiet time, to work or to be alone, or to be with her animals. And she resents any human intrusions.

There are dogs and cats all over the property, which is hidden from view by a thick wood, and a paddock where she keeps a couple of horses and a donkey and some goats and some sheep. Nearby there is a pet cemetery – a final resting place for the company she's kept. On little markers she has written their names.

Beyond the house, half way up the hill, along a narrow dirt path that cuts through the woods, there is a tiny chapel – Notre Dame de la Garrigue – which she built in quasi-Mexican style. Saint Anne guards the door. Inside, there are four prayer stools and a small pile of prayer books. The whitewashed stucco walls are decorated with pictures of saints, photos of animals past and the single photo of a young girl whom Brigitte supported while she was dying of cancer.

The chapel is only one room. But then it needn't be anything more. Because this isn't a cathedral for a movie star, it is the private house of God of a woman who is, perhaps, not as consciously religious as she is overtly spiritual.

No one is sure exactly how many animals live here with her, least of all Brigitte herself. The cats come and go, and odd ones have a tendency to show up around mealtime. But that doesn't matter. If you happen to be a cat or a dog, it's always open house at the Bardot ranch.

The one thing that all the animals who live with her share is that they have each been saved from some sort of horror – the horses from the butchers, the dogs and cats from owners who mistreated them.

She knows them all. And they all know her. And when they see her arrive, they go wild. The dogs race up to her and the cats do too. The horses neigh and the donkey brays and even the goats start calling out to her. They come to the edge of the paddock and wait for her, calling and neighing and braying in an amazing cacophony of joy, showing how they hunger for her attention.

Clearly, it's a two-way street.

Unlike La Madrague, this house is well protected from onlookers. There's a tiny beach at the bottom of a steep walk down the hill through the forest, but from the shore you can't see her property. She loves to walk her dogs there. But she only ever does it very early in the morning, before people start coming down to swim, or late in the afternoon, once they're gone. These days she avoids most contact, if she can.

Yet, here too, the invasion continues. A few summers ago, someone actually tried to land their helicopter on her property.

In recent years, she has got into the habit of spending most mornings at La Madrague, reading, doing her mail, working on her Foundation, then coming here in the afternoon. Whether she sleeps at La Garrigue or back at La Madrague depends entirely on her whim at the moment.

'I never organize my future,' she says. 'That's the surest way to forget living in the present.' And more than once Olga Horstig-Primuz has found herself explaining that, for Brigitte, 'even a dinner date arranged a week in advance is a prison sentence. She will live only for the moment.'

After all the years of tumult, she has forged out her own peace and quiet. This is a woman who has known the highest of highs and the lowest of lows – a woman who, at least for a time, mistook life for stardom – and has, ever since, desperately sought to find some equilibrium.

·　　·　　·

Her son Nicolas has cut out a life for himself in Oslo with his wife and daughters.

Her niece Camille lives in Paris.

In 1962, Mijanou married Patrick Bauchau, a young Belgian film director and actor. For many years, she ran a soft furnishings business on the Left Bank in Paris. She now lives in the Norwegian chalet of her youth, surrounded by artist friends who paint in her living room and a bunch of very large dogs who welcome guests with loud barking and muddy paws.

'After Brigitte became an important star, after *Et Dieu Créa la Femme*, I was always known as Brigitte Bardot's sister. And I got sick of being asked to imitate her. I went to Hollywood with offers of a seven-year contract and the first thing they did was dress me up to look like her. I came home. But I didn't give up the idea of being in films until someone in Italy asked for my autograph and told me to sign it, "BB's sister". Still, in many ways, I think I've been luckier than Brigitte. I was always broke. I never had the kind of money that Brigitte had. But I could walk through the streets alone, or go to a café or do anything I wanted to. I had freedom. She didn't. She was trapped by her fame.'

Brigitte's long-time agent Olga Horstig-Primuz is retired. Her long-time friend Christine Gouze-Renal is still making movies.

Roger Vadim is still making movies too. A few years ago he married actress Marie-Christine Barrault.

'I haven't seen Brigitte for several years. She's another person. When we were together, her contradictions were only inside herself. She could be wonderful, joyous, happy, dynamic, and, from time to time, completely depressed, which provoked disputes. But she didn't express those contradictions the way she does today. She's two completely different people. She's not the woman–child I knew, who was drunk with life, a bit of an anarchist, who didn't care about material things, who mocked anything and everything official and, above all, who walked around with that air of complete indifference. She's not the same person. And nobody's told her the truth for the past 10 years. As soon as someone doesn't say yes to her, she finds a reason to get rid of them. The last of her friends, the ones who were sincere, she got rid of them. The ones who are left, they don't dare to tell her the truth. She thinks people come around only because they're interested in something, because they want something. It only serves to reinforce her loneliness. But that's nothing new. In the old days, even when someone did tell her the truth, she wouldn't hear it. No one could ever tell her anything. She might not have been the only woman who counted in my life, but she was one of the three. The other two? Jane Fonda. And my wife now. Marie-Christine Barrault. I've finished with the best.'

Jacques Charrier lives in Paris and is a grandfather. After he quit acting, he produced a few films. But these days he's returned to his first love, painting.

Gunter Sachs married a beautiful Swedish woman named Mirja Larsson in 1969. They have two children, in addition to Gunter's son from his first marriage. He too is a grandfather. Based mainly in Munich, he lives in houses scattered all over the world. 'I think it's 25, although it might be 27, I can't remember. It's a real problem when I have to figure out which key goes to which house.' He spends mornings handling his investments and running his various businesses, and afternoons at his photography studio. His pictures are exhibited in galleries and published in books.

Bob Zagury married a young American model he met in Paris and they have twin daughters. Allain Bougrain-Dubourg is still making television programmes about animals. Mirko, the sculptor, lives in Burgundy part of the year and the rest of the year he's back in the mountains.

Her old chums Christian Brincourt, Philippe Letellier, Philippe d'Exea and Eddie Barclay are alive and well and living in Paris. They spend summers in St Tropez but haven't seen her in years.

Jicky Dussart lives next door to her at La Garrigue. He paints. Anne Dussart lives in Paris. She's in the magazine business.

Jo de Salerne is still plugging away, keeping St Tropez honest.

Sacha Distel is happily married and still crooning.

Louis Malle is married to Candice Bergen and still making films.

Serge Marquand is acting in Paris. Christian Marquand is there too.

André Pousse is now in his early 70s, still acting, still running his restaurant, still complaining when he loses a game of *pétanque*, still as mean as ever.

Mike Sarne makes films in London. Christopher Wedow lives in the States.

Jean-Louis Trintignant was once married to the Marquands' sister Nadine but they split up and he is now is semi-retired. Sami Frey is still acting. Serge Gainsbourg is dead.

Many of the others have simply faded away, gone to live their lives with whatever memories they have of the time they spent with her.

. . .

'Every day, I thank God,' she says. 'I don't know if he has a large beard. I don't know who he is. But I thank him that I'm alive each day. He doesn't owe me anything.'

There have been plenty of times in both her lives when she's been happy to be Brigitte Bardot. But now in her second life that comes a lot more often than it ever did in her first. 'For me, the cinema is linked to such confusion in my life that I never wish to hear about it again.'

What her life is all about now, she says, is the love she sees in the eyes of her dogs and the purring of her cats and the soft muzzle of the mare she saved from the knackers yard. It's about all the little goats and all the little lambs who won't wind up as a *gigot d'agneau* or on a barbecue spit. It is, she says, about having found a love that lasts.

One night, many years ago, out with friends in St Tropez, she overheard a passing tourist who recognized her and remarked, '*Qu'elle est moche*' – She looks ugly. She let it drop, until the tourist was out of earshot and then she reminded her friends, 'I'm not ugly, I'm Bardot.'

For many people, she will always be Bardot.

She will always epitomize 20th-century womanhood.

Powerfully secure in her appearance. Unbearably beautiful. Terrifyingly secure in her own sexuality. Physically as perfect as any woman could be. Everything about her was perfect. The colour of her hair. Her skin. Her teeth. Her legs. Her fingernails. Her eyes. Her cheekbones. The way she walked. The way she smelled. The way she slept. Her laugh. Her pout.

She was better than perfect. She was unique.

But then, there are those who believe that she is Vadim's

victim. That a long time ago he sold her the wrong bill of goods. That, in the final analysis, women must behave like women and when you turn a woman into a man – when she starts thinking like a man and living like a man – you take something so basic away from her.

She has always refuted that idea. 'Vadim didn't create me. I existed as I'd decided to exist, with my own convictions solidly based on my own thinking. If I didn't enjoy doing something, I didn't do it. That's my little girl side. He never ever made me do anything. It's always been me who's decided everything. The mistakes too.'

Yet before Vadim, some people reason, she was still Brigitte Bardot – much the same way that Mickey was still a nice little mouse who ate cheese. Then Walt Disney came along. It took Vadim to merchandise her and he did it brilliantly. Vadim was the ambitious one. Vadim was her Disney.

All these years later, she could look like the most spectacular 60 year old in the world, with her hair done perfectly and great clothes and great shoes and everything in place. And that is precisely what she refuses to do. She still has the silhouette of a 20 year old, those narrow hips and wonderful legs. But her face is heavier now than it was then.

She still permits herself to be photographed, but generally only by those few photographers whom she trusts. They say she does not permit close-ups.

On those occasions when an old friend has dared to bring up the subject of face lifts – usually in reference to someone else – she categorically dismisses such talk as utter nonsense. She is fundamentally against such things. She says she looks the way she looks and refuses to fall into the trap of trying to look 30 years younger.

And in the end, why not. Her eyes are still wonderful and those lips are still wonderful and her skin is unbelievably soft.

Kissing that face – even if it's just once on each cheek, the way the French do – is a heady experience, totally intoxicating, well worth the price of admission.

There is little doubt but that she and France are inseparable. She's like the Eiffel Tower or the Louvre. On 4 July 1986, to celebrate the 100th birthday of the Statue of Liberty, Jacques Chirac, as prime minister, presented the United States with a figurine of a nude Bardot in the pose of the Statue of Liberty. So in a very real sense, yes, she will always be France.

But none of that means anything to her, unless she can use it to help her work with animals.

The word myth makes her angry.

She should be the queen of St Tropez. But there have never been more than a dozen locals who have supported her Foundation. At one point there were only six, and one of them was so angry at her that he was refusing to renew his subscription.

Considering that so many people in the town lived off her back for so long, to have fewer than 12 supporters out of a population of nearly 5,000 is a pretty pathetic response. She's right when she says that Tropezians should be ashamed of themselves.

Yet, these days she's a difficult friend, even at the best of times, and a terror at the worst of times, and the remains of broken and bloodied friendships are littered for miles around. So people tread softly, always afraid to provoke the least little crack in her humour. Only those few who are really sure of themselves, who know they have nothing to prove to anyone and who make a point of never being at her mercy, manage to stay the course.

'She can turn people with a smile, a laugh, a pout,' notes one old friend. 'It doesn't matter if you've been angry with her or she's been angry with you, people always come back to her. You can't stay away from Brigitte forever.'

In so many ways, the unbelievable adventure that has been her life has been about being loved, about finding love.

And when you tell her that even those people she no longer sees, even those people who are angry with her for a caprice or some misunderstanding – when you tell her how all of them say, even though we don't see her any more, there is still a bit of us that loves her — when you tell her that she is loved, her eyes light up and she asks, '*C'est vrai?*' Is it true?

And when you tell her, '*Oui, c'est vrai,*' yes, it's true, for one brief instant you see the little girl who's trapped inside a 60-year-old woman whose life was stolen by fame and who, in the end, really only wanted to be loved.

Appendix

BRIGITTE BARDOT — FILM APPEARANCES

Where a film has more than one English-language title, the British title precedes the American title. Where films have kept their own title in translation, no other is listed. In the case where well-known actors also appeared, they too are listed.

1952
LE TROU NORMAND
    (The Norman Hole; Crazy for Love)
    Directed by Jean Boyer
    Starring Bourvil
MANINA, LA FILLE SANS VOILE
    (The Lighthouse Keeper's Daughter; The Girl in the Bikini)
    Directed by Willy Rozier
LES DENTS LONGUES
    (The Long Teeth)
    Directed by Daniel Gélin
    Starring Daniel Gélin and Daniele Delorme
    Walk-on appearances by Brigitte Bardot and Roger Vadim

1953
LE PORTRAIT DE SON PERE
    (The Image of His Father; His Father's Portrait)

363

Directed by André Berthomieu
Starring Jean Richard
ACT OF LOVE
(French title of US production: Quelque Part dans le Monde)
Directed by Anatole Litvak
Starring Kirk Douglas and Dany Robin
SI VERSAILLES M'ETAIT CONTE
(If Versailles Could Talk; Versailles)
Written and directed by Sacha Guitry
Starring Sacha Guitry, Jean Marais, Georges Marchal, Claudette
Colbert and Micheline Presle. There is a brief appearance by
Orson Welles as Benjamin Franklin.

1954
TRADITA
(French title of Italian production: Haine, Amour et Trahison)
(Hate, Love and Treachery; Night of Love)
Directed by Mario Bonnard
HELEN OF TROY
Directed by Robert Wise
With Sir Cedric Hardwicke
LE FILS DE CAROLINE CHERIE
(The Son of Caroline Cherie)
Directed by Jean Devaivre
Starring Jean-Claude Pascal

1955
FUTURES VEDETTES
(Sweet Sixteen)
Screenplay by Roger Vadim and Marc Allégret
Directed by Marc Allégret
Starring Jean Marais
DOCTOR AT SEA
(French title of British production: Rendezvous à Rio)
Directed by Ralph Thomas
Starring Dirk Bogarde
LES GRANDES MANOEUVRES
(Summer Maneuvers)

Directed by René Clair
Starring Michele Morgan and Gérard Philipe
LA LUMIERE D'EN FACE
(The Light across the Street)
Directed by Georges Lacombe
CETTE SACREE GAMINE
(Mam'zelle Pigalle; That Darned Kid)
Screenplay by Roger Vadim
Directed by Michel Boisrond

1956
MIO FIGLIO NERONE
(French title of Italian production: Les Week-ends de Neron)
(Nero's Big Weekend)
Directed by Stefano Vanzina
Starring Alberto Sordi, with Vittorio de Sica and Gloria
Swanson
EN EFFEUILLANT LA MARGUERITE
(Mam'zelle Striptease; Please Mr Balzac)
Screenplay by Roger Vadim and Marc Allégret
Directed by Marc Allégret
With Daniel Gélin
ET DIEU CREA LA FEMME
(And Woman . . . Was Created; And God Created Woman)
Screenplay by Roger Vadim and Raoul Levy
Directed by Roger Vadim
With Curt Jurgens, Jean-Louis Trintignant and Christian
Marquand
LA MARIEE EST TROP BELLE
(The Bride Is Too Beautiful; The Bride Is Much Too Beauti-
ful)
Directed by Pierre Gaspard-Huit
With Louis Jordan and Micheline Presle

1957
LA PARISIENNE
(Parisienne)

Directed by Michel Boisrond
With Charles Boyer
LES BIJOUTIERS DU CLAIR DE LUNE
  (Heaven Fell That Night; The Night Heaven Fell)
  Screeplay by Roger Vadim
  Directed by Roger Vadim
  With Stephen Boyd
EN CAS DE MALHEUR
  (Love Is My Profession)
  Directed by Claude Autant-Lara
  Starring Jean Gabin

1958
LA FEMME ET LE PANTIN
  (A Woman Like Satan; The Female)
  Directed by Julien Duvivier

1959
BABETTE S'EN VA-T-EN GUERRE
  (Babette Goes to War)
  Directed by Christian-Jaque
  With Jacques Charrier
VOULEZ-VOUS DANSER AVEC MOI?
  (Come Dance with Me)
  Directed by Michel Boisrond
  With a small part played by Serge Gainsbourg
LE TESTAMENT D'ORPHEE
  (Cocteau's Surrealistic Fantasies)
  Directed by François Truffaut
  Brief appearance by Brigitte Bardot

1960
L'AFFAIRE D'UNE NUIT
  (It Happened at Night)
  Directed by Henri Verneuil
  Walk-on appearances by Brigitte Bardot, Jacques Charrier and
    Christine Gouze-Renal

LA VERITE
  (The Truth)
  Directed by Henri-Georges Clouzot
  With Charles Venal, Paul Meurisse and Sami Frey

1961
LA BRIDE SUR LE COU
  (Please Not Now; Only for Love)
  "Artistic Direction" by Roger Vadim
  With brief appearances by Claude Brasseur, Mireille Darc and
    Serge Marquand
LES AMOURS CELEBRES.
  (Famous Loves)
  Directed by Michel Boisrond
  With Alain Delon, Pierre Brasseur and Jean-Claude Brialy
VIE PRIVEE.
  (A Very Private Affair)
  Directed by Louis Malle
  With Marcello Mastroianni and a brief appearance by Louis
    Malle

1962
LE REPOS DU GUERRIER
  (Warrior's Rest; Love on a Pillow)
  Directed by Roger Vadim
  With Robert Hossein and, briefly, Michel Serrault

1963
LE MEPRIS
  (Contempt)
  Directed by Jean-Luc Godard
  Starring Jack Palance, with Michel Piccoli and brief appear-
    ances by Fritz Lang and Jean-Luc Godard
PAPARAZZI
  Documentary shot in Italy during *Le Mépris*
  Directed by Jacques Rozier
  With Jean-Luc Godard and Michel Piccoli as themselves

367

TENTAZIONI PROHIBITE
  (Forbidden Temptation)
  Documentary shot in Italy during *Le Mépris*
  Directed by Oswoldo Civirani
UNE RAVISSANTE IDIOTE
  (A Ravishing Idiot)
  Directed by Edouard Molinaro
  With Anthony Perkins

1964
MARIE SOLEIL
  Directed by Antoine Bourseiller
  Starring Daniele Delorme and Jacques Charrier with a brief
    appearance by Brigitte Bardot

1965
DEAR BRIGITTE
  Directed by Henry Koster
  Starring James Stewart, Glynis Johns and Fabian, with one
    scene featuring Brigitte Bardot as herself
VIVA MARIA.
  Directed by Louis Malle
  With Jeanne Moreau and George Hamilton
MASCULIN-FEMININ
  (Masculine-Feminine)
  Directed by Jean-Luc Godard
  With Chantal Goya and Marlène Jobert and a walk-on
    appearance by Brigitte Bardot

1966
A COEUR JOIE.
  (Two Weeks in September)
  Directed by Serge Bourguignon
  With Laurent Terzieff and Mike Sarne

1967
HISTOIRES EXTRAORDINAIRES
  (Tales of Mystery; Spirits of the Dead)

Directed by Louis Malle
With Alain Delon

1968
SHALAKO
Directed by Edward Dmytryk
Starring Sean Connery with Stephen Boyd, Jack Hawkins and
Honor Blackman

1969
LES FEMMES
(The Women)
Directed by Jean Aurel

1970
L'OURS ET LA POUPEE
(The Bear and the Doll)
Directed by Michel Deville
With Jean-Pierre Cassel
LES NOVICES
(The Novices)
Directed by Guy Casaril
With Annie Girardot
BOULEVARD DU RHUM
(Rum Boulevard)
Directed by Robert Enrico
Starring Lino Ventura

1971
LES PETROLEUSES
(The Legend of Frenchy King)
Directed by Christian-Jaque
With Claudia Cardinale and Michael J. Pollard

1973
DON JUAN 1973; SI DON JUAN ETAIT UNE FEMME
(If Don Juan Were a Woman)

Directed by Roger Vadim
With Jane Birkin and Robert Hossein
L'HISTOIRE TRES BONNE ET TRES JOYEUSE DE COLINOT
TROUSSE CHEMISE
(The Edifying and Joyous Story of Colinot, the Skirt Puller)
Directed by Nina Companeez

Acknowledgements

While writing this book, many people have shown personal kindness and friendship, for which I would like to say thank you. Old pals such as Maggie Koumi, Nadia Lacoste, Jo and Dee Lustig, and David Thieme.

At Simon & Schuster, I am, as ever, endlessly grateful to Nick Webb for his compassion and enthusiasm. I also wish to thank Carol O'Brien, Mary Pachnos, Cathy Schofield, Sian Parkhouse and, in fact, everyone there, not merely for what they've done on my behalf, but especially for making me feel so much at home.

Thanks as well to my faithful copyeditor, Liz Paton, and to my agent, the legendary Mildred Marmur, in New York. Thanks, as well, to the inimitable, Don Fine.

Needless to say, there is also, as always, the wonderful La Benayoun.

For technical help with Brigitte Bardot's film career, my thanks to: the Centre Nationale de Cinéma, and especially Mme René Laudrin; Agence France Press; the British Film Institute; the Press Association and Eugene Weber; Mme Françoise Fernandez; L'Institut National Audio-Visuel; *Nice Matin*; Radio France, and especially Mme Barbry; *Paris Match*; the auctioneers Ader Picard Tajan; *Var Matin*, and especially Colette Oliver; and the office of the late Paul-Emile Victor.

371

For two large and important collections of documents and letters concerning Brigitte Bardot (one official and one private) that were made available to me, I wish my benefactors to know that I am in their debt.

*   *   *

At this point, I would like to add a few words about the Brigitte Bardot Foundation.

The story of how it came about is to be found in the text. One of the points I sincerely hope I've clearly made is the great importance of its work. This is not just about saving baby seals or banning ivory imports. It's about trying to make life better for all the living beings with whom we share this planet.

The young men and women who carry on this task – Brigitte's soldiers, if you will – are genuinely dedicated to what they're doing. They share her fears and her passions and her vision of the future. What's more, their faith and their commitment and their resolve to make a difference are so compelling that one could be forgiven for thinking that, in fact, the planet will indeed survive.

The Brigitte Bardot Foundation is located at 45 rue Vineuse, 75116 Paris, France (tel: 331-45-05-14-60; fax: 331-45-05-14-80).

*   *   *

Generally speaking, three categories of sources are used in book research: primary sources, in other words, the people who were there at the time; secondary sources, which usually mean newspaper, magazine, film, television or radio accounts made at the time; and tertiary sources, which are books or articles written by people who weren't there. Because one can never count on its accuracy, the use of third source research is akin to shaking hands with the man who shook hands with the man.

Authors short on primary sources – which includes any author too lazy to seek them out or otherwise unable to convince them to talk – generally find themselves forced to rely on those second and third categories. Unfortunately, that method is extremely dangerous.

In the specific case of books that have already been written about Brigitte Bardot, none of them was written with cooperation from her. In fact, none of them was written with cooperation from any of the most important primary sources. Most of them were what is known in the trade as 'paste-ups'.

It begins with someone going through newspaper and magazine cuttings, and compiling what has already been published into what he or she then terms a biography. In reality, it has little to do with ligitimate biography, and more to do with typing. On the whole, whatever errors of fact appeared in those cuttings are simply repeated.

The problem compounds itself when the next biographer comes along, and quotes, as his or her source, that first book.

By the time someone decides, for the fifth or sixth time, to do a book on the same subject, he proudly lists as his sources – to impress the reader with the quality of his research – all that has gone before. He lists all the books and all the newspaper cuttings and all the magazine cuttings, as if to say, aren't I a good fellow for having done my homework. Except, of course, the result of his homework is that not only has he repeated all the previous errors of fact, he has almost certainly, added some of his own.

To protect himself with the reviewers, so that they don't accuse him of doing a paste-up, a common trick is to add a note thanking friends and neighbours for their time. You can tell it's a phony because none – or at best very few – of the people they thank ever seems to end up in the index. I sometimes wonder if they haven't included the milkman. One author, in researching Bardot's life, actually thanked her own astrologer.

In the case of this book, there is no bibliography, and that is for one straightforward and simple reason: no tertiary sources have been used. In places where secondary sources have been used, they have been used only after having been checked with a primary source.

In all other cases, this book is based on hundreds of hours of first-hand interviews. May I therefore express my gratitude to these people.

To begin with, very special thanks for the time given me by Brigitte Bardot's three ex-husbands: Roger Vadim, Jacques Charrier and Gunter Sachs. I enjoyed their company enormously and they couldn't have been more charming or more gracious.

In St Tropez: Andrée Anselmi, Etienne Astegiano, Eddie Barclay, Pierrot Bonnet, Simone Bouquin, Patricia Brigaud, Madelaine and Antoni Clavé, Patrice de Colmont, Jean-Michel Couve, Ghislain (Jicky) Dussart, Michel Luccioni, Jean-Pierre Manivet, Gérard Montel, Jean-Claude (Coco) Robert, Louisette and Jean Robert, Michel Simon, and Jocelyne and Alain Spada. Plus, an added 'merci' to Jo de Salerne, the undisputed king of St Tropez.

In Paris: Paul Albou, Camille Bauchau, Robert Benayoun, Jane Birkin, Juliette Boisriveaud, Irène and Claude Bolling, Allain Bougrain-Dubourg, Christian and Annie-Claude Brincourt, François Challais, Nina Companeez, Philippe d'Exea, Sacha Distel, Gilles Dreyfus, Anne Dussart, Louis Feraud, Christine Gouze-Renal, Olga Horstig-Primuz, Dominique Jacob, Philippe Letellier, Louis Malle, Serge Marquand, Jeanne Moreau, Alice Morgaine, Joss and André Pousse, Jean Robin, Françoise Sagan, André-Pierre Tarbes, Odette Ventura, Marie-France de la Villehuchette, and Robert Zagury.

Elsewhere in France: Jean-Louis Bousnous, Miroslav (Mirko) Brozek, Leslie Caron, Alain Carré, Jean-Noel Grinda, Gabriel Natta, and Madelaine Venant.

In addition: His Highness Prince Sadruddin Aga Khan, Betty Box, Allan Carr, Nicolas Charrier, Mercedes (Zavka) Fonda, Richard Lester, Malcolm Peters, Pierre Salinger, Mike Sarne, Jean-Claude Simon, Christopher Wedow, and Gretchen Wyler.

Acknowledgements

Finally, there are three people to whom I will forever be indebted.

The first is Brigitte's current husband, Bernard d'Ormale. He came into her life recently and, in spite of the media attention he's attracted, has ceaselessly tried to create the kind of calm and quiet life that they both seek. For that, he has my enormous respect. Having so very generously opened doors for me that have, until now, always remained firmly shut, he has my heartfelt thanks.

The second is Marie-Jeanne Bauchau Bardot – the wonderful Mijanou – Brigitte's sister. What a special human being. She is warm, sensitive and deeply caring – the kind of person one meets so rarely – a woman who, I hope, will be our friend for many years to come.

And then there is the lady about whom this book has been written.

Dear Brigitte, thank you, *mille fois merci,* for talking to me, for feeding me, for walking on the beach with me and for letting me see you laugh. When you laugh your eyes light up and the world is suddenly a much sunnier place. Aline and I wish you *un coeur remplit de jours ensoleillés.*

JR/1995)

375

Index

BB = Brigitte Bardot

377

Index